OECD Development Pathways

Multi-dimensional Review of Uruguay

VOLUME 2. IN-DEPTH ANALYSIS AND RECOMMENDATIONS

OECD

dev
DEVELOPMENT CENTRE

Please cite this publication as:
OECD (2016), *Multi-dimensional Review of Uruguay: Volume 2. In-depth Analysis and Recommendations*, OECD Development Pathways, OECD Publishing, Paris.
http://dx.doi.org/10/1787/9789264251663-en.

ISBN 978-92-64-25165-6 (print)
ISBN 978-92-64-25166-3 (PDF)

Series: OECD Development Pathways
ISSN 2308-734X (print)
ISSN 2308-7358 (online)

Photo credits: Cover © design by the OECD Development Centre based on images of isac babel, ElOjoTorpe/Moment Open/Getty Images and VikaSuh, Chaikovskiy Igor, taraki, Toniflap/Shutterstock.com.

Corrigenda to OECD publications may be found on line at: *www.oecd.org/publishing/corrigenda.*

Foreword

Within the framework of the Strategy on Development, the OECD launched the first Multi-dimensional Country Review (MDCR) in 2013, a new series that looks at economic development along the lines of inclusive growth, examining patterns of growth that are equitable, sustainable and improve the overall well-being of citizens. The series aims to identify key constraints to broad-based development, and to formulate appropriate policy recommendations accordingly.

OECD Development Pathways is a new series that looks at multiple development objectives beyond an exclusive focus on growth. The report recognises that well-being is part of development and aims to help countries identify and overcome binding constraints to more equitable and sustainable growth. Governments trying to achieve economic, social and environmental objectives need to understand the constraints they face and to develop comprehensive and well-sequenced strategies for reform. MDCRs take a cross-cutting perspective, which allows for the discussion of policy interactions and trade-offs.

Uruguay is the second country to undertake a multi-dimensional review, and the first one in Latin America. The report is timely as, after a decade of economic prosperity, Uruguay is currently facing new challenges, some of them similar to those of OECD countries. The first volume of the review served to identify the binding constraints to Uruguay's development. Several dimensions of the country's economic and social development, including productivity outcomes, patterns of inequality and macroeconomic policies, were analysed. With this basis, the second volume of the review provides an in-depth analysis and recommendations to tackle Uruguay's critical constraints to development. While the recommendations in this report are intended primarily to support public policy action by Uruguay's national authorities, the findings are also beneficial for academics, the private sector and civil society.

The MDCRs are composed of three distinct phases: diagnosis, in-depth analysis of the binding constraints, and implementation. This phased approach allows for a progressive learning process about the country's specific challenges and opportunities. A participatory workshop, two missions and discussions with authorities, private sector representatives and academia allowed for the preparation of the analysis and recommendations within this second report. Analytical work is based on available statistics on Uruguay, including macroeconomic and structural data, household and labour market surveys and other domestic and international sources.

Acknowledgements

Multi-dimensional Country Reviews are the result of a collaborative effort between the OECD and the country under review. Work on the first phase of the Multi-dimensional Review of Uruguay was carried out jointly by the OECD Development Centre, the OECD Economics Department and the OECD Statistics Directorate, with support from the Ministry of Economy and Finance of Uruguay. The second phase was co-ordinated by the OECD Development Centre, with the participation of the Directorate for Financial and Enterprise Affairs (DAF), the Directorate for Education and Skills (EDU) and the International Transport Forum (ITF).

The Multi-dimensional Country Review process is led by Jan Rieländer, Head of the MDCR Unit and Angel Melguizo, Head of the Latin America and Caribbean Unit, both at the OECD Development Centre, under the direction of Mario Pezzini, Director of the OECD Development Centre, Martine Durand, OECD Chief Statistician and Catherine Mann, OECD Chief Economist.

The second phase of the review was co-ordinated by Rolando Avendaño (OECD Development Centre), and drafted by Iza Lejarraga and Leona Verdadero (Directorate for Financial and Enterprise Affairs), Rolando Avendaño, Anna Jankowska and Rosaura Quiñones (OECD Development Centre), Dejan Makovsek (International Transport Forum) and Mihaylo Milonavovitch (European Training Foundation, previously at the OECD Directorate for Education and Skills). Significant inputs were provided by Natalia Ferreira, Cecilia Llambí, Marcelo Perera and Marcel Vaillant in the form of background papers. Statistical assistance was provided by David López, Sammy Libos and Nathalie Peñaranda and administrative support was provided by Ana Gonzalez and Diane Raillard. Rita da Costa co-ordinated communication with the Uruguayan authorities on behalf of the Director's Office. Gabriel Papa (Ministry of Economy and Finance -MEF) co-ordinated the work with OECD authorities throughout the project and Pedro Keuroglian and Carolina Sena (MREE) served as liaison with OECD in Paris. Additional inputs were provided by Virginia Robano (Centre for Entrepreneurship, SMEs and Local Development), Ian Hawkesworth and Camila Vammalle (both at the Public Governance and Territorial Development Directorate), Andrea Goldstein (Directorate for Financial and Enterprise Affairs), Nathalie Peñaranda and Juan Vazquez Zamora (OECD Development Centre), Heike Buss, Valerio Barbantini and Gregory de Paepe (Centre for Tax Policy and Administration). The authors are grateful for insightful comments and inputs by Céline Colin, Rebecca Lavinson, Sebastián Nieto-Parra, José Ramón Perea (OECD Development Centre), Christian Daude (OECD Economics Department), Daniel Blume, Hans Christiansen, Héctor Lehuedé (Directorate for Financial and Enterprise Affairs) and Paulo Santiago (OECD Directorate for Education and Skills).

The authors are grateful to the Uruguayan institutions that participated in the interviews and consultations for the elaboration of this review, including Graciela Altruda (MEF), Cecilia Alemany (Red Sur), Verónica Amarante (ECLAC), Ignacio Bartesaghi (ALADI-Asia Pacific Observatory), Luis Bermudez (Ministry of Foreign Affairs – MFA), Marcelo Breton (Abengoa),

Luis Caligari (UDELAR), Juan Pedro Cantera (Central Bank of Uruguay), P. Eduardo Casarotti (Catholic University of Uruguay), Luis Costa (Pension Fund Administrator Republica – AFAP), Cleila de la Fuente (European Union), Julio Durante (ANMYPE), Daiana Ferraro (MFA), Mariana Ferreira (Uruguay XXI), Natalia Ferreira (MEF), Fernando Figueira (ECLAC), Luis Garibaldi (Ministry of Education and Culture – MEC), Pablo Gutierrez (National Corporation for Development – CND), Isidoro Hodara (Zona America), Pedro Keuroglian (Ministry of Foreign Affairs), Andrés Lopez (University of Buenos Aires), Martin Larzabal (AFAP), Rafael Laureiro (CND), Andrés Masoller (MEF), Carlos Matyszczyk (AFAP), Edith Moraes (Teachers' Training Council), Gabriel Oddone (CPA-Ferrere Consulting), Luisa Olivera (Ministry of Economy and Finance), Alvaro Ons (CIACEX – Ministry of Foreign Affairs), Rosa Osimani (MEF), Nicole Perelmuter (CAF-Development Bank for Latin America), Sebastián Perez (Chamber of Industry of Uruguay), Julio Pivel Garicoits (OPP), Pedro Ravela (INEED), Ricardo Rocca (UDELAR), Rodolfo Silveira (LATU), Beatriz Tabacco (National Logistics Institute), Ines Terra (MEF), Marcel Vaillant (UDELAR), Andrea Vignolo (MEC), Emma Zafaronni (MEC). The team is particularly grateful to Enrique Iglesias and the Fundación Astur for their support throughout the project.

The following ministries and agencies provided useful support during the production of the report: Central Bank of Uruguay, Ministry of Economy and Finance, Ministry of Industry, Energy and Mining, Ministry of Health, Ministry of Education and Culture, Ministry of Labour and Social Security, Ministry of Foreign Relations, Ministry of Housing and the Environment, Ministry of Social Development, Ministry of Transport and Public Works, Plan Ceibal, National Agency for Research and Innovation, National Institute of Logistics, National Statistics Institute, Office of Planning and Budget, Banco de la República, National Institute for Education Assessment, National ad-hoc Accreditation Board, Laboratorio Tecnológico del Uruguay, Pension Fund Administrator República (AFAP), National Corporation for Development (CND), Council of Secondary Education, Teachers Training Council, SEGIB, Fundación Astur, Inter-American Development Bank, World Bank, UNICEF Uruguay, CAF Uruguay, ILO-CINTERFOR, Ferrere Consulting, Abengoa-Teyma and CINVE.

The team is grateful to Fiona Hinchcliffe for editing the manuscript and to the OECD Development Centre's Communications and Publications Unit, especially Delphine Grandrieux, Aida Buendía and Elizabeth Nash for their support in editing, laying out and producing the report.

Table of contents

Tables

Figures

Boxes

Acronyms and abbreviations

AFE	State Rail Administration
ALADI	Latin American Integration Association
ANEP	National Administration for Public Education
ANII	Agencia Nacional de Investigación e Innovación (National Research and Innovation Agency)
APEC	Asia-Pacific Economic Co-operation
BCU	Banco Central del Uruguay (Uruguay Central Bank)
BEPS	Base Erosion and Profit Shifting
BIT	Bilateral Investment Treaty
BPO	Business Process Outsourcing
CAF	Development Bank of Latin America
CAPEX	Capital expenditures
CEIP	Council of Early and Primary Education
CEQ	Commitment to Equity Project
CES	Council of Secondary Education
CFA	OECD Committee on Fiscal Affairs
CFE	Council of Educational Training
CGS	Credit Guarantee Scheme
CIACEX	Inter-Ministerial Commission for Foreign Trade Affairs
CIAT	Inter-American Center of Tax Administrations
CIT	Corporate Income Tax
CND	National Development Corporation
CODICEN	Central Boarding Council
CoG	Centre of Government
COMAP	Commission for the Implementation of the Investment Law
CUTI	Chamber of Uruguayan Information Technologies
CVU	Road Corporation of Uruguay
DNTF	National Directorate of Rail Transport
DNV	National Road Directorate
ECLAC	Economic Commission for Latin America and the Caribbean
EIS	Engineering Intensive Sectors
EIU	Economic Intelligence Unit

EU	European Union
FAO	United Nations Food and Agricultural Organization
FATS	Foreign Affiliate Trade Statistics
FDI	Foreign Direct Investment
FEE	Fondo de Estabilización Energetica
FIRB	Australian Government's Foreign Investment Review Board
FOB	Free on Board
FTA	Free Trade Agreement
FTZ	Free Trade Zone
GATT	General Agreement on Tariffs and Trade
GDP	Gross Domestic Product
GHG	Greenhouse Gas
GVC	Global Value Chains
ICTs	Information and Communication Technologies
IDB	Inter-American Development Bank
ILO	International Labour Organization
IMESSA	Impuesto Específico a los Servicios de Salud (Specific Tax for Health Services)
IMF	International Monetary Fund
INE	Instituto Nacional de Estadística (National Institute of Statistics)
INEED	National Institute of Educational Assessment
INEFOP	Instituto Nacional de Empleo y Formación Profesional (Institute for Labour and Professional Training)
IPA	Investment promotion agency
IPR	Investment Policy Reviews
IPRs	Intellectual Property Rights
ISCED	International Standard Classification of Education
ISDS	Investor-state dispute settlement
ISEP	International Society for Education Planning
JASPERS	Joint Assistance to Support Projects in European Regions
LAC	Latin America and the Caribbean
LPI	Logistics Performance Index
MEC	Ministry of Education and Culture
MEF	Ministerio de Economía y Finanzas de Uruguay (Ministry of Economy and Finance of Uruguay)
MFN	Most Favoured Nation principle
MSITS	Manual on Statistics of International Trade in Services
MTOP	Ministry of Transportation and Public Works
NAFTA	North American Free Trade Agreement

NTB	Non-tariff Barriers to Trade
OECD	Organisation for Economic Co-operation and Development
OPEX	Operational Expenditures
OPP	Presidential Office for Planning and Budget
PAC	Community Classroom Programme
PFI	Policy Framework for Investment
PFIs	Public Financial Institutions
PIAAC	Programme for the International Assessment of Adult Competencies
PISA	Programme for International Student Assessment
PPP	Purchasing power parity
PPPs	Public-Private Partnerships
PTA	Preferential Trade Agreement
R&D	Research and Development
RAB	Regulated Asset Based Model
RBC	Responsible Business Conduct
RCA	Revealed Comparative Advantage
SACU	Southern African Customs Union
SAFI	Sociedades Financieras de Inversion (Financial Investment Enterprises)
SELF	Rail and Logistics Services
SEP	Chile's System of Public Enterprises
SIGA	Sistema Nacional de Garantías (National System of Guarantees Enterprises)
SMEs	Small and Medieum-sized Enerprises
SNC	National Competitiveness System
SNIP	National Public Investment System
SOEs	State-owned Enterprises
TFP	Total Factor Productivity
TIFA	Trade and Invesment Framework Agreement
TOCAF	Accounting and Financial Administration Text
TPES	Total Primary Energy Supply
TPP	Trans-Pacific Partnership
TRIMS	Trade-related Investment Measures
TRIPS	Trade-related aspects of intellectual property rights
UCU	Catholic University of Uruguay
UDE	University of the Enterprise (Universidad de la Empresa)
UDELAR	University of the Republic
UI	Unemployment Insurance
UNIDO	United Nations Industrial Development Organization
USTPO	United States Patent and Trade Office

UTEC	Universidad Tecnológica del Uruguay (Technological University of Uruguay)
UTU	University of Work of Uruguay
VAT	Value-added Tax
WCO	World Customs Organization
WEF	World Economic Forum
WTO	World Trade Organization

Multi-dimensional Review of Uruguay
Volume 2. In-depth Analysis and Recommendations

Executive summary

In recent years, Uruguay has made remarkable progress in strengthening its macroeconomic management and implementing an ambitious agenda of social reforms. For over a decade, economic growth has been solid and the remnants of the economic crisis in the early 2000s have been mitigated. Stable macroeconomic policies and a favourable external environment have contributed to these accomplishments. Uruguay's progress is also reflected in improvements across various dimensions of well-being. As one of the few high-income countries in Latin America, and with the lowest levels of poverty and income inequality on the continent, Uruguay currently benefits from above-average outcomes in areas such as life satisfaction, environmental quality, health, trust, perception of government and air quality. At the same time, there are impending challenges stemming from the country's vulnerability to external shocks, its undiversified economic structure, and its limitations in the provision of human capital and infrastructure.

This second volume of the Multi-dimensional Review of Uruguay provides an in-depth analysis of Uruguay's critical development constraints and makes recommendations for addressing them. Although challenging external conditions risk curbing the rapid pace of economic growth, Uruguay's strong institutional capital should allow it to address the challenges of its relatively exposed economy. Constraints identified in the education and infrastructure sectors stress the need for a long-term perspective in implementing reforms. The high trust in government, low perceptions of corruption and well-developed social capital can support Uruguay in constructing the solid long-term policy framework required. The report identifies three main policy areas for future action to put Uruguay on a more sustainable development pathway: designing a well-functioning strategy for international integration, overcoming the barriers to infrastructure development, particularly in the transport sector and addressing the challenges within the education and skills systems that are costly from both an economic growth and a social perspective.

Towards deeper global integration

Uruguay has made important progress in its integration into the global economy, participating more actively in global production chains and creating the conditions for attracting foreign investment to contribute to the country's sustained productivity growth. However, the current regional context and the changing nature of global demand mean that Uruguay's integration model needs to be upgraded and reinforced. The export sector, which has doubled in size over the last decade, remains an important pillar of the economy. Although well-designed regional and plurilateral agreements can allow the country to strengthen links with its neighbours, new challenges emerge today when defining a more ambitious integration strategy and forging trade ties with commercially relevant partners outside Mercosur.

Low diversification, a rigid regulatory framework and a sub-optimal use of trade arrangements are all putting the brakes on Uruguay's integration into global markets. The country should focus on diversifying trade across new markets and sectors, while introducing greater flexibility into its regulatory profile, especially for its service sector. Uruguay has yet to introduce modern, behind-the-border disciplines that are essential for sustaining the development of global value chains and consolidating the institutional framework for a truly "deep integration" agenda. These include addressing barriers in competition policy, intellectual property rights, investment and regulatory coherence. Finally, the regional context, in particular Uruguay's participation in Mercosur, highlights the need for better use of current international trade and investment agreements.

Supporting trade with good quality infrastructure

Poor infrastructure can undermine Uruguay's international integration ambitions by hindering trade and investment. With almost 97% of commercial cargo in Uruguay transported by road, poor infrastructure conditions can have a significant impact on economic activity. Uruguay's infrastructure gap, which is more visible in its quality rather than its coverage, needs to be addressed.

Uruguay needs to upgrade a range of infrastructure development areas, from planning and management to delivery and operation. Creating a National Transport Plan, as well as a clear strategy for how the infrastructure sector should be organised, should be the first step. Project programming and prioritisation can be strengthened by improving co-ordination and clarifying responsibilities among the various bodies involved in the infrastructure cycle. Once Uruguay has adopted a holistic view for how its infrastructure sector should be planned and organised, it will be in a position to consider private participation in delivery. Current regulations, in particular for public-private partnerships, need to be extended and brought into line with a National Transport Plan. Prioritisation and procurement decisions should be carried out by separate entities to avoid potential bias. Such improvements to the infrastructure cycle will disentangle the process and execution of projects.

Building the skills required for a dynamic economy

Strengthening Uruguay's human capital and skills remains a central challenge for the country over the coming years, with enormous potential for enhancing Uruguay's competitiveness on the global stage. Inequalities in the access to and quality of education, particularly secondary schooling, need to be addressed urgently. Grade repetition and dropout rates are high in both secondary and higher education. Uruguay's public expenditure on education is low for OECD standards, and socio-economic disparities in attainment and performance are significant. The country can do more to tackle the current challenges in the sector, including the inequality in learning conditions for students, the variability of student assessment frameworks, the lack of proper student support schemes and the low status of the teaching profession.

Policies focused on student support and flexibility are key to solving these problems. Redefining assessment procedures can allow schools to identify the areas in which students are struggling. In secondary schools, teaching conditions should be upgraded to improve work-time flexibility, strengthen school leadership and autonomy and enhance job security. Individualising the learning process and introducing peer-learning among secondary schools can be effective measures to improve learning outcomes. In higher education, students need a more supportive and flexible academic environment to thrive. Allowing mobility within tertiary institutions, institutionalising self-help groups as an instrument of academic preparation and improving coherence between secondary and tertiary education are recommended to improve higher education outcomes. Finally, the potential benefits of technical education should be expanded and actively involve the private sector from the beginning to better align courses with the needs of the labour market.

Multi-dimensional Review of Uruguay
Volume 2. In-depth Analysis and Recommendations

Chapter 1

Assessment and recommendations

In recent years, Uruguay has made remarkable progress in strengthening its macroeconomic management and improving its people's well-being. The recovery from the Argentinian and Uruguayan crisis in 2001-02 saw the country begin its most extended period of economic growth. For most of the 2001-10 decade, stable macroeconomic policies and the favourable external environment allowed for solid growth and counteracted the devastating effects of the crisis. This is reflected in improvements in different dimensions of well-being. The country's achievements are remarkable both by regional and OECD standards. As one of the few high-income countries in Latin America, and with the lowest levels of poverty and income inequality on the continent, Uruguay scores highly in areas such as life satisfaction, environmental quality, health, trust, perception of government and air quality (Figure 1.1). Nevertheless, some challenges remain, including unequal access to education (particularly secondary), youth unemployment and social exclusion.

While Uruguay's growth path is currently stable, its history of economic fluctuations urges caution. Over the past decades, Uruguay's growth performance has seen external conditions and domestic living standards fluctuate rapidly. Volatility in growth rates has been high compared to OECD countries, with Uruguay swinging between periods of strong economic growth, economic crises and subsequent recoveries. Such inherent volatility has increasingly challenged Uruguay's capacity to maintain previous living standards. Between 1961 and 2014, per capita gross domestic product (GDP) grew by 1.8% annually, significantly below the 2.2% average for OECD economies with similar income levels. Today, the macroeconomic policy framework is solid, but external conditions risk curbing economic growth. Uruguay needs to address the structural issues driving economic and social vulnerability.

This second volume of the Multi-dimensional Review of Uruguay provides an in-depth analysis of Uruguay's critical constraints to development. It extends the analysis completed in the initial assessment (OECD, 2014a), taking it a step further and proposing concrete recommendations for key policy issues (Box 1.1). The initial assessment stressed the role of Uruguay's institutional capital in constructing a solid policy framework to deal with external and domestic challenges. These include reducing external vulnerabilities, diversifying the economic structure and preserving a social agenda. Uruguay's institutional strength – witnessed by high public trust in government, low perceptions of corruption and well-developed social capital – suggests that the country is well-placed to undertake important long-term reforms. Constraints in education and infrastructure underline the need for a long-term perspective in implementing reforms.

The in-depth analysis contained in this report focuses on three key areas for intervention: First, Uruguay's need to improve its **international integration** strategy, by harnessing new opportunities in global value chains, improving the investment framework and developing its services sector (Chapter 2). Second, the present state of **infrastructure development** in Uruguay, and the existing institutional barriers to improving the national transport system (Chapter 3). Third, the current challenges for consolidating the **education**

and skills systems, the economic and social costs of current deficiencies and the education policies required to improve performance, equity and other educational outcomes (Chapter 4). This chapter reviews these constraints and summarises the main policy recommendations identified to mitigate them.

Figure 1.1. **Well-being in Uruguay compares favourably to the rest of the world**

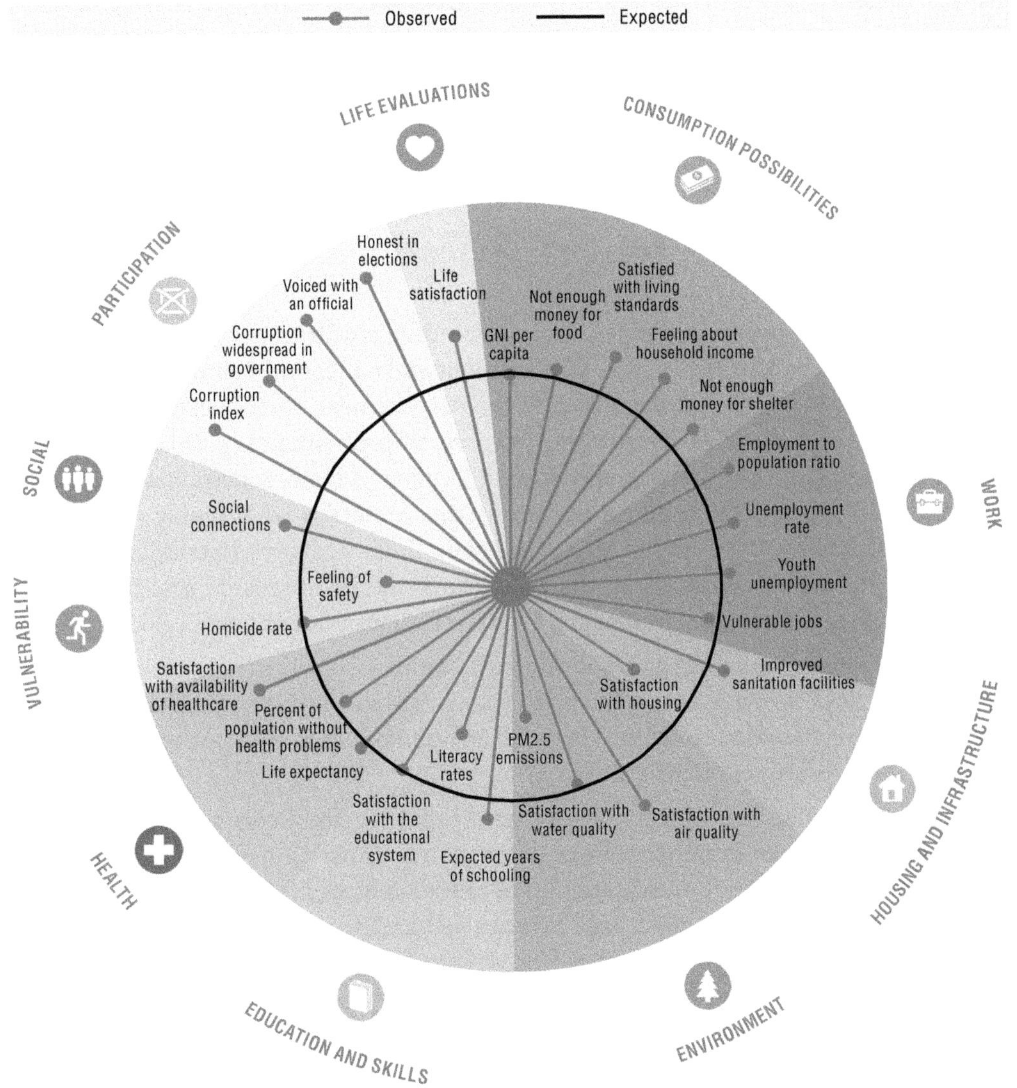

Note: Bivariate regressions were run with the relevant well-being measures as the dependent variable, and GDP per capita as the independent variable, to estimate a coefficient for the relationship between GDP and the outcome in question. The coefficient was then applied to Uruguay's actual GDP per capita to produce an expected value for the outcome. Uruguay's actual well-being outcome is expressed as a ratio of the expected outcome measured in standard deviations. PISA: Programme for International Student Assessment; GNI: gross national income.

Sources: OECD calculations based on Gallup Organization (2013), *Gallup World Monitor* (database); UNDP (2015), *International Human Development Indicators* (database), *http://hdr.undp.org/en/data*; UIS (2015), *UIS Data Centre* (database), *http://data.uis.unesco.org/*; World Bank (2015), *World Development Indicators* (database), Washington, DC, *http://data.worldbank.org*; PISA 2009 data.

StatLink http://dx.doi.org/10.1787/888933329967

Box 1.1. What do multi-dimensional country reviews involve?

The OECD multi-dimensional country reviews are carried out in three phases, which constitute the basis for an exchange with policy makers: The first phase, or *initial assessment*, provides a general diagnosis of the country's development model and identifies its main constraints. The second phase, *in-depth analysis and recommendations*, tackles the most binding constraints identified and examines them in greater depth. Taking into account linkages, trade-offs and synergies across policies, the in-depth analysis provides a series of policy recommendations to overcome these structural barriers. Finally, the third phase of *strategy building and implementation* incorporates recommendations into a coherent development strategy, proposing an appropriate sequencing for the implementation of policies.

Building stability through better international integration, infrastructure and education

The initial assessment found that Uruguay's binding constraints were in the areas of international integration, infrastructure development and education. "Binding constraints" are defined as those with the largest effect on the development outcomes under analysis. As a first step, the *Better Life* framework,[1] an overall assessment of Uruguay's living standards, allowed for a preliminary appraisal of Uruguay's main constraints. The initial assessment also focused on three dimensions: the evolution of Uruguay's structural trends and productivity, the patterns of inequality (in income, access to public goods and employment) and the sustainability of the current macroeconomic and fiscal framework. All things considered, three policy areas for future action were identified:

1. International integration, through trade and investment. Uruguay's reliance on exporting goods and services, its involvement in various intraregional platforms and its willingness to develop new economic sectors and become a regional hub should put the integration agenda at the forefront of public policy.
2. Infrastructure development, especially in the transport sector. Uruguay's infrastructure gap could be putting an important brake on economic growth. Its efforts to strengthen its transport network reflect its ambition to become a logistics focal point in the region. Despite a high coverage of road and railroad networks, quality improvements and a consolidated long-term national plan for transport will be critical for fulfilling the country's productive and integration strategy.
3. Education, especially secondary and post-secondary education. A better-performing and more equitable education system can provide more opportunities to broader segments of the population, strengthening the country's human capital and skills, reducing pervasive inequalities and favouring social mobility.

Low diversification, a rigid regulatory framework and the sub-optimal use of trade arrangements hinder Uruguay's integration in global markets

Uruguay is an open, liberalised economy with an investor-friendly regime and is increasingly participating in international trade. The country's recent record of solid economic growth has been partially driven by its dynamic external sector. Doubling in less than a decade, Uruguay's export sector remains an important pillar of the economy, with about one third of GDP embodied in exports, while the same share of jobs depend on external demand (Ferreira and Vaillant, 2014). Nonetheless, the benefits from Uruguay's trade and investment profile are still relatively limited compared to other economies. This suggests that there is considerable scope for stronger integration and greater competitiveness in new sectors. For this, as stressed in the initial assessment, Uruguay's integration model needs to be reinforced. Until recently, regional and plurilateral agreements have allowed the country to strengthen links with its neighbours. Today, however, new challenges demand a more ambitious integration strategy. Global value chains (GVCs) have reconfigured the patterns of international trade – harnessing new opportunities to participate in them has become a priority. In addition, the regional context, with a more uncertain macroeconomic environment means it is critical for Uruguay to forge trade ties with commercially relevant partners outside Mercosur. Uruguay is therefore increasingly inserting itself beyond the region through its services sector, including transportation, tourism and business services, but existing barriers to international integration in services could undermine this process (Figure 1.2).

Figure 1.2. **FDI restrictions by sector in Uruguay remain high in some sectors, 2013**

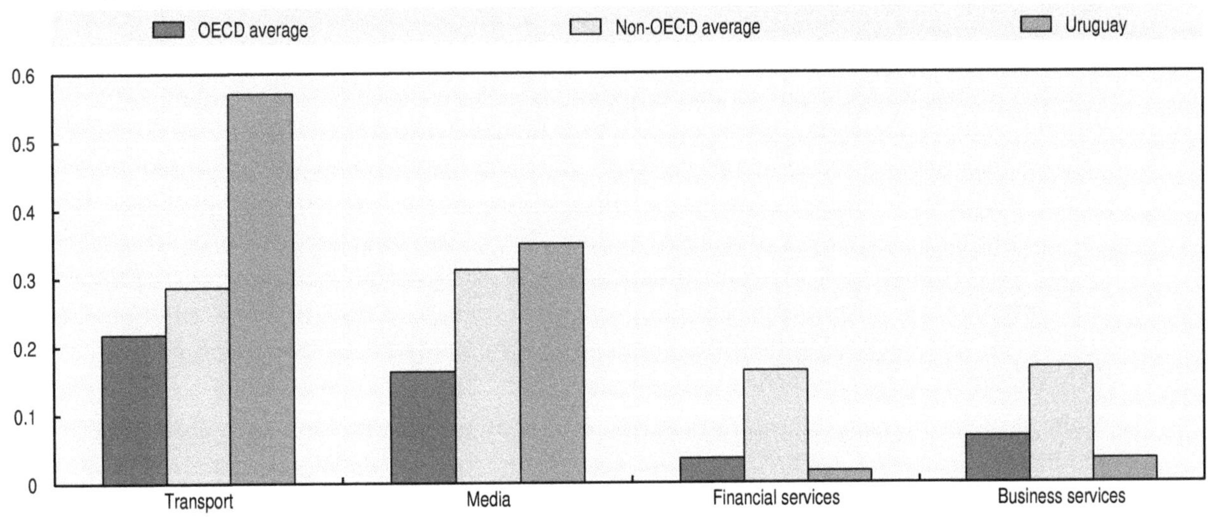

Note: OECD 2013 FDI Regulatory Restrictiveness Index: closed = 1, open = 0.

Source: Authors' elaboration based on OECD (2015), *FDI Regulatory Restrictiveness Index*, *www.oecd.org/investment/fdiindex.htm*.

StatLink http://dx.doi.org/10.1787/888933329971

Low diversification, a rigid regulatory framework and the sub-optimal use of trade arrangements could hinder Uruguay's integration in global markets. Uruguay's capacity to diversify its trade towards new markets and sectors remains an important challenge. The recent development of a "global services" sector, less sensitive to distance and economic downturns, is a move in the right direction. However, Uruguay's regulatory profile for domestic services remains relatively restrictive, undermining other sectors of the economy and hampering its connectivity to world markets. Besides regulation in the services sector, Uruguay has yet to tackle modern, behind-the-border disciplines (or rules) essential for sustaining the development of GVCs and consolidating the institutional framework for a truly "deep integration" agenda. Finally, the regional context, in particular Uruguay's commitments in Mercosur, highlights the need for better use of current international trade and investment agreements.

Recommendations: towards more strategic international integration, investment and services

- **Deepen engagement in trade and investment.** Uruguay needs to collaborate closely with its Mercosur partners to strengthen integration. It will need to deepen and upgrade disciplines, notably advancing services negotiations and including comprehensive disciplines on competition, state-owned enterprises, intellectual property rights and regulatory coherence. To ensure that current agreements are compatible with its overall strategy for further integration, Uruguay should ensure that these agreements are conducive to the development of regional and global value chains. This involves the revision and accumulation of rules of origin and other flexibilities; and adapting regional trade agreements to include disciplines that cover issues such as intermediates trade, free flow of capital, global demand for services across chains, international movement of skills, and protecting the knowledge and technology that accompany production. These measures, aimed at increasing coherence in regulatory regimes across countries, will be critical to Uruguay's GVC participation. For this purpose, Uruguay could establish a committee in Mercosur to identify and review good practices emerging from new disciplines in 21st century agreements, with a view to assess their relevance and to tailor them to the Mercosur context.
- **Look to new markets, in particular Asia.** Uruguay should take advantage of any flexibilities within Mercosur to diversify its markets and forge new agreements with commercially important partners, including fast-growing economies in emerging regions (e.g. Asia). It should align its trade partnerships with existing and emerging global production networks (including with countries home to the headquarters of multinational enterprises) (OECD/CAF/ECLAC, 2015). The first step is to develop a market diversification strategy for those GVCs and other products for which Uruguay has comparative advantages. Pursuing opportunities to plug into new emerging initiatives, and deepening ties with members of the Trans-Pacific Partnership, could help to further these diversification efforts.
- **Maintain and intensify efforts to participate in bilateral negotiations and plurilateral platforms.** Uruguay should continue to diversify its current dialogue platforms, and ensure the successful conclusion of key negotiations, notably the Mercosur-European Union agreement. At the same time, Uruguay should continue unilateral service reforms, evaluate the potential benefits of plurilateral negotiations, such as the Trade in Services Agreement (TiSA) and, depending on the assessment, re-consider its participation. The country should also consider full membership of the Pacific Alliance. To increase its participation in these bodies, Uruguay's task is two-fold: 1) identify prevalent regulatory barriers to exports to target markets, to develop a clear request list for these negotiations; and 2) identify ongoing and priority areas of reform, to shape the proposals it can put forward in negotiations.
- **Aim for more comprehensive trade and investment agreements with partners.** To do this, Uruguay could adopt a suitable model agreement to use as a base, containing flexible and cumulative rules of origin; GATS Plus practices with respect to rules governing services; and open accession clauses, substantially covering all trade, competition disciplines and TRIPS Plus provisions. The country should set up a working group to propose elements that should systematically be considered for inclusion in a model Bilateral Investment Treaty (BIT) and Free Trade Agreement (FTA) for Uruguay, drawing

on the most progressive existing agreements (i.e. with Chile and Mexico), as well as international best practices.

- **Consider undertaking unilateral reforms in services sector regulations** to decrease restrictiveness in key sectors and to enhance compatibility with regional partners. The effective harmonisation of regulations would foster greater competitiveness in services sectors where regulatory barriers play a fundamental role. This will require establishing a centralised unit that ensures coherence in national regulations, particularly in services; and to review good practices in regulatory coherence and co-operation, such as those in the Trans-Pacific Partnership and other negotiations. One example is efforts to facilitate the movement of people through the Visa Program between the Pacific Alliance and Mercosur.
- **Adopt a supply-chain approach to trade and investment promotion.** Strengthening export and investment promotion goes beyond targeting specific sectors and products towards investment and trade promotion activities that take into account upstream and downstream activities. For this, Uruguay could develop programmes that promote the competitiveness of services that are embedded or embodied in the country's comparative advantages. This can be accomplished by creating tailored programmes and instruments for services and goods that are complementary to Uruguay's key exports. The current portfolio of Uruguay XXI, the country's investment promotion agency, could be expanded, and new instruments could be tailored to the internationalisation of services. Several OECD examples, discussed in Chapter 2, can offer guidelines. Uruguay should also consider working together with Mercosur or Pacific Alliance members to group export and investment promotion activities. This allows for greater impact and efficiency in asset use.
- **Reinforce programmes to integrate small and medium-sized enterprises (SMEs) into global services activities** and facilitate their access to integration mechanisms, such as free trade zones. Uruguay's free trade zones have contributed to a more diversified export basket, and the value added they have created accounts for around 4% of GDP. To better integrate them with the rest of the economy, Uruguay can reinforce programmes targeting SMEs to integrate them into global services activities and facilitate their access to these integration mechanisms. To achieve this, the government needs to co-ordinate and centralise all existing programmes for SMEs in the service sector.
- **Strengthen the institutional framework and inter-ministerial co-ordination for fostering competitiveness in services.** This can be done through the pursuit of a National Services Strategy, which brings together relevant actors across ministries in order to enhance coherence and effectiveness of adopting public policies relevant to service sector regulation and support. The example of Jordan is illustrative for this purpose.
- **Finally, improving information systems, particularly in the services sectors, is crucial.** Uruguay should put in place efficient services data collection mechanisms meeting MSITS (Manual on Statistics of International Trade in Services) 2010 norms, and should centralise services data collection institutions. At the same time, the National Statistics Office or Central Bank should establish a census of the channels through which services exports take place (cross-border, e-commerce, movement of persons, establishment, etc.). Uruguay could exchange practices and technical assistance with countries that have collected services data at the firm level (e.g. Colombia and New Zealand).

Transport infrastructure and planning are holding back Uruguay's growth

The initial assessment concluded that Uruguay has a significant infrastructure gap in the transport sector. Strong economic growth over the last decade has placed greater stress on the country's transport infrastructure, and today Uruguay's transport endowments are insufficient to meet the needs of the economy. Uruguay faces challenges in a number of areas of transport infrastructure, from planning and management to delivery and operation. Uruguay lacks a National Transport Plan, as well as a clear strategy for how its infrastructure sector should be organised. This makes project programming and prioritisation difficult. The initial assessment also stressed Uruguay's need to improve the co-ordination of the infrastructure sector (OECD, 2014a). The lack of co-ordination among the different bodies involved in the infrastructure cycle is significant, and challenges in the distribution of responsibilities are evident. In addition, current regulations, in particular for executing public-private partnerships (PPPs), are lacking.

While the quality of ports, electricity supply and telecommunications is good, the quality and coverage of Uruguay's roads are not. In 2012, up to 55% of roads were considered to be in "mediocre or bad" condition (Figure 1.3). As almost 97% of commercial cargo is transported by road in Uruguay, poor conditions can have a significant impact on economic activity. Moreover, Uruguay's performance on logistics is only 30% that of Germany, and is largely held back by the quality of its infrastructure and customs procedures, hindering its capacity to become a logistics hub.

Figure 1.3. **Road condition in Uruguay by management type**

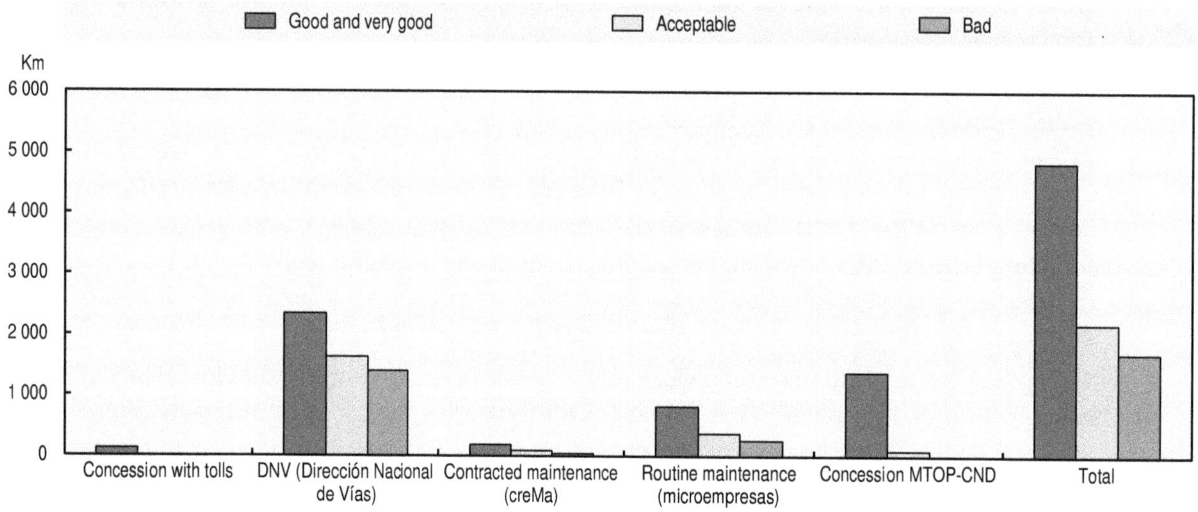

Source: CAF (2010), Análisis del sector transporte. Serie informes sectoriales. Infraestructura. Serie Informes sectoriales. Infraestructura. *http://publicaciones.caf.com/media/1131/IS_URUGUAY.pdf.*

StatLink *http://dx.doi.org/10.1787/888933329986*

Recommendations: Overcoming the barriers to transport infrastructure development

- **Create a National Transport Plan.** This could be achieved by upgrading the existing transport, infrastructure and logistic plan developed by the Ministry of Transport and Public Works to reflect best practice in national transport planning. Such a plan should be adopted at the highest political level and provide a clear roadmap to the relevant line ministry.

- **To improve infrastructure delivery, Uruguay needs to adopt a holistic view on how its infrastructure sector should be planned and organised.** Although the country appears to be focusing on PPPs to close the gap, only after proper foundations have been secured should private participation be considered. At present, given the lack of a national transport plan, PPPs should only be considered where there is a critical and clear present need. Moreover, infrastructure projects developed as PPPs need to be aligned with the National Transport Plan. Also, the prioritisation and procurement decisions should be carried out by separate entities to avoid potential bias on the project evaluation process. Uruguay should enforce and strengthen the current regulations, avoiding off balance sheet PPP execution. Clearer regulations should be set in place for PPPs' contract renegotiation.
- **Re-organise the governance of infrastructure.** To improve transport performance, Uruguay needs to corporatise its infrastructure management (especially the road sector). This involves the creation of an institution responsible for publicly reporting performance indicators on the condition and financial viability of infrastructure projects. Where such governance already exists (e.g. in the rail sector), performance contracts should be established between the Ministry of Transport and Public Works and the infrastructure managers.
- **Design a proper regulatory framework for all actors involved in the infrastructure sector.** This will initially require a regulator attached to the government. Once the economic regulator develops sufficient capacity, Uruguay may wish to consider detaching the institution to create an independent economic regulator. This may be desirable for ensuring fair access to infrastructure and allowing a more transparent approach to financing. This approach should cover rail and roads once the full corporatisation of road infrastructure management is completed. Given Uruguay's relatively small pipeline of infrastructure projects, one economic regulator could cover several sectors.
- **Avoid relying on public private partnerships (PPPs) for infrastructure.** Although the country appears to be focusing on PPPs to close the infrastructure gap, private participation should only be considered once proper foundations have been secured. At present, given the lack of a national transport plan, PPPs should only be considered where there is a critical, clear and urgent need. Future infrastructure projects delivered as PPPs need to be aligned with the National Transport Plan.
- **Ensure that decisions to execute a project and decisions on the procurement method are made by separate entities.** It is recommended that Uruguay revise the roles of the Ministry of Economy and Finance (MEF) and the Office for Planning and Budget (OPP) in this process and assign responsibility according to the nature of their work and the investment framework currently in place.
- **Ensure PPP projects are part of both the national and sub-national budgets.** PPP expenditure should systematically be included in the national budget in the same way as traditional expenditure, so as to avoid implicit bias in procurement decisions. Where PPPs are implemented by a state-owned enterprise and the budgetary framework does not require a detailed budget line for its expenditure, the Central Budget Authority or responsible entity should put in place a reporting and evaluation mechanism, independent of the PPP unit. An independent body should also be in charge of PPP management.
- **Establish clear regulations for PPP contract renegotiation.** Uruguay should adopt mandatory guidance, involving detailed descriptions, stating when renegotiations of PPP contracts are allowed and to what extent. Responsibility for the supervision/administration of renegotiations should be devolved to a body seen to be independent

(e.g. the competition authority, or supreme audit institution). The substance and economic impact of renegotiations should be made publicly available. Considering the complexity of PPPs, an independent competition/arbitrage committee with specialised staff should be created to resolve any disputes. Alternatively, the competition authority may be tasked with this function.

Insufficient human capital and skills are key obstacles to growth and social inclusion

Inequalities in access to and the poor quality of education, particularly secondary schooling, remain a critical challenge for Uruguay. Uruguay's basic education provision is good: adult literacy is almost universal and access to pre-primary and primary education is among the highest in Latin America. The educational path, however, tends to get narrower the further students progress through the education system. Attainment and learning outcomes at more advanced levels of education are worrying. As illustrated by the Programme for International Student Assessment (PISA) 2012 results, performance is low (Figure 1.4). Uruguay's secondary school graduation rate has changed little in the last two decades, and dropout and repetition rates are among the highest in Latin America. A consensus has emerged on the need to improve the provision of Uruguay's secondary schooling.

Figure 1.4. **Repetition rate in lower secondary education, selected PISA economies, 2012**

Results based on students' own responses

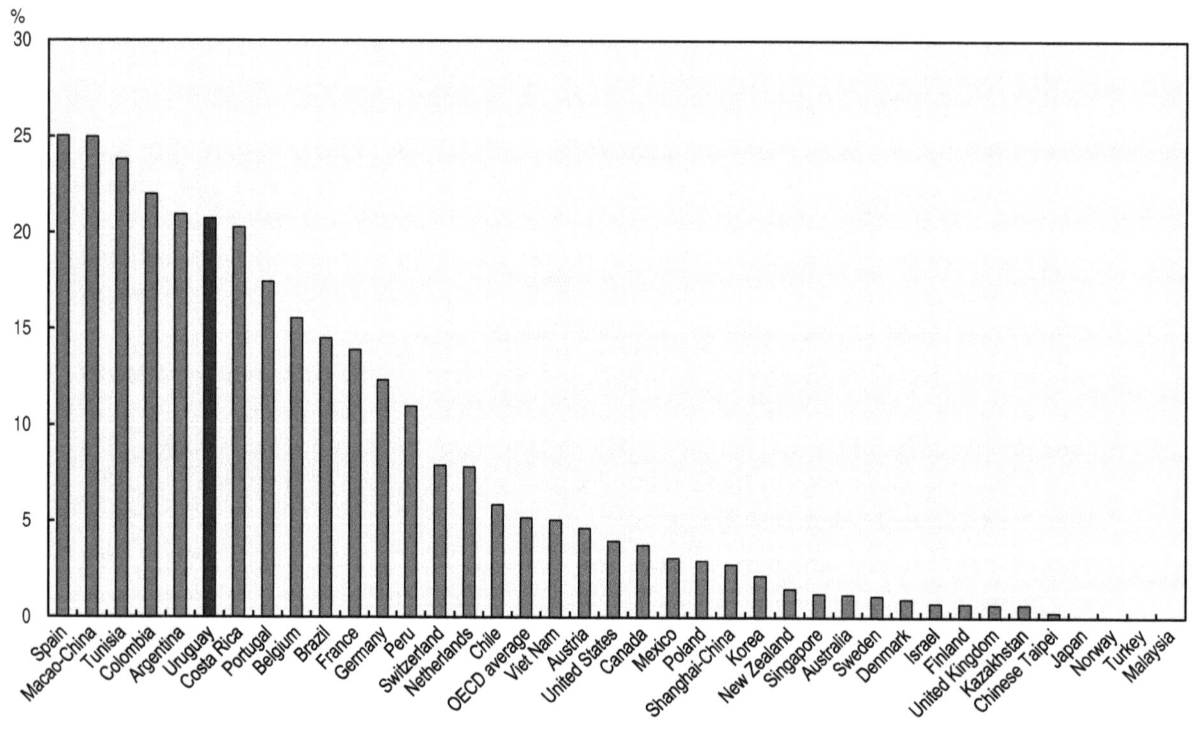

Note: Percentage of students reporting that they have repeated a grade once in lower secondary school.

Source: OECD calculations based on PISA 2012 database, Table IV.2.18, *http://pisa2012.acer.edu.au/*.

StatLink http://dx.doi.org/10.1787/888933329995

Today, the insufficient provision of human capital and skills is considered one of Uruguay's main obstacles to growth and social inclusion. As Uruguayan exports become more skills-intensive, and the situation of young people not in education, employment or training more critical, the challenge of improving Uruguay's education and skills systems is more urgent (OECD/CAF/ECLAC, 2014). Various learning outcomes and labour-market indicators stress that improving the quality and relevance of Uruguay's education system is a priority. Nearly 30% of Uruguayan firms identify an inadequately educated workforce as a major constraint to their activities, compared to only 15% in OECD countries (Melguizo and Perea, 2016). Uruguay's public expenditure on education is low by OECD standards, and disparities in attainment and performance by socio-economic background are significant. In 2010, only 25% of 15-17 year olds in the lowest-income quintile completed lower secondary education, compared to 85% in the highest quintile (OECD, 2014a). Key weaknesses in several areas of education policy explain the current situation: the variability of student assessment frameworks, the inequality in learning conditions, the lack of proper student support schemes and the low status of the teaching profession.

Public higher education in Uruguay faces similar equity challenges as the rest of the public education system. Access rates are in stark contrast with success rates, especially for disadvantaged students. Ways are needed to create a more supportive academic environment which meets students' learning needs and is flexible enough to allow for adjustments in their academic career. Learning opportunities could be better tailored to meet with the employment needs and Uruguay's international integration objectives.

Recommendations: Strengthening education and skills

- **Improve methods for identifying students in need of support.** To give every student in the country a fair chance not only of enrolling, but also of graduating, effective support mechanisms are needed. Education authorities need to improve classroom assessments by specifying assessment procedures and creating objective criteria to guide teacher-led assessments. The choice of criteria should allow students' success or failure to be tracked over time, knowledge and skills gaps to be identified, and the information on success and failure to be communicated clearly to parents and students. The use of assessment results for formative purposes regarding the students should also be encouraged. OECD experience highlights that students' performance not only indicates individual success or failure, but can also indicate problems and necessary adjustments for the teaching and the learning environment.
- **Combine classroom assessments with external standardised examinations for a fuller picture of students' needs.** The National Learning Assessment administered at the primary level is a good, home-grown example of the information potential of standardised testing built on a rich, externally maintained pool of multiple-choice and open-ended questions, complemented by questionnaires on students' socio-economic context. Teachers should be encouraged to use the external test for developing their classroom assessments.
- **Improve the conditions for teaching.** The importance of teachers in the education process cannot be overstated. It is essential to improve the conditions of the teaching profession by giving teachers in secondary schooling more time and stability with a group of students, primarily by curbing the detrimental practice of teaching multiple shifts in different schools. In this direction, long-term education reforms should develop a realistic plan for scaling-up the full-time school model nationwide.
- **Create incentives for teaching.** Current teaching reforms call for a package of measures tailored to the expectations and needs of young teachers without a teaching license, providing them with incentives to obtain one and to stay in the profession. The incentives

could be both financial (e.g. a salary premium upon licensing) and other, such as work-time flexibility, a greater degree of autonomy in developing the curriculum, and greater job security. In higher education, promoting student mobility by initiating a revision of the *carrera* system in favour of a modular approach to study content and awarding credits is recommended to increase responsiveness to student needs. Overall, a more comprehensive assessment of the profession is needed.

- **Increase the autonomy of schools.** Standardised international tests suggest that schools with greater autonomy and leadership to adjust curricula and teaching perform better (OECD, 2014b). Experiences from OECD countries also confirm that a certain degree of autonomy to adjust the organisation of instruction time, class composition and teaching can lead to more personalised and effective learning environments which benefit disadvantaged students (OECD, 2012). Strong school leadership can also lead to significant school improvements. Encouraging peer learning among secondary schools on experiences with greater teaching and curricular autonomy could help to set guidelines for balancing student-centred instruction with aligned curricular and assessment practices.
- **Facilitate mobility in higher education.** International practice points towards a growing awareness of the benefits of more flexible student pathways and student mobility within and between tertiary institutions. Universities in several OECD countries offer a modular approach in which students can accumulate transferable academic credits for each successfully attended course. Allowing for a certain degree of mobility within tertiary institutions in Uruguay will allow students to change or fine-tune their initial study choices and concentrate on subjects of real interest. Promoting student mobility implies a need to revise the *carrera* system in favour of a modular approach to study content and award credits.
- **Strengthen support for students in higher education, especially for students' own initiatives to improve learning.** Universities should devote more attention to self-help groups by fostering a stronger connection and better co-ordination between them and the "official" academic world at the National University (UdelaR). Uruguay could recognise these groups as academic instruments and institutionalise them by providing them with content and instructions sanctioned directly by the faculty, and requesting that the faculty take ownership and responsibility for their respective self-help groups.
- **Improve the coherence between secondary and tertiary education levels.** The divide between upper secondary and tertiary levels of education means misalignments between their curricula, diverging expectations of schools and universities regarding the preparedness of secondary school graduates and a lack of information in schools about university courses and professional career paths. Transitioning support schemes to reduce the information gap between both levels, and to introduce induction and remedial courses for first year students are recommended.
- **Do more to match higher education provision with employers' needs.** Uruguay's new Technical University (UTEC) is a key initiative for addressing some of the higher education issues in Uruguay. Ensuring UTEC fulfils its potential will require it to become, from its inception, suitable and attractive for private sector participation (OECD, 2014a; Melguizo and Perea, 2015). UTEC must offer relevant and up-to-date curricula, and promote innovation in the study process, while avoiding emulating the National University (UdelaR) and its research outlet. This can be done by preserving a more technical, labour market-oriented character and formalising arrangements for inter-institutional teacher and student transfers between UTEC and UdelaR.

The synergies between these three policy areas, integration, transport and education and skills, should be exploited. Uruguay's current constraints to development require specific, closely inter-related policy responses for improvements in the areas of education and infrastructure to best respond to integration challenges. Regarding education, the composition and quality of the country's human capital will be determinant of its capacity to integrate internationally and develop niches in the service sector. As a key driver of the country's global value chain participation in services, an adequately trained population, with the necessary language and communication skills, cultural affinity and internationally recognised qualifications will be critical for Uruguay. This requires a whole-of-government framework to strengthen education systems, activate the skills supply and develop relevant skills for the labour market. The emphasis on talent development by the *Global Services for Exports Programme* is a good example. In a similar manner, infrastructure development will be critical for Uruguay's trade competitiveness and potential for integration. Uruguay has invested in industrial parks, put in place important logistics infrastructure projects and consolidated a relatively high-quality technological infrastructure. However, transport challenges are limiting its successful insertion into global value chains. Reducing these gaps in education and infrastructure will be an essential step towards the consolidation of a real integration strategy.

Note

1. See *www.oecd.org/statistics/better-life-initiative.htm.*

References

Ferreira, N. and M. Vaillant (2014), "Uruguay's trade policy and specialisation over two decades: A gradual and permanent path to trade openness," background paper, mimeo.

Gallup Organization (2013), *Gallup World Monitor* (database).

Melguizo, A. and J.R. Perea (2016), "Mind the skills gap! Regional and industry patterns in emerging economies", *OECD Development Centre Working Paper*, No. 329, OECD Publishing, Paris.

OECD (2015), *FDI Regulatory Restrictiveness Index*, *www.oecd.org/investment/fdiindex.htm.*

OECD (2014a), *Multi-dimensional Review of Uruguay: Volume 1. Initial Assessment*, OECD Development Pathways, OECD Publishing, *http://dx.doi.org/10.1787/9789264209459-en.*

OECD (2014b), *PISA 2012 Results: What Makes Schools Successful? (Volume IV): Resources, Policies and Practices*, PISA, OECD Publishing, Paris, *http://dx.doi.org/10.1787/9789264201156-en.*

OECD (2013), *PISA 2012 Results: What Makes Schools Successful? Resources, Policies and Practices (Volume IV)*, PISA, OECD Publishing, *http://dx.doi.org/10.1787/9789264201156-en.*

OECD (2012), *Better Skills, Better Jobs, Better Lives: A Strategic Approach to Skills Policies*, OECD Publishing, Paris, *http://dx.doi.org/10.1787/9789264177338-en.*

OECD/CAF/ ECLAC (2015), *Latin American Economic Outlook 2016: Towards a New Partnership with China*, OECD Publishing, Paris, *http://dx.doi.org/10.1787/9789264246218-en.*

OECD/CAF/ECLAC (2014), *Latin American Economic Outlook 2015: Education, Skills and Innovation for Development*, OECD Publishing, Paris, *http://dx.doi.org/10.1787/leo-2015-en.*

UIS (2015), *UIS Data Centre* (database), UNESCO Institute for Statistics, *http://data.uis.unesco.org/.*

UNDP (2015), *International Human Development Indicators*, (database), United Nations Development Programme, *http://hdr.undp.org/en/data.*

WEF (2014), *World Competitiveness Report 2014-2015*, World Economic Forum, Geneva.

World Bank (2015), *World Development Indicators* (database), Washington, DC, *http://data.worldbank.org.*

Multi-dimensional Review of Uruguay
Volume 2. In-depth Analysis and Recommendations

Chapter 2

International integration, investment and services in Uruguay

Uruguay has consistently pursued an investor-friendly regime, making remarkable progress in attracting FDI and achieving sustained productivity growth. The uncertainty in regional markets, however, and the changing nature of global demand pose new challenges for its international integration strategy. This chapter outlines steps that Uruguay could take to harness new opportunities in global value chains (GVCs) and to diversify to markets with fast-growing economies, particularly Asia. Uruguay should continue to pursue efforts to position itself as an exporter of business services, for reduced sensitivity to distance to final markets and economic downturns. Its regulatory profile in domestic backbone services, however, remains relatively restrictive, hampering competitiveness and the ability to capture segments of GVCs. In addition, Uruguay could make better use of international trade and investment agreements by forging modern, behind-the-border disciplines. In this regard, the chapter provides some guidance on how to develop GVC-friendly Regional Trade Agreements. Given the widening remit of this "deep integration" agenda, institutional co-ordination could be improved to maximise the effectiveness of its policy efforts.

The statistical data for Israel are supplied by and under the responsibility of the relevant Israeli authorities. The use of such data by the OECD is without prejudice to the status of the Golan Heights, East Jerusalem and Israeli settlements in the West Bank under the terms of international law.

Introduction

Uruguay has shown remarkable progress in attaining greater trade and financial integration and increasing its participation in new sectors. Its strong economic performance over the past decade (5.2% growth between 2006 and 2014) attests to a sound macroeconomic framework and a favourable external environment, helping to make the Uruguayan economy one of the most dynamic in the region. However, within a changing external environment, and confronted with several structural constraints to integration, Uruguay will be challenged to sustain its recent performance.

This chapter argues that as a small economy, Uruguay needs to increase its global integration in order to sustain growth and poverty alleviation. Uruguay is already an open, liberalised economy, but while its participation in global value chains has been increasing and has coincided with a period of strong national growth, the overall benefits of this participation are still relatively limited compared with other countries and regions. This suggests that there is considerable scope for stronger integration, to diversify its trade partners and maximise the competitiveness of its service sectors. This chapter takes stock of Uruguay's services trade performance and proposes an action plan for enhancing regional and international integration. It begins with an overview of Uruguay's trends in and strategies for integration, before taking a closer look at Uruguay's services trade. The third section explores the regulatory and administrative barriers to trade in services, with a particular focus on those barriers to investment which may be hindering market access. The fourth section examines the role of Regional Trade Agreements and Bilateral Investment Treaties as mechanisms for fostering deeper integration across partners, and in the service sectors. The final section discusses strategies for fostering deeper integration and enhancing services exports.

Uruguay's pool of trade and investment partners is growing, with a higher participation of Asian and some Latin American economies in particular (Figure 2.1). Mercosur remains the main trade destination for Uruguayan goods, accounting for an average share of around 30%.[1] However, Asia is gaining ground (12.4% for the period 2010-12). While Uruguay's trade in services is opening new avenues for diversification, trends in the composition of merchandise exports suggest that a certain amount of commodity-dependence still persists in the Uruguayan economy. The share in exports of primary and natural resource-based products has increased (from 60% in 1997-99 to 75% in 2010-12), with the share in low-technology exports decreasing from 25% to 12% over the same period. This signals the importance of continued diversification efforts (OECD/ECLAC, 2014).

The potential for further integration is demonstrated by the share of value added generated by Uruguay relative to the size of its economy. Domestic value added as a share of gross domestic product (GDP) increased slightly between 1995 and 2011 (from 13% to 16%), indicating a simultaneous increase in both participation and domestic value added. While this share is equal to the regional average, it falls short of the global average (22%) as well as that of transition economies (30%) (UNCTAD, 2013). This suggests that Uruguay benefitted from increased engagement in certain value chains during this period, but that its benefit compared with other countries and regions remains at the lower end of the spectrum, with significant room for deeper integration.

Figure 2.1. **Evolution in Uruguay's export and import partners, 2000-13**

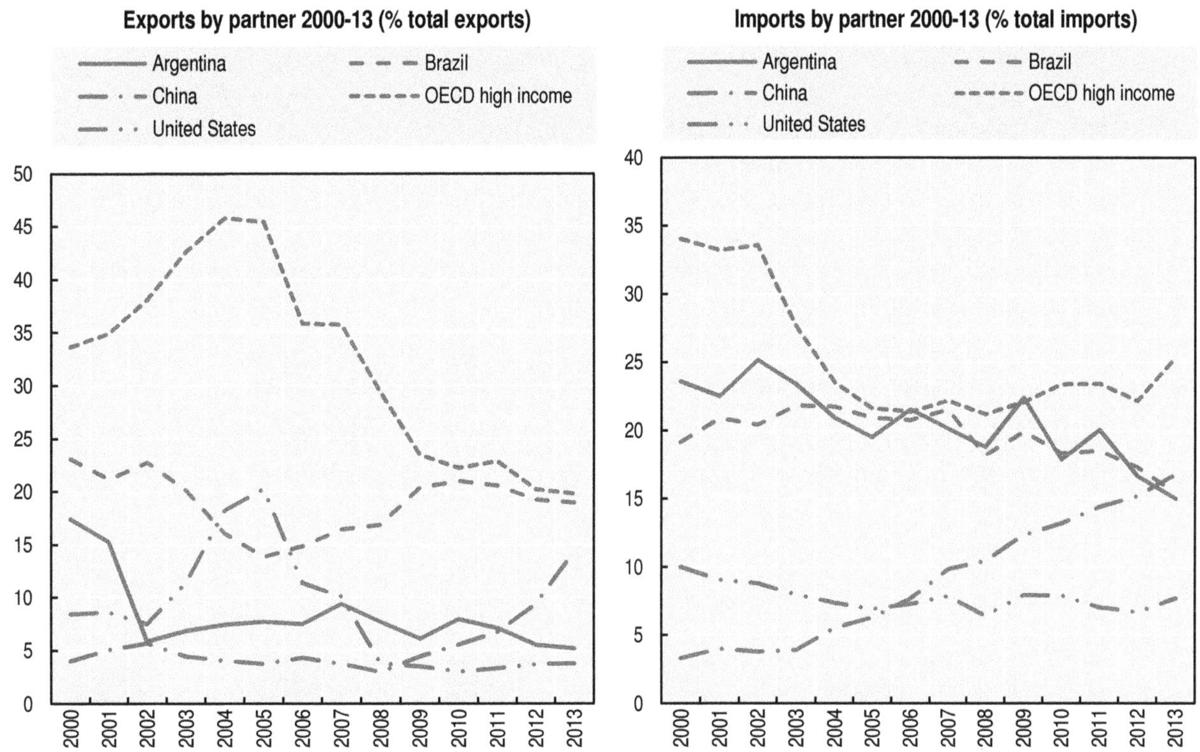

Source: Authors' calculations based on United Nations (2015a), *United Nations Commodity Trade Statistics (Comtrade)* (database), *http://comtrade.un.org/.*

StatLink http://dx.doi.org/10.1787/888933330008

To maintain the inertia in its export-based growth, Uruguay needs to capitalise on this moment by overcoming structural barriers to economic integration. Overall, external conditions are likely to be more restrictive in the medium term, with Latin America slowing down as a whole, and external financial conditions tightening. In addition, the scenario of a potential "growth normalisation" in some emerging economies, including the People's Republic of China, could also hinder Uruguay's growth performance in the years to come. With an average 7.3% growth in 2014, China continues to drive global growth (2.6% in 2014). Uruguay's current integration with China is notable, particularly when compared with its Mercosur partners. Its exports to China increased by 7% in 2014, showing higher resilience than Argentina and Brazil, both of which experienced significant contractions (19% and 12%, respectively) in their exports to China.

Trade in services is the key to resilient growth

International integration has had a decisive impact on the way goods and services are produced, resulting in increasing levels of fragmentation and geographical dispersion. The emergence of global value chains means that production of most goods now involves distinct stages of production, each in a different country. This phenomenon is driven by firms which use advances in communication and regulation to optimise their sourcing strategies through geographic re-organisation and the separation of production stages. This new separation provides countries with the opportunity to integrate into global value chains at a specific stage, enabling participation in new sectors through specialisation in concrete tasks.

This productive fragmentation has also effectively blurred the lines between goods and services trade. Services are increasingly important, acting as the "glue" which binds stages of production together and embeds value along these chains. Recent OECD work on the Trade in Value Added (TiVA) database has demonstrated that service activities such as transport, logistics and warehousing, banking, business and professional services, as well as communications services, contribute more than 30% of total value added in manufacturing industries (OECD, 2014b; Figure 2.2). This suggests that not only are service value chains important avenues for integration, they are also crucial for enhancing competitiveness in goods trade by ensuring that components are transported efficiently and by providing various inputs required throughout the value chain.

Figure 2.2. **Services value added in manufacturing, 2009**

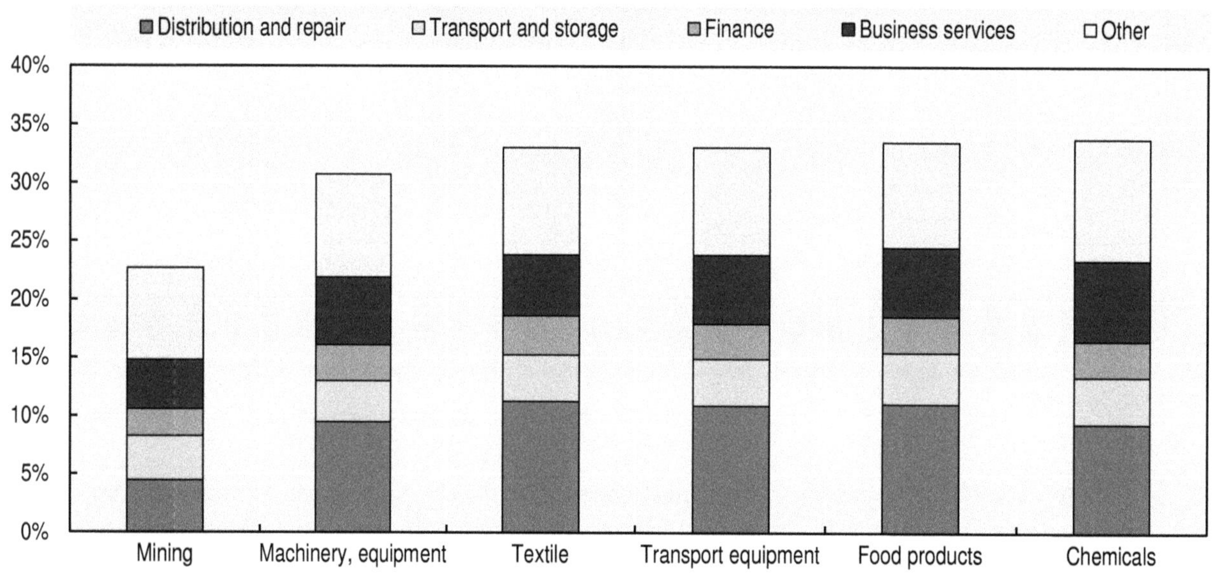

Source: Authors' calculations based on OECD/WTO (2013), *Trade in Value Added (TiVA)* (database), *www.oecd.org/sti/ind/measuringtradeinvalue-addedanoecd-wtojointinitiative.htm.*

StatLink http://dx.doi.org/10.1787/888933330019

The service sector offers considerable potential for Uruguay to diversify its trade patterns, improve labour productivity and increase economic resilience. Services are playing an increasingly important role in Uruguay, particularly within the dynamic segments known as global services (Figure 2.3). Services accounted for 32% of Uruguay's GDP in 2012 (MEF, 2013) and global trade in services has been increasing considerably. According to the most recent available data for 2013 (though see Box 2.1), Uruguay exported over USD 3.1 billion in services, accounting for 26% of its total exports. Over three-quarters of its services exports were in the travel and transport sectors, with non-traditional sectors accounting for nearly one-quarter (Figure 2.4). Non-traditional services sectors such as financial services, wholesale and trade services, telecommunications, as well as the range of business services included in global services which are offshored from company headquarters, experienced some of the fastest rates of export growth. Computer and information services grew by over 25% every year between 2000 and 2013. Other business services followed suit, at over 22% growth every year over this period, compared to the 8% annual growth rate of services exports overall.

Figure 2.3. **The evolution of trade in services**

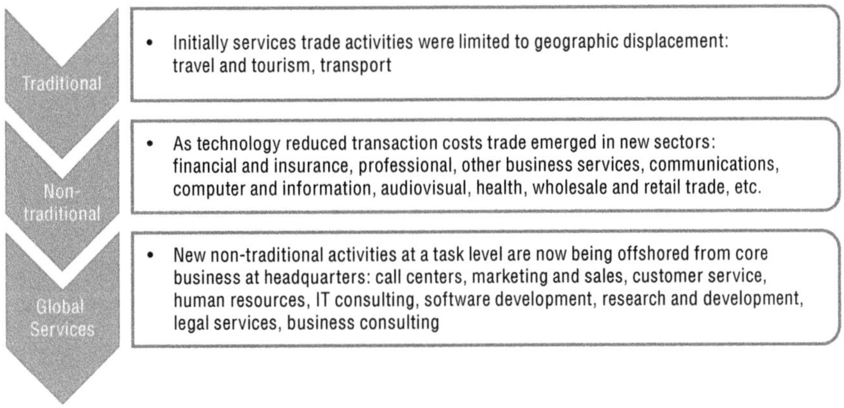

Box 2.1. **The challenges of compiling services trade statistics**

Measuring services trade is critical for understanding its role in the economy and for designing strategic instruments for export promotion, maximising market access and fostering competitiveness. Nevertheless, accurately capturing services trade through the four possible GATS modes of supply continues to be a statistical challenge for many countries. Despite international efforts to standardise reporting – such as the 2010 Manual on Statistics of International Trade in Services (MSITS) – services trade presents difficulties in bringing together comprehensive information on cross-border trade, tourists' consumption abroad, commercial presence of foreign affiliates, and the temporary movement of service providers. The lack of a centralised authority for data collection, and the differences in firm transaction reporting and the information needed by statistical agencies create particular challenges, especially for small providers.

In the case of Uruguay, the Central Bank of Uruguay reports electronic balance of payments information to the International Monetary Fund in the BPM6 format, but these statistics do not capture the significant services trade activities taking place in the Special Economic Zones, or the Foreign Affiliates Trade statistics providing information about services rendered through commercial presence. Putting in place the appropriate systems for enhancing services trade reporting requires maintaining an accurate register of businesses within the economy, an appropriate legal mandate for confidential data collection, as well as service industry surveys which will capture transactions in line with the norms presented in the 2010 MSITS.

Furthermore, different areas of trade-related statistics can be divided across different ministries of government institutions complicating the compilation and validation processes. For instance, in many countries diverse institutions, such as the National Statistics Office, Central Bank and Customs Agency can be involved in collecting inward foreign affiliate trade statistics (FATS), outward FATS, foreign direct investment, trade in goods, trade in services, and business registries. However, in the case of Ireland, for instance, the government has unified reporting responsibilities to the National Statistics Office to ensure timely and coherent information, particularly in recording the activities of multi-national enterprises within the country's borders. In Uruguay, most statistics on trade in goods and services as well as investment are compiled by the Central Bank (albeit with a significant time lag), and complemented with the Census of the Free Trade Zones. FATS data are not currently available.

Source: Connolly, M. (2012), *UN Manual on Statistics of International Trade in Services 2010.*

Figure 2.4. **Services exports from Uruguay, 2013**

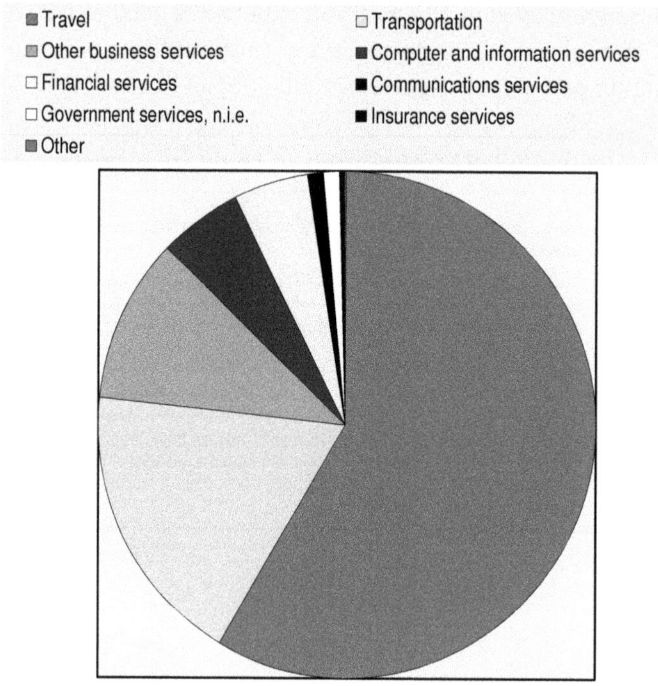

Source: Authors' calculations based on United Nations (2015b), *Service Trade Statistics* (database), *http://unstats.un.org/unsd/servicetrade/default.aspx.*

StatLink http://dx.doi.org/10.1787/888933330026

Export destination markets for these fast-growing services segments are diversified across core markets in the United States, European Union (EU) and within Latin America. Within this category of non-traditional services, 35% were exported to the US, 23% to Latin America (outside of Mercosur), 15% to Mercosur, followed by 12% to the EU (Uruguay XXI, 2013). Global services represent around 75% of export in non-traditional sectors, with an important share being supplied from Uruguay's Free Trade Zones. Services exports from Free Trade Zones totalled USD 602 million in 2010, or around 19% of Uruguay's total services exports that year. By encouraging investment in new sectors, these zones have also been crucial for the diversification of Uruguay's services exports (Lalanne and Vaillant, 2013; Ferreira and Vaillant, 2014). Exports from these zones tend to be more concentrated in financial, professional, business and IT services (accounting for roughly two-thirds of exports in 2010). The export destination of services firms based in Free Trade Zones follow broadly similar trends to the country as a whole. The US and EU are important destinations for financial and professional services, accounting for over 50% of exports from Uruguay in these sectors. Mexico and the US are key destinations for business services exports (Lalanne and Vaillant, 2013; Blyde, 2014). Argentina and other regional partners dominate as key exports partners for other service sectors, including trading and commercial intermediation and logistics services.

The productivity of the service sector has also been improving. Between 1997 and 2012, the average productivity growth rate in the service-related sectors of transport, storage and communications (7.2%) was considerably higher than the economy average (0.9%). This demonstrates the important role that expanding services exports can play in diversifying dependence on external markets, as well as contributing to structural change and development. Furthermore, following the 2008 crisis, the fall in service trade was considerably less than for goods, indicating the relative resilience of such trade. Given Uruguay's small and open economy, bolstering its economic resilience remains a priority.

Uruguay's competitiveness in services trade is influenced by many factors. These include its market size, geography, infrastructure, business climate and labour force, as well as regulatory and institutional factors (Box 2.2). Despite its limited domestic market size, Uruguay is working towards becoming a regional gateway to the Mercosur area. The country benefits from relatively high-quality technological infrastructure in the areas of mobile and fixed telephony penetration, Internet bandwidth and power supply. Furthermore, Uruguay has invested in industrial parks to enhance access to quality infrastructure, and has also put in place important logistics infrastructure, such as cold supply chains. Uruguay's geographic location allows its services to reach markets in the United States, as well as

Box 2.2. **Uruguay is well placed to grow its service participation in global value chains**

Global value chains in services present certain advantages for countries at the periphery of manufacturing hubs to reach distant markets and expand their exports due to the diminished role of distance to manufacturing hubs and the advances in technology and the relative portability of services via ITC (Information, Technologic and Communications) technology. Thus, the growing tradability of new services areas, as demonstrated by the global explosion in the trade of business services, provides growing opportunities for suppliers who are capable of providing certain fundamental base conditions. Five fundamental factors have been identified as key determinants:

Human capital	Numerous studies have shown that the quality and quantity of adequately trained human capital is the key driver of global value chain participation in services. Education levels, language skills, cultural affinity and internationally recognised qualifications are important determinants. Rapid growth in offshore services can sometimes cause upward pressure on wages which can affect competitiveness, particularly in BPO (Business Process Outsourcing) sectors.
Standards and certifications	Putting in place the appropriate regulations to meet data privacy standards is critical. Furthermore, financial and accounting services chains are particularly demanding of data protection, often requiring compliance with standards such as the ISO 27001 Information Security Management System.
National innovation system	National innovation systems play an important role in fostering knowledge and technology advances, particularly in more knowledge-intensive and higher value added sectors such as computer services, software development, and entertainment services, among others. This requires the concerted co-operation of leading firms, government and educational institutions to support and encourage movements toward the technological frontier.
ITC infrastructure and services	Broadband Internet availability, download speed, and cost are important factors in facilitating trade in these sectors, with direct implications for trade costs. Many companies require back up services with multiple providers and international gateways.
Geographic location	Proximity to large markets such as the US and EU, as well as time zone compatibility, can be pertinent in selecting offshore destinations.

Uruguay's performance in these five factors is higher than its regional peers. With high quality communications infrastructure, a strategic geographic location for US and EU markets, growing capacities in R&D in many areas as well as stringent data privacy standards, Uruguay is strongly poised to benefit from offshore opportunities. The recent reforms for setting up a proper National Innovation System (ANII) have shown promise for strengthening the country's capacity in this area. While Uruguay's labour pool is relatively shallow, recent initiatives to adapt qualifications through finishing schools (see below) and create registries of skill levels and certifications among qualified professionals could be a useful step towards developing its talent pool. Furthermore, putting in place mutual recognition agreements with key partners could increase labour flexibility and help address skill shortages in high-demand sectors. The medium-term success in ensuring that skills meet the labour market demands will rely on a more broad-based incorporation of service-specific skill needs into the education and skills national agenda.

Source: Bamber et al. (2014), "Connecting local producers in developing countries to regional and global value chains: Update", *OECD Trade Policy Papers*, No. 160, *http://dx.doi.org/10.1787/5jzb95f18851-en*.

in Europe (due to small differences in time zones). The country's macroeconomic stability and attractive business climate are further strengths for fostering competitiveness and attracting new services outsourcing opportunities.

Uruguay is integrating globally through its services

Uruguayan exports have experienced significant growth from a value-added perspective in recent decades, with export values tripling between 1995 and 2011. Services accounted for 21% of total value added exports in 2011. Uruguay's regional and international insertion can be seen in the increasing share of foreign value added in its exports. In 2011, foreign value added accounted for 28% of total value added, up from 11% in 1995, signalling the growing importance of Uruguay's backward linkages (foreign value added in a country's gross exports). Uruguay's international insertion was 44% in 2011,[2] just above the Latin American average for both goods and services in 2011. Uruguay's global value chain participation takes place predominantly through stronger backward linkages (Figure 2.5). Since 1995, Uruguay's global value chain participation has increased at an average rate of 13% every year, slightly above the regional average, with backward linkages growing faster than forward linkages. This growth in backward linkages tends to be associated with stronger GDP per capita growth and diversification, unlike forward linkages which tend to be associated with the supply of natural resources and commodities at the beginning of a value chain (AfDB/OECD/UNDP, 2014; Klinger and Lederman, 2006).

Figure 2.5. **The share of forward and backward linkages in global value chains, selected economies, 2011**

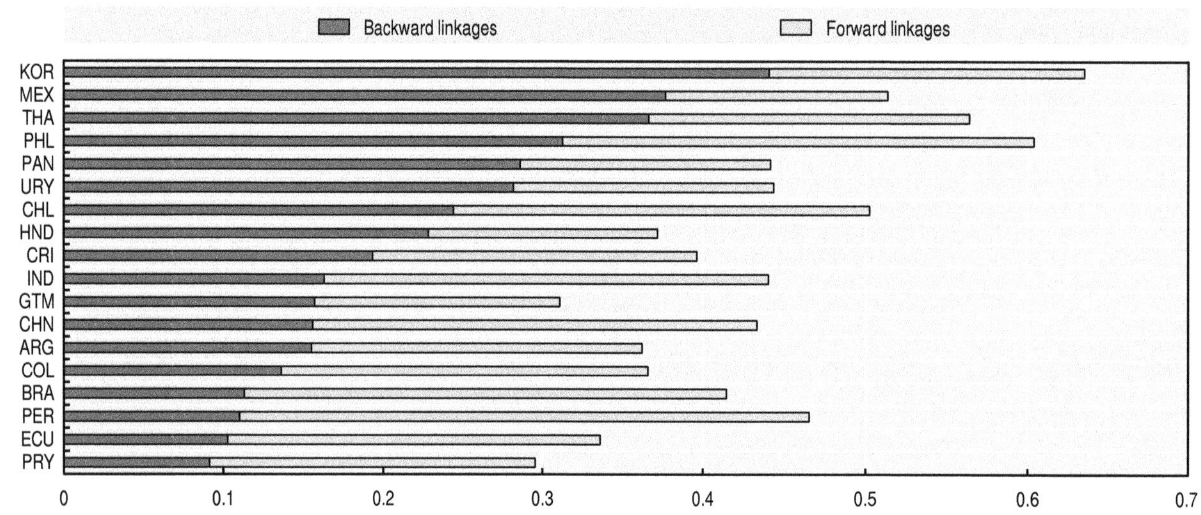

Source: UNCTAD-EORA GVC database (2015), *The Eora Multi-Region Input-Output Database*, *http://worldmrio.com*; UNCTAD (2013), *World Investment Report - Global Value Chains: Investment and Trade for Development*, United Nations Conference on Trade and Development, *http://unctad.org/en/publicationslibrary/wir2013_en.pdf*.

StatLink http://dx.doi.org/10.1787/888933330032

Imported inputs into Uruguayan exports come primarily from Latin America, Europe and North America, although the share coming from China has been increasing in recent years. This pattern underscores the importance of regional integration as a source of inputs, as well as the strategic importance of the trade relationship with Europe. Europe plays an even stronger role in re-exports containing Uruguayan value added than Latin America, with over 40% of re-exports occurring from the European region (Figure 2.6).

Figure 2.6. **Origins of backward linkages and forward linkages**

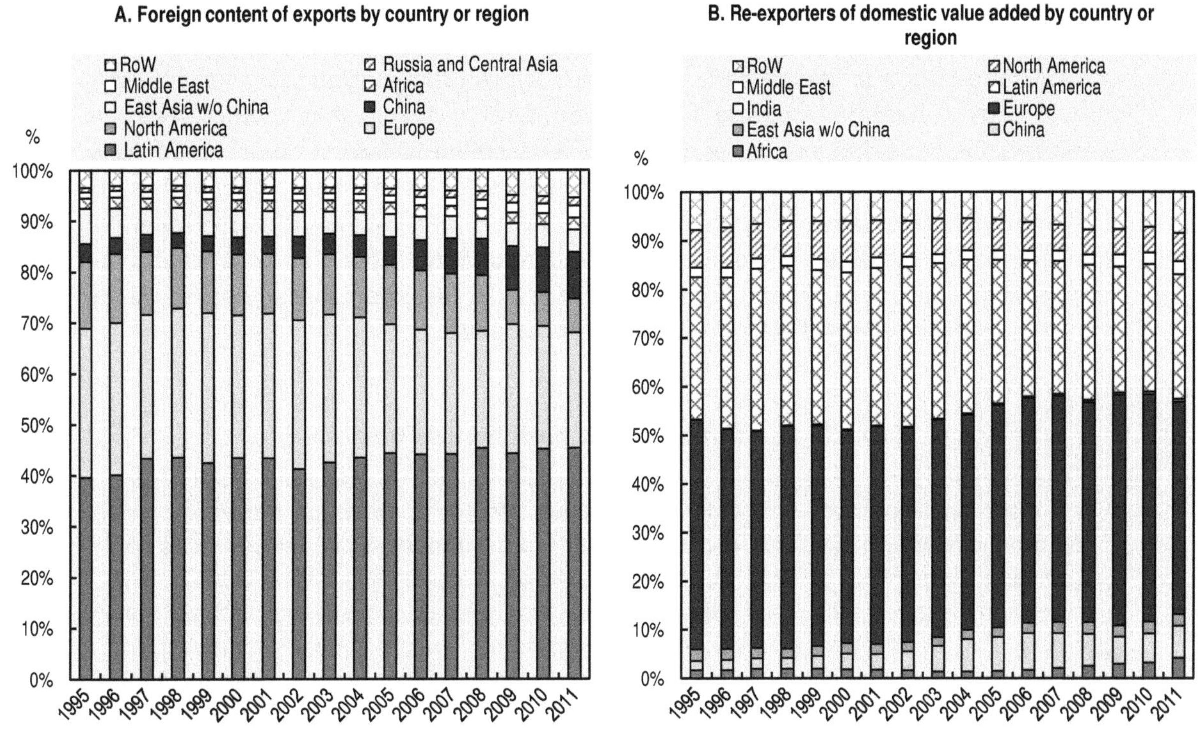

Source: Authors' calculations based on UNCTAD-EORA GVC database (2015), *The Eora Multi-Region Input-Output Database, http://worldmrio.com.*

StatLink http://dx.doi.org/10.1787/888933330043

Uruguay's trade and investment policy framework is taking shape

Uruguay's international economic integration policy rests on two main pillars: the creation of an inter-ministerial body to improve co-ordination (the Inter-Ministerial Commission for Foreign Trade Affairs (CIACEX) and the strengthening of Uruguay's main investment promotion agency, Uruguay XXI. Together these two pillars aim to promote an open regionalism and an active role for public policy in diversifying trade and investment partners, maintaining Uruguay's investment grade in international financial markets and close co-ordination with multilateral organisations. Meanwhile, the reform of the Customs Code has aimed to facilitate and improve the overall system performance by introducing changes to the internal structure, incorporating risk models and professionalising staff.

Created in 2005, CIACEX defines the main strategies in international trade integration, international negotiations, trade and investment promotion.[3] It comprises the ministers of foreign affairs; economy and finance; livestock, agriculture and fisheries; energy and mining; and tourism and transport. Although CIACEX was initially created to improve co-ordination among ministries and government agencies, for some government actors this role has been undermined by its size and structure. Although it works well at the technical level and provides valuable dialogue with the private sector, the general perception is that it lacks the capacity for co-ordination at the political level.

Uruguay's Executive Branch is formed by the Presidency, vice-Presidency and the Council of Ministers, and co-ordinates strategy-setting and the implementation of national policies. The CIACEX services this type of Committee structure, with the participation of several civil servants in simultaneous positions. Formalising the capacity of centre of government

(CoG) bodies like CIACEX is essential for this purpose (OECD, 2013c). The OECD highlights some of the functions that these bodies require, including a) a leadership function, which enables the Commission to speak for the Head of Government and work with ministries who are contributing to foreign trade activities, b) a co-ordination function, which allows the CoG body to harness resources across government to ensure that Cabinet decisions are made coherently and ex-post performance assessment is carried out, c) an advisory function, which enables the Commission to advise the Cabinet on the validity and utility of different initiatives, and d) a communication function, which allows the government to report internally and externally and improve accountability. These functions need to be formalised in order to be effective. To attain its objectives, the Commission needs to clearly define the responsibilities of each Commission participant.

Box 2.3. **The National Competitiveness System**

The bill for creating a National Competitiveness System (SNC), that will be part of the new institutional configuration, aims to strengthen Uruguay's systemic competitiveness and productivity and highlights the increasing need for improving the government's co-ordination capacities. The SNC will be in charge of co-ordinating several institutional bodies and integrating their activities into a long-term, over-arching strategy, with the aim of designing, implementing and evaluating programmes for productive transformation. Together with the Competitiveness Cabinet, the system includes several agencies (ANII, ANDE, Uruguay XXI, INEFOP, INACOOP, CND, INIA, National System to address Climate Change). The absence of an institutional framework for the services sector could be addressed in this new configuration. The bill must also advise on appropriate public policies in conjunction with improvements in the innovative sector including resource utilisation and international economic integration. The SNC will be regulated at the national level, with input from local counterparts. The productivity, innovation and foreign trade cabinets will be combined and streamlined through the establishment of a secretariat.

A commission is being formed to analyse the proposed changes to the bill to best meet the objectives of improved competitiveness and inclusive growth. There are several areas for improvement, the primary focusing on the bodies involved with the development of human capital and capacity building. In this direction, the Ministry of Education and Culture (MEC) and the LATU could be considered to participate in the framework, to involve all stakeholders in the process. Also, as in the case of some OECD countries, more emphasis on innovation and a stronger connection between the science, technology and innovation sectors is needed (OECD/ECLAC, 2014). The goals, policies and strategies proposed by this bill could enhance Uruguay's capacity to maintain productivity, improve product quality and secure competitiveness in the long run.

The second pillar of Uruguay's trade and investment strategy is the consolidation of its investment and trade promotion agency, Uruguay XXI. As the focal investment agency, Uruguay XXI's main objective is to support the internationalisation process of the economy through investment and export promotion, within the framework established by the national government. As a non-governmental organisation subject to private law, the agency has a small, professional structure, including public and private actors. Its board includes representatives of the Ministry of Foreign Affairs and Economy and Finance, as well as various chambers (industry, commerce, etc.).

One of Uruguay XXI's main initiatives to develop the services sectors is the Global Services for Exports Programme (2590/OC-UR), set up in March 2012 with the support of the Inter-American Development Bank. This programme aims to increase exports in global services, facilitate foreign direct investment (FDI) attraction, and stimulate further employment for dynamic services segments. The programme has a strong emphasis on the development of human resources in global services, with the implementation of a new talent portal to match the supply and demand of skilled labour. It is also establishing finishing schools which organise tailored programmes for industry-specific training. Furthermore, the programme will also target the regulatory framework and explore strategies for supporting strategic sectors in services with promising growth potential. The programme has prioritised four main sectors of activity: 1) consulting processing services (call centres, back office, human resource management, financial services, consulting); 2) information technology services (software development, data management); 3) pharmaceutical-industry services; and 4) logistics services.

What are the barriers to greater international integration through trade in services?

Unlike the trade in goods, services trade is significantly influenced by investment restrictions and behind-the-border measures. Accordingly, trade in services is greatly facilitated by regulatory coherence between trading partners. Diverse types of regulations will have differing but often cumulative impacts on foreign provider market access. Such regulations include restrictions on foreign ownership or market entry, limitations on the movement of people, barriers to competition and public ownership, regulatory transparency and administrative requirements as well as adherence to international standards and other discriminatory measures. OECD work on services trade restrictiveness based on sector expert consultations is finding that restrictions on foreign ownership and market entry – such as foreign equity limits and quotas for licenses – are generally regarded as the most restrictive, followed by barriers to competition. However, it is important to bear in mind that sector specificities play an important role in the relative restrictiveness and that other types of restrictions can also be significant. Given the trade-restricting influences of certain regulations, steps should be taken to evaluate their impacts and to ensure that they achieve their objectives while minimising trade restrictive effects and ensuring appropriate competition and safety standards, among other objectives.

According to the World Bank *Services Trade Restrictiveness* database, Uruguay's overall services restrictiveness profile is higher (i.e. more restrictive) than Latin American and EU averages (Table 2.1). Nevertheless, this relatively high score masks significant heterogeneity across sectors. Although Uruguay ranks quite high in regulatory restrictiveness in telecommunications and financial services, in sectors such as professional services and retail trade, its regulatory profile is one of the most open in the world. In the following sections, we examine Uruguay's regulatory profile by sector, with a particular focus on investment-related measures as they often have the most significant market entry impacts.

Foreign direct investment is restricted in certain key sectors

Trade in services and investments are inextricably linked because commercial presence plays an important role in the provision of services in many sectors. In 2013, 53% of global FDI was in the service sector, with a notable 20% increase in services greenfield investments over 2012 (UNCTAD, 2014). FDI into Mercosur amounted to 6% of global FDI flows (UNCTAD, 2014). In the case of Uruguay, inward FDI flows have increased significantly in recent years, reaching USD 2 796 million in 2013: a 4% increase over the previous year. Uruguay ranks second after Chile in terms of its FDI flows as a share of GDP (5%). Uruguay's FDI stock as a share of GDP was 37% in 2013, exceeding the shares in Argentina, Brazil, Colombia and Peru (Uruguay XXI, 2014; Figure 2.7).

Table 2.1. **Uruguay's ranking in its restrictiveness of services sectors**

Sector	Country ranking (out of 104 countries)	Services restrictiveness score (max 100)
Overall	66	28.4
Telecommunications services	96	62.5
Retail trade	1	0
Transportation services	76	41.4
Professional services	1	11
Financial services	92	45.4

Source: Authors' calculations based on World Bank (2015), *Services Trade Restrictiveness* (database), *http://data.worldbank.org/data-catalog/services-trade-restrictions.*

Figure 2.7. **Inward foreign direct investment in Uruguay, 2005-13**

USD million and as a share of GDP

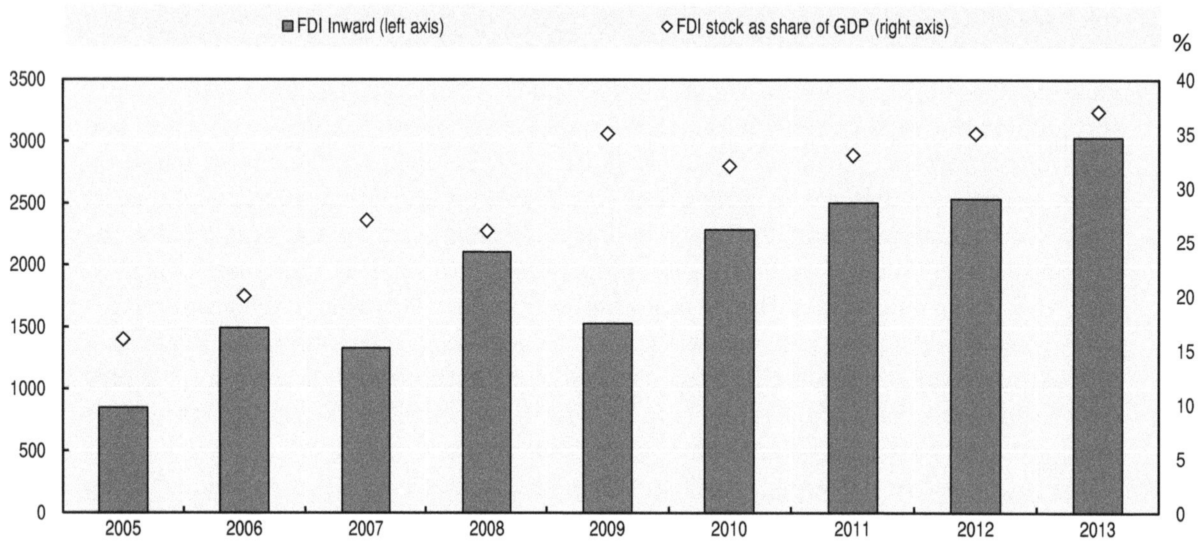

Source: Authors' calculations based on Banco Central del Uruguay (2015), "Inversión Extranjera Directa en Uruguay", *www.uruguayxxi.gub.uy/informacion/wp-content/uploads/sites/9/2015/07/IED-en-Uruguay-Uruguay-XXI-Julio-2015.pdf.*

StatLink http://dx.doi.org/10.1787/888933330057

In 2012, over 65% of Uruguay's FDI came from South America and Europe (Figure 2.8). Argentina, Brazil and Spain were the top three countries of origin and cumulatively accounted for over 50% of Uruguay's inward FDI (Uruguay XXI, 2014; Figure 2.9). The largest share of FDI, nearly 40%, was directed towards the construction sector. Nevertheless, financial, hotel and restaurants, and transport and communication services attracted at least 18% of total FDI. Furthermore, 37% of the inquiries registered by the Investment Agency in 2013 were for service sector investments.

Figure 2.8. **Inward FDI into Uruguay by source region, 2012**

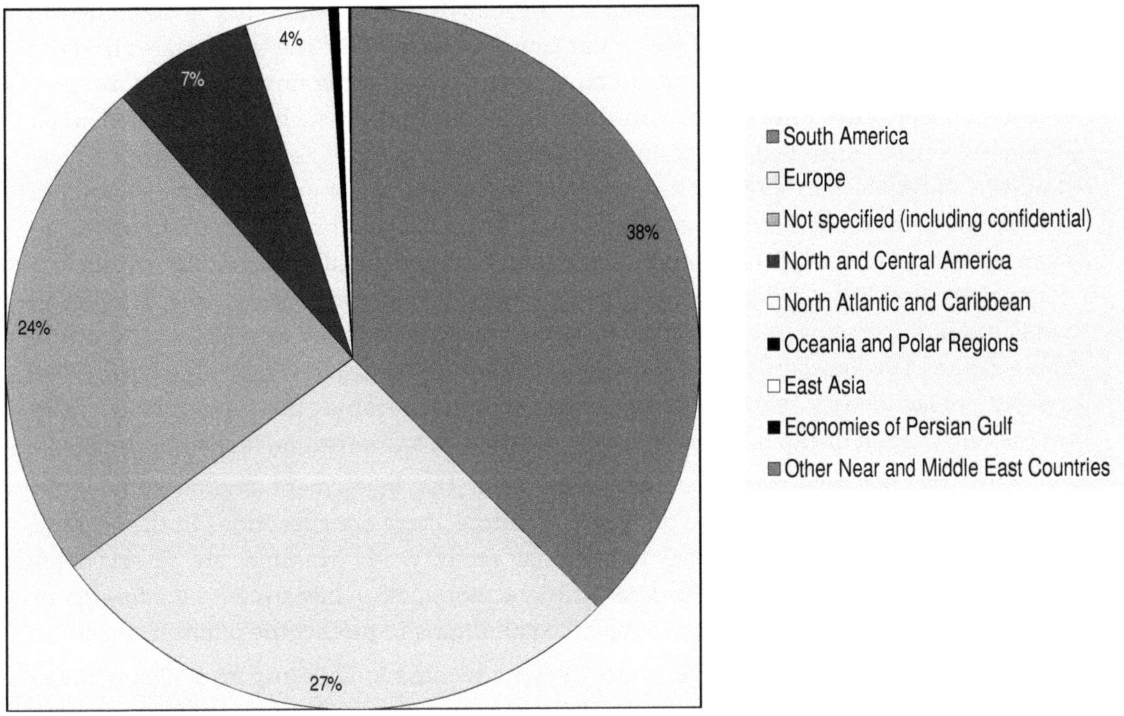

Source: Authors' calculations based on IMF (2015), *Co-ordinated Direct Investment Survey (CDIS)* (database), *http://data.imf.org/?sk=40313609-F037-48C1-84B1-E1F1CE54D6D5&sId=1390030109571.*

StatLink http://dx.doi.org/10.1787/888933330064

Figure 2.9. **Foreign direct investment in Uruguay, 2010-12**

Inward direct investment (% world investment, top 5 economies)

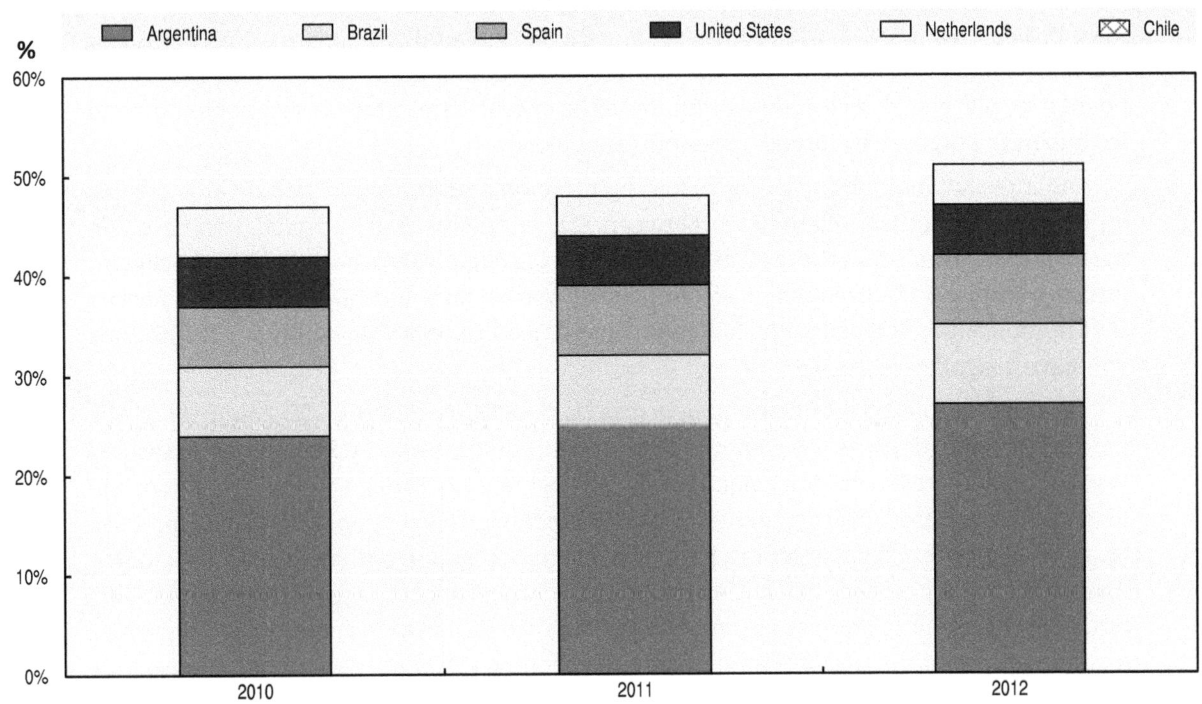

Source: IMF (2015), *Co-ordinated Direct Investment Survey (CDIS)* (database), *http://data.imf.org/?sk=40313609-F037-48C1-84B1-E1F1CE54D6D5&sId=1390030109571.*

StatLink http://dx.doi.org/10.1787/888933330071

In light of the significant impact of investment restrictions on market entry, we begin by examining Uruguay's investment regime. Uruguay's investment policy is embodied in the Protection and Promotion of Investment Law, 7 January 1998.[4] The law declares that the promotion and protection of national and foreign investment is in the nation's interest. It also enshrines the principle of non-discrimination, under which a government must treat enterprises controlled by nationals or residents of another country as favourably as domestic enterprises in similar situations (OECD, 2006). No prior authorisation is required for foreign investment. Foreign companies may act through a branch, a subsidiary or an agency without the need to formally incorporate an independent company within the country. To establish a Uruguayan company, a foreign investor may set up a Uruguayan public limited company or corporation (*sociedad anónima*) and may own up to 100% of the share capital. The *sociedad anónima* is the most commonly established type of company. The investment law also guarantees free movement of capital, meaning there are no restrictions on the repatriation of capital or profits and government authorisation is not required.

Although the investment law prescribes that the investment regime should not discriminate between foreign and domestic investors, there are exceptions in the sectoral legislation. Certain sectors related to national security, for example, are reserved for Uruguayan nationals, while for legal government monopolies, investment by a foreign or domestic investor may be approved subject to conditions to protect the public interest.

According to the OECD FDI Regulatory Restrictiveness Index, Uruguay's FDI regime is generally open, and comparable with the OECD country average (Annex 2.A1). The majority of restrictions in the country are found in the services sectors – transport, media and financial services – as we have seen above. This trend is reflected across most countries in the index, both OECD and non-OECD, where service sectors such as transport, media, real estate, communications and electricity, tend to be the most restrictive. One reason is that these sectors are often deemed strategic or have been subject to state ownership in the past. In contrast, FDI in the manufacturing sector is the most liberalised (Figure 2.10), containing the least number of restrictions, except when a horizontal measure applying across the board is in place, such as screening requirements or restrictions on the acquisition of land for business purposes by foreign investors (see below).

As international production is becoming more organised around global value chains, an examination of the relationship between FDI restrictiveness and global value chain participation reveals that the level of restrictiveness is negatively associated with backward linkages (Figure 2.11). Even when accounting for market size and GDP per capita – factors that influence the degree to which a country will need to seek FDI –statutory restrictions still have a significant impact.

In terms of the type of restriction, across both OECD and non-OECD countries in the Index, FDI restrictions are concentrated in foreign equity limits and screening measures (e.g. national interest tests or economic benefits) (Figure 2.12). Foreign equity restrictions are usually a sector-based measure limiting the extent of foreign ownership allowed in companies or in the aggregate of companies in a particular sector. Screening mechanisms are considered discriminatory when they do not apply to both foreign and national investments. This practice is particularly prevalent in emerging economies as well as in resource-rich countries, including those in the OECD. The rationale for screening FDI is for governments to exclude those that are not in line with the country's overall economic priorities and development objectives. In many cases, screening is becoming more focused, covering only potential threats to national security or investments in strategic sectors such as natural resources.

Figure 2.10. **Restrictions in foreign direct investment in the manufacturing and service sectors, 2013**

2013 OECD FDI Regulatory Restrictiveness Index

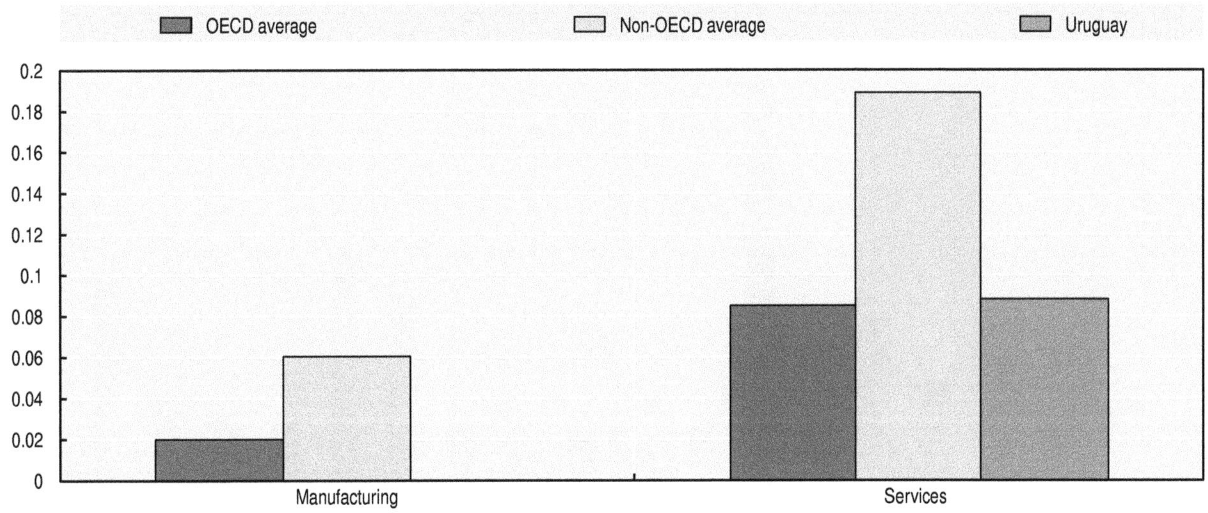

Note: Manufacturing vs services restrictions, average (closed = 1, open = 0).

Source: Authors' calculations based on OECD (2015), *FDI Regulatory Restrictiveness Index* (database), *www.oecd.org/investment/fdiindex.htm*.

StatLink *http://dx.doi.org/10.1787/888933330083*

Figure 2.11. **FDI restrictions limit backward global value chain participation, 2011**

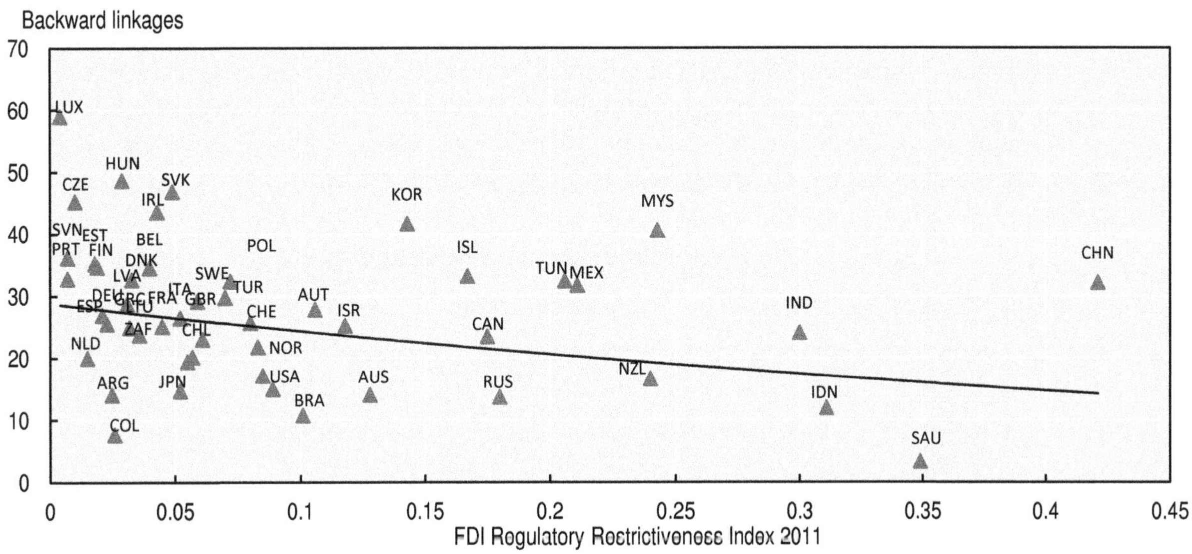

Note: FDI Regulatory Restrictiveness Index measures statutory restrictions on foreign direct investment. Restrictions are evaluated on a 0 (open) to 1 (closed) scale. On the other hand, foreign value added share of gross exports is a reliable measure of "Backward linkages" in analyses of GVCs.

Source: Authors' calculations based on OECD/WTO (2015), *Trade in Value Added (TiVA)* (database), *www.oecd.org/sti/ind/measuringtradeinvalue-addedanoecd-wtojointinitiative.htm* and OECD (2015), *FDI Regulatory Restrictiveness Index* (database), *www.oecd.org/investment/fdiindex.htm*.

StatLink *http://dx.doi.org/10.1787/888933330096*

Figure 2.12. **Types of FDI restrictions in selected OECD and non-OECD countries, 2013**

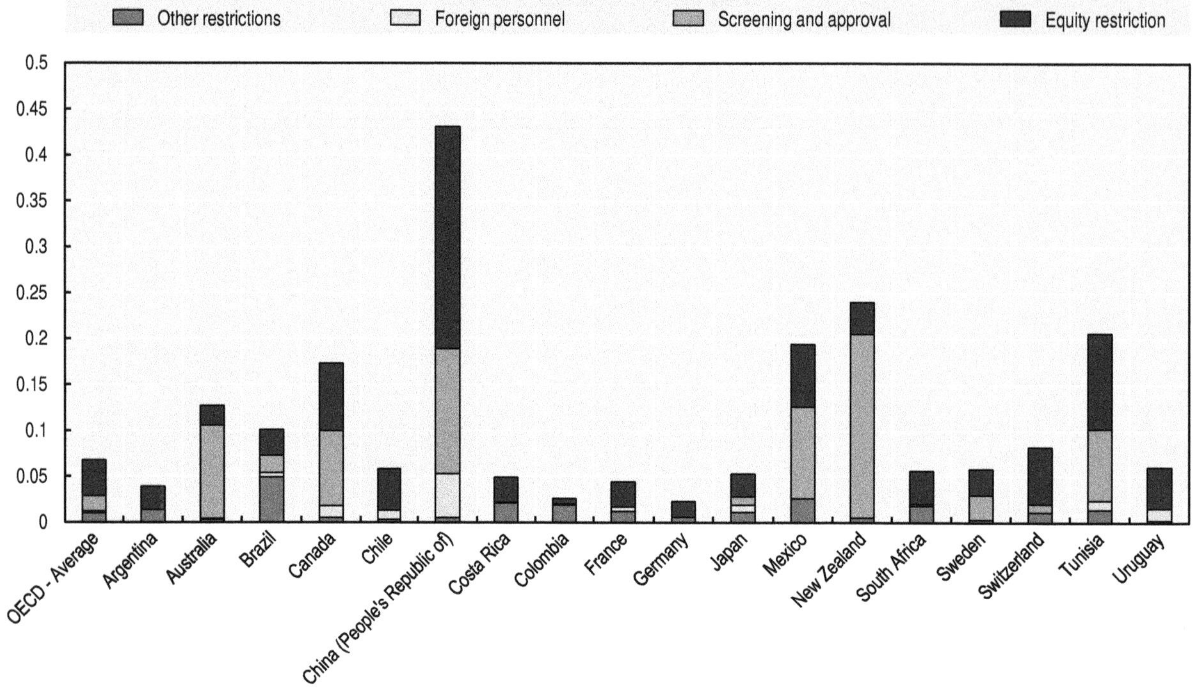

Note: OECD 2013 FDI Regulatory Restrictiveness Index: closed = 1, open = 0.

Source: Authors' calculations based on OECD (2015), *FDI Regulatory Restrictiveness Index* (database), *www.oecd.org/investment/fdiindex.htm.*

StatLink http://dx.doi.org/10.1787/888933330106

In Uruguay, restrictions are focused primarily on equity limits and hiring of foreign key personnel, with some screening mechanisms also in place. The rest of the section examines investment and related regulatory restrictions at the sectoral level, with a focus on sectors where investment barriers are most prevalent (Figure 2.13).

Figure 2.13. **FDI restrictions by sector in Uruguay, 2013**

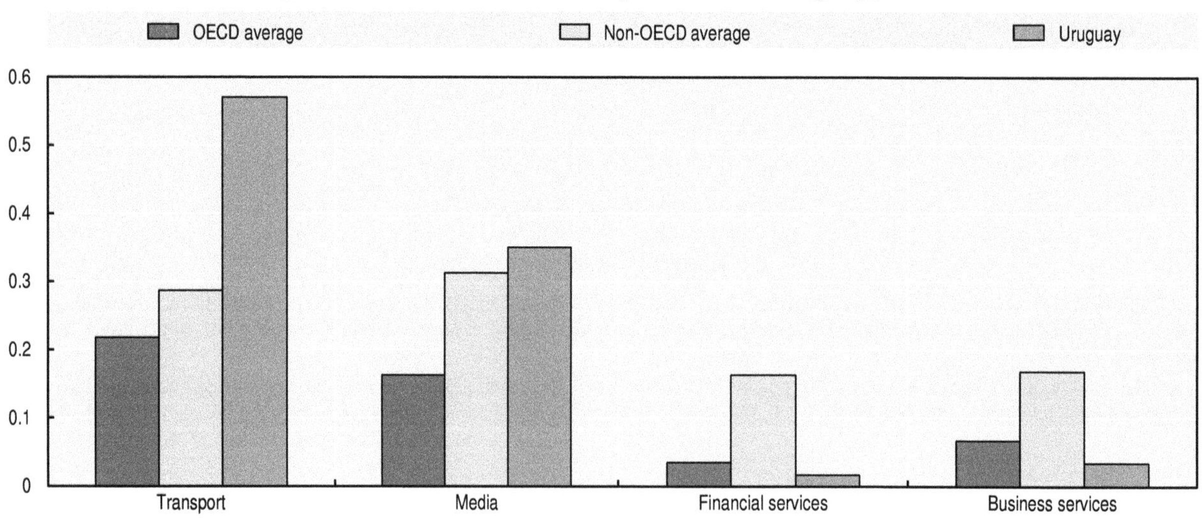

Note: OECD 2013 FDI Regulatory Restrictiveness Index: closed = 1, open = 0.

Source: Authors' calculations based on OECD (2015), *FDI Regulatory Restrictiveness Index* (database), *www.oecd.org/investment/fdiindex.htm.*

StatLink http://dx.doi.org/10.1787/888933330112

Restrictions are high in the transport sector

Overall, Uruguay's transport sector is more restrictive than most countries in the Index (Figure 2.13). The domestic road freight transport sector is subject to several foreign equity restrictions, commercial presence obligations and limitations on concessions, as well as government mandated price ceilings. For international road transport services, an equity restriction of 49% applies, requiring that the controlling stake be held by Uruguayan nationals. The state holds the right to provide regular public national and international passenger transport services (both regularly scheduled and irregularly scheduled), but also grants concessions and permits to private enterprises[5] (but only Uruguayan nationals or enterprises).[6] Uruguayan enterprises are those that are managed, controlled, and in which more than 50% of the capital is owned by Uruguayan nationals domiciled in Uruguay. In addition to equity restrictions and control of licenses and permits, the Ministry of Transport also regulates maximum prices in road freight transport.[7]

Uruguay's rail transport is managed and operated by the State Railway Administration or AFE (*Administración de Ferrocarriles del Estado*), an autonomous state-owned enterprise open to private-sector participation. In order to provide railway passenger and cargo transportation services, a railway operator must obtain a license (*Licencia de Operación Ferroviaria*) from the *Dirección Nacional de Transporte*. Among the requirements for obtaining the license are: a) at least 51% of the paid-in capital of the railway operator must be owned by Uruguayan nationals domiciled in Uruguay or by Uruguayan enterprises that meet the same requirements for paid-in capital; and b) at least 51% of the railway operator's board of directors or managing board must be composed of Uruguayan nationals domiciled in Uruguay. However, current reforms to this sector and the changing institutional landscape make it difficult to assess the degree of regulatory restrictiveness.

Uruguay's regulatory profile in maritime transport resembles that of several OECD member countries, and includes cabotage[8] restrictions, nationality requirements, as well as differential tax benefits reserved for Uruguayan nationals (STRI Transport and Courier Services). Cabotage trade is reserved for Uruguayan-flagged vessels, whose crews (including the captain) are composed of at least 50% Uruguayan nationals. However, waivers permitting foreign-flagged vessels to perform cabotage services may be granted by the Executive Branch when Uruguayan-flagged vessels are not available. Vessels providing cabotage transportation services within Uruguay are subject to the following requirements:

- if owned by natural persons, vessels must be owned by Uruguayan nationals domiciled in Uruguay
- if owned by an enterprise:
  - 51% of the enterprise owners must be Uruguayan nationals
  - 51% of the voting shares must be owned by Uruguayan nationals
  - the enterprise must be controlled and managed by Uruguayan nationals.

Half of all the Uruguayan foreign trade cargo (imports and exports) is reserved for Uruguayan-flagged vessels; however, waivers are granted to foreign-flagged vessels to carry the unreserved portion. Uruguay may impose restrictions on access to foreign trade cargo transportation on the basis of reciprocity. Port services are provided by private operators under concessions given by the state, which owns the ports, within the capped price limits for various services set by the government. Uruguayan-registered vessels are exempt from a number of taxes, including on spare parts, fuel and lubricants. Furthermore, shipping companies operating Uruguayan merchant ships are excluded from income and value-added tax, and the vessel is not included in wealth tax.[9]

The air transport sector faces a larger share of restrictions due to the security-related aspects of the sector. As in most OECD countries, Uruguay restricts foreign equity participation in the sector to less than 50%, as well as nationality requirements for employees (STRI Transport and Courier). Only a national air transportation enterprise (*empresa nacional de transporte aéreo*) may offer a domestic air transportation service (cabotage) and may provide international scheduled and non-scheduled air transport services. Only a national air works enterprise (*empresa nacional de servicios de trabajo aéreo*) may operate aircraft in domestic non-transportation air services. In order to be a national air transportation enterprise or a national air works enterprise, the firm must be 51% owned by Uruguayan nationals domiciled in Uruguay. All crew and other personnel, including management, must be Uruguayan nationals, unless otherwise authorised by the National Civil Aviation and Aviation Infrastructure Directorate (*Dirección Nacional de Aviación Civil e Infraestructura Aeronáutica*).

Media is the second most restrictive sector

In line with observed trends, particularly in non-OECD countries, Uruguay's media sector limits participation by foreign providers (Figure 2.13). Uruguayan law stipulates that free-to-air television and AM/FM radio broadcasting services are closed to foreign ownership and may only be supplied by Uruguayan nationals. All stockholders or partners in broadcasting enterprises in Uruguay, or established in Uruguay, must be Uruguayan nationals domiciled in Uruguay. Senior management, members of the boards of directors, and the responsible director or manager of broadcasting enterprises, must be Uruguayan nationals. The responsible director of a subscription (cable, satellite, MMDS) television enterprise must also be a Uruguayan national.

Financial services are relatively unrestricted

Uruguay is relatively restrictive of foreign entry into the financial services sector through its limitations on licensing. Only a limited number of licenses are granted by the Executive Power and require special authorisation from the Central Bank. In the OECD area, only a few countries, such as Denmark and New Zealand have limitations on branch establishment by foreign companies (World Bank STR database, OECD STRI Regulatory database). Within the country's insurance market, there are no limits on foreign participation in new or existing companies; however, entry through a branch is not allowed. For foreign investors, this implies that insurance companies can be fully owned by foreign shareholders as long as the companies are duly incorporated and registered in the country.

Restrictions are increasing on foreign state purchase of farmland

International investors have long been interested in agricultural investments in South America, attracted by the affordable price of land, policies that encourage foreign investment, and the lack of tariffs on farm exports. Uruguay has a total cultivated area of 16 million hectares. Land transactions have been carried out for 6 million hectares in the last decade. According to the National Institute of Colonization (*Instituto Nacional de Colonización*), 83% of the fields sold in 2010 (approximately 336 000 hectares) were bought by foreign investors from Brazil, Argentina, New Zealand, Korea, the US and Europe.

The growth in demand and interest in Uruguayan agriculture by international investors has driven land prices up by an average of 20% every year since 2002.

While discussions on foreign ownership of land typically involve private actions by profit-driven investors (speculators), a 2011 report from the United Nations Food and Agricultural Organization (FAO) highlighted the problematic nature of land purchases by foreign governments ("land grabbing") to support food production and improve food security in their respective countries. This practice is targeting agriculturally rich countries across all regions. In Latin America, the practice has grown in Argentina, Brazil and Uruguay in particular.

In 2014 Uruguay introduced restrictions on the purchase of agricultural land, to preserve the country's sovereignty over its natural resources. Law No. 19.283 forbids foreign states from owning rural real estate and agricultural exploitations (i.e. a land surface intended for agricultural production). It also prohibits the ownership of rural real estate and agricultural exploitations by corporations (*sociedades anónimas*) or companies limited by shares (*sociedades en comandita por acciones*) which have foreign states or their sovereign funds as shareholders. In taking this action Uruguay has followed the examples of Argentina and Brazil, both of which have enacted laws restricting the amount of farmland that can be owned by foreigners in general, regardless of whether they are individual investors, corporations or foreign governments. However, Uruguay's agricultural land restriction applies only to foreign governments.

Screening mechanisms offer an alternative to equity restrictions in managing land ownership issues (Box 2.4).

Box 2.4. **Screening as a measure to restrict "landgrabbing"**

From March 2015, the Australian Government's Foreign Investment Review Board (FIRB) has adopted a new screening threshold for agricultural land investment. The aim is to increase scrutiny of foreign investment in the agricultural sector. All foreign purchases of agricultural land will be subject to FIRB screening when the cumulative value of agricultural investments by the foreign investor reaches the threshold of USD 15 million. This is a significant reduction from the previous screening threshold, which was USD 252 million.

The New Zealand Government, through its Overseas Investment Office, reviews all foreign investment proposals for "sensitive land" (farm land), which requires consent. Foreign investors – individuals, corporations and governments – must meet certain criteria based on national interest and economic benefit. The transaction must be proven to be beneficial for New Zealand and the relevant overseas person must show intent to reside in the country indefinitely.

Source: OECD (2015).

These examples show that whether it is in the form of equity restrictions or screening mechanisms, recent restrictions introduced in countries with rich agricultural land are becoming more focused and targeted, with the intent to cover potential threats to national security or protect investments in natural resources which are considered strategic. The introduction of new restrictions must be guided by evidence-based processes such as cost-benefit analyses, as well as sound rationale that uphold national development goals.

Administrative barriers are important disincentives

In addition to explicit regulatory obstacles, the administrative procedures related to business establishment and trade facilitation can also influence the competitiveness of services supplied in a country. Uruguay's performance is varied when assessed against indicators related to establishing and running a business. For instance, according to the World Bank Doing Business Indicators, registering a business in Uruguay involves 5 procedures and can be completed in roughly 6.5 days, both of which are below the world average. Nevertheless, the relative cost is considerable, amounting to nearly 23% of Uruguay's per capita income, compared to a world average of 8%. In terms of customs and trade facilitation, Uruguay performs well in the OECD Trade Facilitation Index on ensuring appeal possibilities in administrative decisions taken by border agencies, as well as co-operation with other country authorities. On the other hand, its performance is below the regional and upper middle-income country averages for the publication of trade information, advance rulings, the simplification and harmonisation of documents related to customs and international trade processing, as well as within-Uruguay border agency co-operation (OECD, 2013a). These outcomes suggest that Uruguay can do more to improve the transparency and efficiency of its administrative processes so as to maximise connectivity and competitiveness for both domestic and international suppliers within its borders.

From an overall business perception perspective (financial attractiveness, business environment and the availability and quality of skilled labour), Uruguay ranked 42nd out of the top 50 services outsourcing destinations in 2014 (A.T. Kearney, 2014: Table 2.2). This puts Uruguay below several other Latin American countries, with the limited availability of skilled labour noted as the largest constraint in relative terms. Uruguay's small labour force and higher labour costs than some of its regional competitors, such as Colombia and Costa Rica, are challenges for capitalising on certain outsourcing opportunities (Uruguay XXI, 2013). Furthermore, the obligations for salary increases over time and the strengthening of the currency may also drive up labour costs. Nevertheless, in terms of city attractiveness, Montevideo scored higher than many of its Latin American cities as a destination for services outsourcing (Tholons, 2015: Table 2.1).

Table 2.2. **Uruguay's ranking for services outsourcing**

Country	A.T. Kearney rank Global Services Location Index 2014	Tholons Top 100 Outsourcing Cities 2015
India	1	1
China	2	10
Mexico	4	40
Thailand	6	85
Philippines	7	2
Brazil	8	24
Viet Nam	12	18
Chile	13	28
Costa Rica	24	11
Panama	30	99
Argentina	38	33
Uruguay	42	25
Colombia	43	45

Sources: AT Kearney (2014), *A Wealth of Choices: From Anywhere on Earth to No Location at All: The Global Services Location Index 2014, www.atkearney.com/fr/research-studies/global-services-location-index/full-report#sthash.G2ygB6TH.dpuf;* Tholons Top 100 Outsourcing Cities 2015. December 2014. New York. Available at: *http://www.tholons.com/TholonsTop100/.*

Trade and investment agreements offer unexploited opportunities for deepening and diversifying integration

International trade and investment agreements can be useful vehicles for strengthening integration. Uruguay could make better use of international agreements – particularly with more advanced economies – in order to accelerate its alignment with international regulatory standards. While most of the reforms negotiated in international agreements can be taken unilaterally, these may prove difficult to achieve within the domestic political processes. For this reason, many countries have used international negotiations as an external "anchor" for driving domestic policies, making reforms with a complicated internal political economy more feasible as the result of a commitment to a larger partner or group of partners in an external process. Similarly, international agreements can provide a "lock-in mechanism" that dissuades policy reversals in the future which may come with changes in government. Finally, international negotiations can be a means to acquire technical knowledge on prevailing international standards (related to transparency, technical barriers, etc.) and offer platforms for exchanges of information with regulatory authorities in other countries.

Uruguay has forged limited trade ties with commercially relevant partners outside of Mercosur

Uruguay has not fully reaped the benefits from international agreements, and has yet to exploit new ties with commercially relevant trading partners. In total, Uruguay has forged preferential trade partnerships with 21 countries. Over half of these trade partners are Latin American countries, in particular members of Mercosur and ALADI (Latin American Integration Association). The majority of its remaining trade partners are in Africa and the Middle East (Figure 2.14). In particular, it has established regional trade agreements (RTAs) with the five countries that are members of the Southern African Customs Union (SACU) and selected countries in North Africa and the Middle East, including Egypt and Morocco. Beyond these two regions, it has concluded one RTA with India, but does not have trade partnerships with other Asian countries, despite this being a growing destination for its exports. Neither does it have any accords with North America, after its efforts to negotiate a bilateral free trade agreement (FTA) with the United States were abandoned. There have been long-standing negotiations between Mercosur and the European Union, and the conclusion of this accord could bring important opportunities for Uruguay.

Uruguay's pattern of insertion into the global economy has been embedded in its integration within the Mercosur bloc. With the exception of the Uruguay-Mexico FTA, Uruguay's bilateral trade negotiations have been conducted as part of the Mercosur bloc, rather than being part of an autonomous strategy. In any case, the selection and nature of Uruguay's trade ties appears to be more politically than commercially motivated. The majority of existing agreements are with countries with which Uruguay does not have strong commercial interests, and often constitute distant markets with high tariff barriers. As a result, the number and composition of existing trading partners provides limited opportunities for increased trade, both in terms of export markets and import (input) sources. Hence, although there are clear advantages to negotiations as part of a larger bloc – in terms of increased negotiating leverage, coherence of agreements, economies of scale –, the resulting configuration of RTAs with non-Mercosur patterns is not commercially meaningful. The exception to this is, of course, the agreement with the EU; failure to conclude this agreement may lead to lost opportunities, particularly as other countries obtain preferential access with the EU.

Beyond the agreement with the EU, Uruguay could benefit from greater market diversification, particularly with high-income and high-growth economies where the opportunities for dynamic learning and technological spillovers may be higher. Only two of its RTA partners are high-income OECD countries, Chile and Israel, although these are relatively small markets with a low level of technological sophistication in their productive structure. Similarly, the level of demand and degree of consumer sophistication in other large middle-income markets with which Uruguay has RTAs is not very strong. Given that Uruguay has a small internal market, the profile of demand in its external markets can critically influence the sophistication of its export basket. Forging agreements with larger markets, as well as markets with higher purchasing power and more diversified consumer preferences, could allow Uruguayan firms to discover more sophisticated activities. In this sense, market diversification can support a productive diversification strategy. To this end, Uruguay should consider strategies for plugging into intra-regional initiatives such as the TPP (Trans-Pacific Partnership), which could offer opportunities for greater market diversification.

Figure 2.14. **Uruguay's RTA partners, by region and income level**

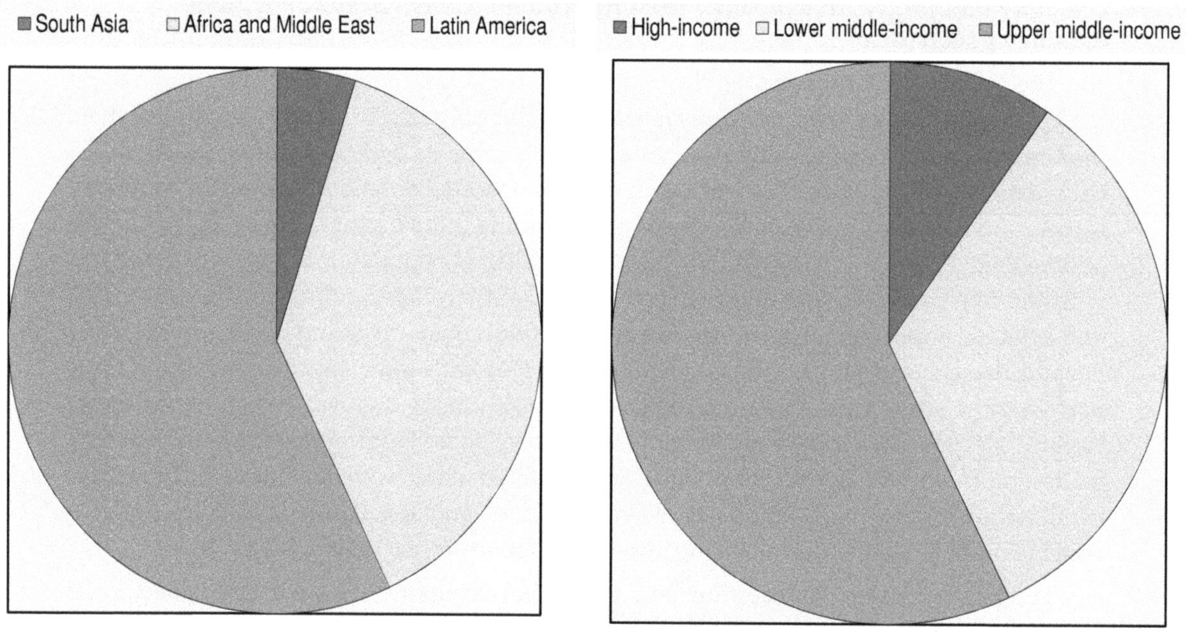

Source: Authors' calculation, based on texts of RTAs and RTAs database, *www.oecd.org/tad/benefitlib/regionaltradeagreements.*

StatLink http://dx.doi.org/10.1787/888933330123

Uruguay has a large scope for expanding and diversifying its trade partnerships

Overall, Uruguay's composition of trade partners may not be aligned with its best commercial interests. At present, only 40% of Uruguay's trade is covered by the network of its RTAs, and the bulk of this relates to intra-Mercosur trade. Trade with non-Mercosur trading partners represents only 9% of exports, and 6% of imports (Figure 2.15). This suggests that Uruguay could still benefit from endowing its main export markets with better legal and regulatory frameworks, so as to facilitate market access of more exporters and investors, particular SMEs, and provide more diversified and efficient sources of inputs for domestic producers and cheaper goods for consumers.

Figure 2.15. **Share of trade covered by Uruguay's trade agreements**

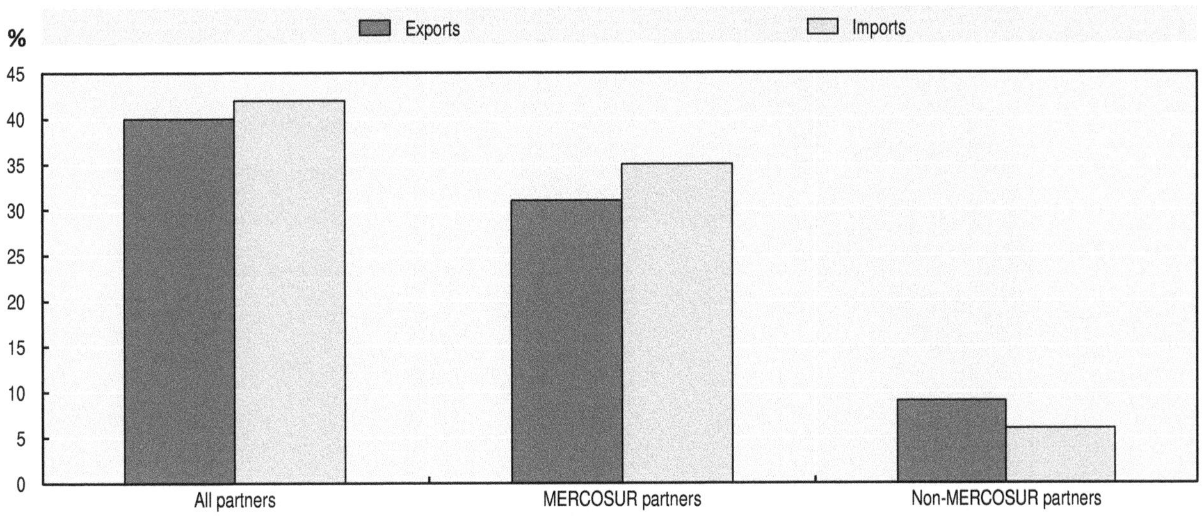

Source: Authors' calculation, based on texts of RTAs and RTAs database, *www.oecd.org/tad/benefitlib/regionaltradeagreements*.

StatLink http://dx.doi.org/10.1787/888933330139

Part of Uruguay's challenges in its negotiating strategy lie with the Mercosur policy to negotiate as part of the bloc, giving Uruguay limited leeway to negotiate agreements independently. While Uruguay should continue to deepen its integration in Mercosur, which remains its main trading partner, it could also consider agreeing with Mercosur members on certain flexibilities to pursue commercial opportunities that are of particular interest to Uruguay and that do not conflict with the commitments undertaken under Mercosur. It should consider what level of flexibility is appropriate for conducting other negotiations, particularly in the areas of services and investment that are not at odds with the Common External Tariff. This may call for a more flexible interpretation of Mercosur's Article 32, concerning the scope of unilateral negotiations with third parties. In effect, Uruguay's negotiations with Mexico serve as a precedent for pursuing a more variable geometry. Uruguay's exports to Mercosur have not been very dynamic, whereas it has seen significant export growth to other areas with which it does not enjoy the benefit of an agreement, notably in Asia.

Uruguay has made limited strides in "deep integration" agreements

Apart from the relatively small network of trade partnerships under RTAs, the contents of Uruguay's agreements are of limited scope and coverage. Only one-quarter of Uruguay's RTAs represent fully-fledged trade agreements. Figure 2.16 displays all the trade agreements signed by Uruguay, ranging from those of more limited scope (framework agreements) to those of most comprehensive coverage (economic integration agreements). Only seven of the agreements signed by Uruguay (27% of its total agreements) are considered to be comprehensive regional trade agreements: free trade agreements, customs unions, and economic integration agreements. On the other hand, 34% are partial scope agreements, notably within the ALADI framework and its Mercosur accords, which generally cover a few sectors, such as the automobile industry, agro-industry, or selected services. Similarly, over one-quarter of these accords are Framework Agreements signed by Mercosur which establish the basis for negotiations leading to the establishment of future FTAs. The remaining three agreements pertain to preferences Uruguay has conferred on a non-reciprocal basis.

Figure 2.16. **Taxonomy of Uruguay's trade agreements**

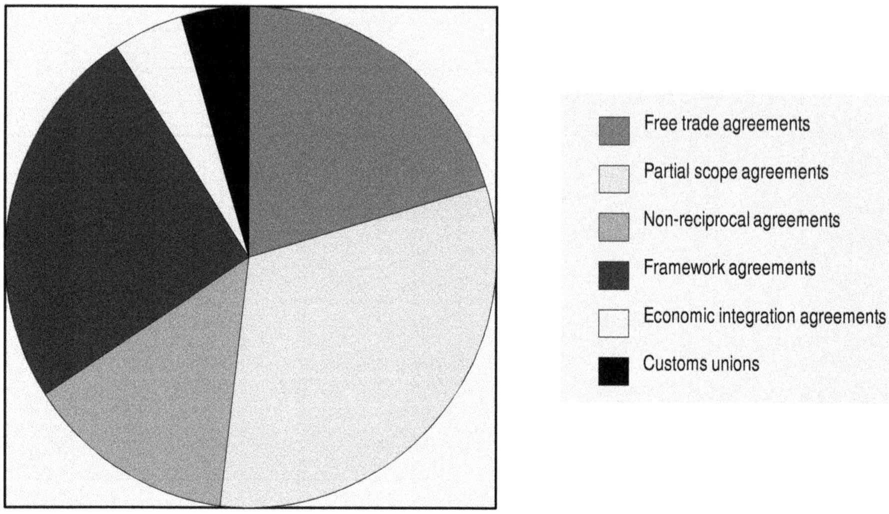

Note: Share of the total for each type of agreement.

Source: Authors' calculation, based on texts of RTAs and RTAs database, *www.oecd.org/tad/benefitlib/regionaltradeagreements*.

StatLink *http://dx.doi.org/10.1787/888933330148*

Uruguay's RTAs are also characterised by the limited coverage of so-called 21st century disciplines. Compared to other countries of similar size and development, Uruguay has signed a high share of "shallow RTAs".[10] Only two of its RTAs – with Mercosur and Mexico – are considered to contain "deep" integration disciplines, governing non-tariff measures of a domestic regulatory nature (see Table 2.5 below). Of these, only the FTA with Mexico covers disciplines related to investment, intellectual property rights, services and competition issues. Other small countries in the region – such as Costa Rica or Panama – have signed the same number of agreements as Uruguay, but have pursued a strategy of deep integration in the majority of their accords (Figure 2.17). Even economies that have signed fewer RTAs, such as Malaysia or Hong Kong, China, have nevertheless focused on deep integration disciplines. Hence, although Uruguay has signed a reasonable number of RTAs, these are largely confined to traditional trade barriers, with limited coverage of domestic regulatory reforms.

Quality is more important than quantity of RTAs

Not all RTAs are equal, and not all of them have the same effects on the pattern and benefits derived from integration. A recent stream of empirical work is showing that RTA heterogeneity – namely, variations in the design and contents of the agreement – plays an important role in explaining different effects and outcomes from existing agreements (Ahcar and Siroen, 2014; Di Comite, Nocco and Orecife, 2014; Christian, 2013). As the scope of issues negotiated in trade agendas has been widening, and new partners have become active players in the new regionalism wave, the diversity of RTAs has also increased over time. There is significant variation in the nature of these arrangements, including the scope and depth of the agreements, the design and nature of specific commitments and obligations, and the overall modalities of negotiation and implementation, as well as the institutional architecture. Many of these dimensions are being shown to influence the economic outcomes. Moreover, the number of signatories, their economic size and distance between them, as well as the level of economic development and economic growth, can also play a role.

Figure 2.17. **Share of RTAs with deep integration coverage**

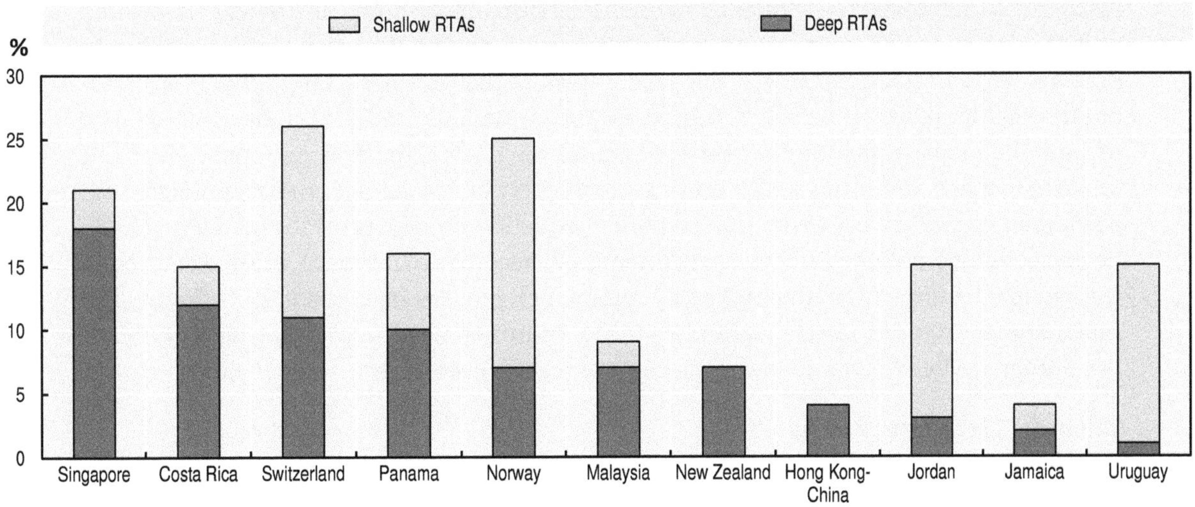

Note: RTAs comprises partial scope agreement, free trade agreements, customs unions and economic integration agreements; it excludes framework agreements and non-reciprocal agreements, as well as bilateral investment treaties.

Source: Authors' calculation, based on texts of RTAs and RTAs database, *www.oecd.org/tad/benefitlib/regionaltradeagreements*.

StatLink http://dx.doi.org/10.1787/888933330154

Despite the opportunities for RTAs to facilitate insertion into global value chains, they also have risks when they are poorly designed. Poorly designed trade agreements can hinder the development of global value chains, increasing fragmentation and diverting trade and investment. In particular, it is important to consider the potential negative effects of uncoordinated RTAs on production sharing, and the risks of inconsistent regulations on global value chains (Feridhanusetyawan, 2005) leading to a "spaghetti-bowl" effect created by the overlapping of different rules of origin (Zhang and Shen, 2011; Baldwin, 2008). In other cases, however, regional agreements have had no effect on the development of global value chains, particularly when the formation of partners has been politically rather than commercially driven. The policy question for Uruguay and other economies considering to expand their integration strategy is not so much whether to pursue new RTAs, or how many of them, but which type of RTAs to pursue.

Deep integration is essential for the development of global value chains

Recent research on global value chains suggests that there is often a strong regional basis underpinning the development of global value chains. Some authors argue that supply chain trade is not global, but mostly regional (Baldwin and López-Gonzalez, 2013). In effect, a high share of foreign value added comes from countries that are geographically close, suggesting that distance and congruity/geographical proximity can play a determinant role. The regional dimension, however, appears to be stronger for manufacturing-based global value chains than for natural resources and services. Indeed, natural resources and services have seen the emergence of international (extra-regional) supply chain trade. As noted above, not only are Uruguay's RTAs largely concentrated in the region, but they are also largely confined to goods trade. Establishing a favourable regulatory regime for cross-border services activities is a promising area of reform. As technology increasingly enables a growing range of services to be traded, there will continue to be opportunities to capture high-value added services activities along international supply chains.

This suggests that "deep" and comprehensive RTAs, particularly those containing disciplines that cover the "trade-investment-services-know-how" nexus, are associated with a higher degree of insertion into global value chains. For global value chains to emerge, RTAs need to address a new set of issues that are associated with the cross-border fragmentation of production processes, such as intermediates trade, the free flow of capital, the global demand for services across the chains, the international movement of management and other skills, and the protection of knowledge and technology that accompanies production. Given that a whole production process is established abroad, the degree of behind-the-border regulatory integration becomes paramount. After all, although the benefits for firms from unbundling the production process are evident, the risks are also much higher. In order to attenuate these risks, countries need to provide higher behind-the-border predictability and lower the costs of divergences in regulatory regimes.

Towards 21st century RTAs

The so-called "21st century" RTAs could represent relevant areas of international co-operation for Uruguay. The WTO-plus or WTO-beyond elements are key features of these RTAs, involving a degree of liberalisation and/or rule-making that goes beyond the commitments made by countries in the WTO. These RTAs provide for a range of behind-the-border domestic policies, such as services, investment, intellectual property rights, competition policy, and regulatory transparency (Table 2.3). Modern RTAs also contain provisions that have helped reforms at a sectoral level, notably in telecommunications and financial services. Unlike the agreements under the World Trade Organization, free trade

Table 2.3. **Disciplines negotiated in modern regional trade agreements**

WTO-beyond areas	Illustrative commitments in RTAs
Transparency	Commitment to ensure advance notice/publication and public comment process open to foreign parties (government and private sector) before introducing new regulations
Regulatory coherence	Commitment to maintain or establish a national, inter-ministerial co-ordination body to ensure coherence in regulatory measures; commitment to conduct regulatory impact assessments for regulatory measures exceeding a threshold of economic impact
Anti-corruption	Obligations to penalise corruption, apply sanctions to public and private entities, and provide for whistle-blower protection
Competition policy	Maintenance of measures to proscribe anti-competitive business conduct; harmonisation of competition laws; establishment or maintenance of an independent competition authority
State-owned enterprises	Establishment or maintenance of an independent competition authority; non-discrimination regarding production and marketing condition; provision of information; affirmation of Art XVII GATT provision
State aid	Assessment of anti-competitive behaviour; annual reporting on the value and distribution of state aid given; provision of information
Public procurement	Progressive liberalisation; national treatment and/or non-discrimination principle; publication of laws and regulations on the Internet; specification of public procurement regime
Innovation	Participation in framework programmes; promotion of technology transfers
Intellectual property rights (IPRs)	Harmonisation of standards; enforcement; national treatment, most-favoured nation treatment Accession to international treaties not referenced in the TRIPs (Agreement on Trade-Related Aspects of Intellectual Property Rights) Agreement
Data protection	Exchange of information and experts; joint projects
Research and technology	Joint research projects; exchange of researchers; development of public-private partnership
Education and training	Measures to improve the general level of education
Investment	Information exchange; development of legal frameworks; harmonisation and simplification of procedures; national treatment; establishment of mechanism for the settlement of disputes
Movement of capital	Liberalisation of capital movement; prohibition of new restrictions
Labour market regulations	Regulation of the national labour market; affirmation of International Labour Organization (ILO) commitments; enforcement
Social security matters	Co-ordination of social security systems; non-discrimination regarding working conditions
Movement of persons	Mutual recognition agreements for professional services
SMEs	Technical assistance; facilitation of the access to finance
Environment	Development of environmental standards; enforcement of national environmental laws; establishment of sanctions for violation of environmental laws; publication of laws and regulations; co-operation on climate change

agreements have fashioned a more holistic approach, integrating the movement of goods, services, capital, people and knowledge. This is particularly important for trade associated with global value chains, which requires that production processes – including capital, technology, management – cross borders and are protected in foreign markets.

Countries that pursue regulatory integration in their RTAs are more likely to become part of these production-sharing schemes. Multinational enterprises that are at the core of global value chains are already operating by these new global standards, and will more readily locate in countries that have adopted them in order to minimise transaction costs.

Capturing the more sophisticated and more services-oriented tasks along the international supply chain is likely to lead to knowledge spillovers from global firms to local suppliers, as well as higher income-generating activities. Countries seeking to attract more sophisticated segments of the value chain need to be prepared to embrace and implement a complex package of rules typically embedded in 21st century RTAs, from the protection of intellectual property rights, to data protection and e-commerce. The more sophisticated the economic activities, the more intensively they rely on the regulatory and institutional environment. Similarly, the inherently regulatory nature of most services barriers has placed demands on new components of regional negotiations, such as regulatory co-operation and coherence.

The pursuit of deep integration is no longer circumscribed to a small number of trade partnerships, but has become considerably more widespread. Almost two-thirds (57%) of RTAs signed since the beginning of 2001 display "deep" coverage, as opposed to only 10% of RTAs prior to the WTO (Figure 2.18). By way of contrast, Table 2.4 displays the WTO-plus and WTO-beyond disciplines contained in RTAs signed by Uruguay (via Mercosur).

Table 2.4. **Deep integration components in Uruguay's RTAs**

Free trade agreements (chronological order, earliest to recent)	SPS, TBTs and standards	Services	Movement of people/ visas	Labour market regulation	E-commerce	Investment	Intellectual property right	Data protection	Innovation	Taxation/subsidies	Movement of capital	Competition	State trading enterprises	Regulatory coherence	Transparency
Mercosur	WTO+	GATS+	WTO+	??	--			--	WTO+		WTO+			--	
Merscosur-Chile	WTO+	GATS+	--	--	--	TRIMS=	TRIPS=	--	WTO+	WTO+	--			--	WTO-
Mercosur-Bolivia	WTO=	GATS=	--	--	--	--	--	--	WTO+	WTO=	--			--	WTO-
Mercosur-Peru	WTO+	GATS=	--	--	--	TRIMS=	TRIPS=	--		WTO+	--			--	WTO-
Mercosur-Colombia, Ecuador, Venezuela	WTO+	GATS=	--	--	--	TRIMS=	TRIPS=	--	WTO+	WTO+	--			--	WTO-
Uruguay-Mexico	WTO+	GATS+	WTO+	--	--	TRIMS+	TRIPS+	--			--	WTO+	WTO+	--	WTO=
Mercosur-Cuba	WTO=	--	--	--	--			--			--			--	WTO-
Uruguay-Venezuela	WTO=	--	--	--	--			--			--			--	WTO-
Mercosur-Israel	WTO=	GATS=	--	--	--			--			--			--	WTO-
Mercosur-India	WTO=	--	--	--							--				WTO-
Mercosur-Egypt*	WTO=	GATS=													WTO-
Mercosur-SACU*	WTO=														WTO-

Notes: *denotes that the agreement has been signed but is not yet in force. The list above excludes framework agreements and those under negotiations.

Figure 2.18. **Coverage of WTO-plus disciplines in RTAs - Percentage of RTAs signed since 2001**

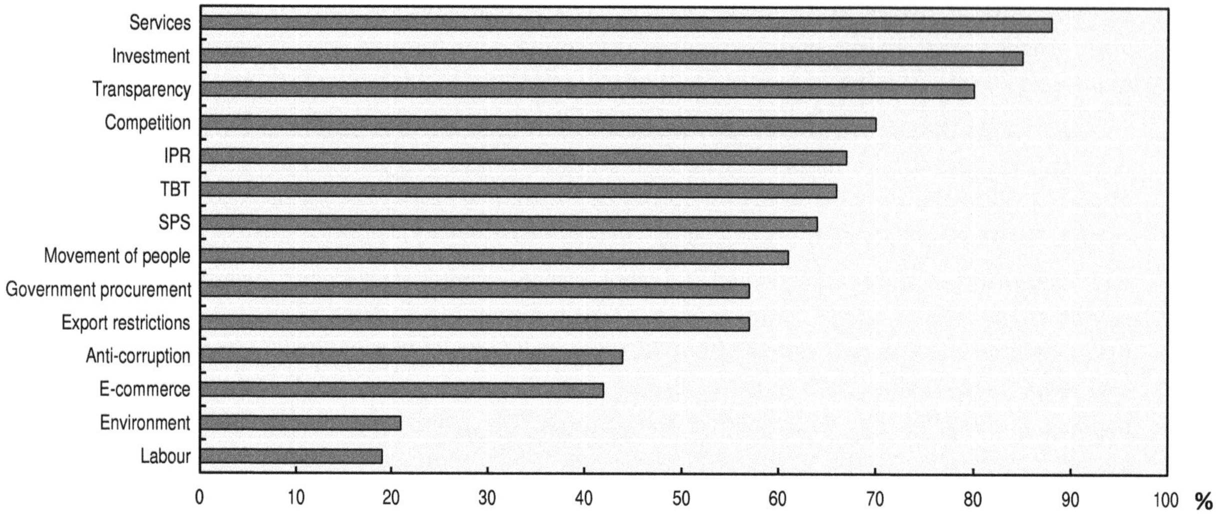

Note: IPR: Intellectual property rights; TBT: Technical barriers to trade; SPS: Sanitary and photosanitary measures.

Source: OECD (2014a), "Part 1 of a report to G20 Development Working Group on the impact of BEPS in low income countries", *www.oecd.org/tax/tax-global/part-1-of-report-to-g20-dwg-on-the-impact-of-beps-in-low-income-countries.pdf.*

StatLink http://dx.doi.org/10.1787/888933330168

RTA coverage of services will increase global value chain participation

An implication of offshoring and the fragmentation of production is that goods and services sectors are increasingly intertwined. Indeed, services have become the "glue" of global value chains. The "servicification" of industry refers to the phenomenon whereby services are embedded, and embodied, in manufacturing and agro-industry products. An increasing share of the value of manufacturing goods is made up of services: domestic and imported services inputs used along the production process account for one-third of the total value of exports in transport equipment, textile, chemicals or food products (OECD, 2013a). As a result of this "servicification" of manufacturing, the competitive nature of services play a crucial enabling role in the development of global value chains. Since services are inputs into the production of goods, the cost of services trade barriers also affects the competitiveness of manufacturing and agricultural supply chain.

In light of the importance of ensuring the competitiveness of services, increasing the coverage and depth of services chapters in RTAs can be a useful strategy for lowering trade costs. In general, trade costs for services tend to be higher than those of goods and more often of a regulatory nature, but RTAs can play a role in bringing down these costs through greater regulatory coherence (Miroudot, Souvage and Sheperd, 2013). Effectively, bringing down services trade costs is also relevant for increasing productivity, as services sectors with lower trade costs tend to have higher rates of productivity growth (ibid.). By lowering these trade costs for services and increasing productivity in these sectors, suppliers in Uruguay could increase their opportunities for fostering competitiveness in manufacturing and agricultural value chains.

Several of Uruguay's trade arrangements provide a framework for trade in services, although the actual progress in market opening and rules development has been limited, except for financial services, where Uruguay assumed GATS-plus commitments under

Mercosur, and to a lesser extent, in telecoms services. The Mercosur Montevideo Protocol on Trade in Services signed in 1997 provided a framework for liberalising services, which was to be undertaken over a period of ten years, by 2007. The Protocol mirrors a GATS template, defining modes of supply, market access rules and national treatment similar to those of GATS. Except for a few sectors, the commitments under Mercosur lock in the schedules under GATS, and in this sense, provide limited liberalisation beyond the multilateral level. Similarly, none of the Mercosur bilateral treaties that cover services (such as Mercosur-Egypt or Mercosur-Peru) go beyond an affirmation of GATS.

Bilateral investment treaties offer good protection to foreign investors

With the global trend towards fragmented production, firms do not just look for increased market access, but more importantly, for favourable conditions for market presence. Firms that unbundle their production across borders face important risks related to the treatment they will receive in the host country. In this context, bilateral investment treaties (BITs) have emerged to promote certain standards of treatment for foreign investors. BITs usually provide for non-discrimination through national treatment, most-favoured nation and fair and equitable treatment provisions, as well as security for investors and protection against expropriation. BITs also usually contain provisions on the transfer of funds. Since the mid-1990s, the inclusion of investor-state dispute settlement provisions in BITs has offered investors recourse to international arbitration to settle disputes with the host country. Where BITs succeed in making the investment framework and environment of signatory countries more predictable, stable and safe for investors, it is expected that they will help countries to attract vertical and horizontal FDI.

Uruguay has been able to pursue BITs independently, concluding agreements with over 30 countries (see Table 2.5). These BITs contain provisions that are commonly encountered in the so-called "first-generation" treaties, given that most of the country's treaties were adopted in the 1990s and 2000s. On average, Uruguay's treaties are 19 years old, which is close to the global average. Older treaties were concluded essentially with European countries – its traditional commercial partners –, while more recent ones have been concluded with countries from a broader geographical scope (Americas, Asia, Australia). Uruguay is also a party to 17 non-BITs agreements that cover investment matters (see Annex 2.A2). In particular, through its membership of Mercosur, Uruguay has concluded, with major partner countries, several international agreements that encompass investment Economic Complementation Agreements; Framework Agreements, and Trade and Investment Framework Agreements.

Between BITs and FTAs with investment coverage, 100% of Uruguay's inward FDI stock is covered by international investment agreements, and around 40% of Uruguay's outward FDI stock is covered.[11] This is a high degree of treaty coverage compared to the global average: less than 20% of global FDI is currently under cover of an international investment agreement.[12] This markedly high level of correspondence between Uruguay's inward FDI counterparts and its BITs might suggest that BITs are an important element of its investment policy, more so than in most other countries where other factors (size of market, geography) could be driving investors to the market. Alternatively, it could reflect the fact that Uruguay has only concluded BITs with its traditional or existing partners, and that there may be unexploited investment opportunities from concluding agreements with non-traditional partners.

These agreements have allowed Uruguay to offer adequate protection to foreign investors. However, the BITs could have a greater impact on both inward and outward direct investment by including market access and other practices to enhance transparency, responsible conduct, and other sustainable development considerations.

Table 2.5. **Bilateral investment treaties signed by Uruguay**

Partners	Status	Date of signature	Date of entry into force
Ecuador	Terminated	31/07/1985	31/07/1985
Germany	In force	04/05/1987	29/06/1990
Netherlands	In force	22/09/1988	01/08/1991
Switzerland	In force	07/10/1988	22/04/1991
Hungary	In force	25/08/1989	01/07/1991
Italy	In force	21/02/1990	02/03/1998
Romania	In force	23/11/1990	29/08/1993
Canada	Terminated	16/05/1991	
Poland	In force	02/08/1991	21/10/1994
United Kingdom	In force	21/10/1991	01/08/1997
BLEU (Belgium-Luxembourg Economic Union)	In force	04/11/1991	23/04/1999
Spain	In force	07/04/1992	06/05/1994
France	In force	14/10/1993	09/07/1997
China	In force	02/12/1993	01/12/1997
Malaysia	In force	09/08/1995	13/04/2002
Chile	In force	26/10/1995	22/04/1999
Czech Republic	In force	26/09/1996	29/12/2000
Venezuela, Bolivarian Republic of	In force	20/05/1997	18/01/2002
Sweden	In force	17/06/1997	01/12/1999
Portugal	In force	25/07/1997	03/11/1999
Canada	In force	29/10/1997	02/06/1999
Panama	In force	18/02/1998	14/08/2002
Israel	In force	30/03/1998	07/10/2004
Mexico	In force	30/06/1999	01/07/2002
El Salvador	In force	24/08/2000	23/05/2003
Australia	In force	03/09/2001	12/12/2002
Finland	In force	21/03/2002	18/06/2004
Armenia	In force	06/05/2002	15/12/2013
United States of America	In force	04/11/2005	01/11/2006
India	Signed (not in force)	11/02/2008	
Viet Nam	In force	12/12/2008	09/09/2009
Korea, Republic of	In force	01/10/2009	08/12/2011
Chile	Signed (not in force)	25/03/2010	

Source: UNCTAD (2016), *International Investment Agreements Navigator*, *http://investmentpolicyhub.unctad.org/IIA*.

The core treaty protection provisions are applicable at the post-establishment phase, while the admission of investment remains subject to national laws. Uruguay's BITs do not provide foreign investors with a right of free establishment in its territory. That is, the standards of treatment that are granted to covered foreign investors, such as guarantees of fair and non-discriminatory treatment, apply to investments that have already been admitted under national regulations, at the post-establishment phase. Uruguay could consider extending these legal protection provisions to the pre-establishment phase, which would provide covered foreign investors with market access, while granting its nationals investing abroad the same market access guarantee in partner countries. For example, BITs agreed between Japan and Korea (2003) and Viet Nam (2005) cover both the pre- and post-establishment phases. Likewise, the Canadian and US model, similar to NAFTA (the North American Free Trade Agreement), applies to the "establishment, acquisition, expansion, management, conduct, operation, management, maintenance, use, enjoyment [...]". Since econometric studies suggest that comprehensive free trade agreements and pre-establishment NT provisions in international investment agreements are positively correlated with greater FDI inflows, Uruguay might consider inserting pre-establishment protection provisions in its future treaties.

Uruguay's international investment agreements promote responsible business

Despite the fact that most treaties are grounded in first-generation practices, Uruguay has been a forerunner in adopting some new practices, particularly the insertion of Responsible Business Conduct (RBC) elements. It is worth noting, in the light of the current global debate on the links between sustainable development goals and investment treaties, that Uruguay is one of the most advanced countries in the use of its international investment agreements to advance its sustainable development policies. An OECD survey of 2 107 investment treaties shows that only 12% of the entire stock of international investment agreements contains language on such matters, while 17% of Uruguay's treaties refer to RBC issues.[13] The issues mentioned in its treaties are environment (in 17% of its treaties) and labour standards (8% of Uruguay's treaties). In addition, references to sustainable development and RBC concerns are made in the preambles to Uruguay's international investment agreements. Although preamble language does not create binding treaty commitments, it is nevertheless important for clarifying the purpose of the treaty as well as the broader context for interpreting the treaty. As such, preamble language can provide essential inputs to the treaty interpretation process. However, Uruguay does not include RBC issues systematically: only 20% of the later treaties contain references to RBC standards. This suggests that it is Uruguay's treaty partners who have called for inclusion of such language, rather than a firm policy stance by Uruguay.

Dealing with tax incoherencies can pay dividends

Closely related to services and investment, Uruguay has also made progress in double taxation treaties and investment (Box 2.5). Agreements do not liberalise investment, but encourage countries to explore bilateral treaties and that joint activities are taken for the promotion. Moreover, in some agreements (i.e. with Mexico and Peru), the parties undertake to explore new agreements for avoiding double taxation. Finally, other agreements (e.g. Mercosur-CAN) involve co-operation over export processing zones and other special regimes.

Intellectual property rights protection will attract high-tech sectors

High-quality intellectual property rights (IPRs) are an increasingly important framework condition for the development of global value chains. Indeed, when firms establish segments of their production in foreign countries, they are also transferring knowledge (and technology) abroad, particularly in more sophisticated segments of the value chain. The implication is that countries that wish to attract production processes that are more sophisticated (e.g. beyond assembly services, etc.) need to ensure adequate IPR protection. The quality of the supply chain segments can be more important than the quantity of value-added segments that locate in the country. The higher the degree of technological sophistication, the more productivity spill-overs it will generate and the higher income-generating activities it will create. The allocation of value depends on the ability of participants to supply sophisticated, hard-to-imitate products or services. Increasingly, the supply of such products or services stems from forms of knowledge-based capital, such as brands, basic R&D and design, and the complex integration of software within organisational structures (OECD, 2013a). IPRs play an important role in allowing the development of such knowledge-based capital. In this context, integrating TRIPs provisions could become a useful component of Uruguay's trade agreement strategy.

Box 2.5. **Uruguay can benefit from global processes to address international tax matters**

The G20 has identified base erosion and profit shifting (BEPS) as a serious risk to tax revenues, sovereignty and fair tax systems worldwide. BEPS enable multinational companies to take advantage of tax rates that are lower than in the country where the profit is made by shifting profits across borders. This activity – which arises from deficiencies in current international tax rules and standards – harms developed and developing countries alike. But for low-income countries, which rely very heavily on tax revenue from multinational companies, profit shifting has a particularly significant effect on vital tax revenues. If the largest and most high-profile taxpayers are seen to be avoiding their tax liabilities, confidence in, and effectiveness of, the tax system is undermined.

The OECD and G20 economies are working together to address BEPS issues, providing consistency for both business and tax sovereignties. In 2013, the OECD launched a 15-point Action Plan to provide governments with the domestic and international tools they need to combat profit shifting (OECD, 2013b). Engagement of developing countries in the OECD/G20 BEPS Project is therefore important, in particular to ensure they receive appropriate support to address the specific challenges they face.

The lack of transfer pricing, comparable data and the granting of wasteful tax incentives have also been identified as areas of particular concern for developing countries (OECD, 2014a). While these issues are not part of the BEPS Project itself, they will undergo further analysis through the G20 and work of the OECD Task Force on Tax and Development.

The engagement of developing countries in designing solutions to counter BEPS has now been scaled up to enable them to participate in the project directly. Since 2015, 13 developing countries have been involved in the Committee on Fiscal Affairs (CFA) and in the relevant Working Parties on BEPS, with Peru and the Inter-American Center of Tax Administrations (CIAT) representing Latin America. In order to engage with a broader group of developing countries, particularly low-income countries which may lack the capacity to participate directly in the BEPS Project, network meetings are organised in five regions, including Latin America and the Caribbean (LAC), in partnership with CIAT. Uruguay participated in the LAC Regional Network Meeting which was held on 26-27 February 2015 in Lima, Peru.

Discussions with the Uruguay Tax Commissioner in 2014 suggested that Uruguay might be interested in Participant status on the CFA. The OECD will encourage Uruguay to consider applying for this status in 2015 to provide the new government with a solid platform for engaging in the BEPS Project and directly in the OECD work on Uruguay's other tax priorities.

Sources: OECD (2013b), *Action Plan on Base Erosion and Profit Shifting*, *http://dx.doi.org/10.1787/9789264202719-en*; OECD (2014a), "Part 1 of a report to G20 Development Working Group on the impact of BEPS in low income countries", *www.oecd.org/tax/tax-global/part-1-of-report-to-g20-dwg-on-the-impact-of-beps-in-low-income-countries.pdf*.

State-owned enterprises need clear governance

Given the large relative weight of state-owned enterprises in domestic demand (see Box 2.6), Uruguay would benefit from inserting competition disciplines into its RTAs. At present, Uruguay is not a member of the Government Procurement Agreement of the WTO. In addition, the only international agreement that includes coverage of government procurement is with Mexico, although its standards and provisions are the most progressive among OECD countries.

Box 2.6. **Improving governance of state-owned enterprises in Uruguay**

State-owned enterprises (SOEs) in Uruguay are prevalent in the finance sector and in a large part of the utilities and infrastructure sectors, such as energy and oil, telecommunications, transport, water and sanitation. They contribute to a substantial share of the country's GDP and employment. According to World Bank estimations (2014), SOEs in Uruguay account for around 2.3% of total employment and 16.8% of employment in the public sector; their aggregate current expenditure amounts to 12% of GDP and total capital expenditures represent 1.7% of GDP. Given that SOEs play a fundamental role in the Uruguayan economy, ensuring transparency and accountability in SOE corporate governance is vital for improving economic efficiency.

Corporate governance in state-owned enterprises has gained prevalence within the OECD in recent years. The OECD Guidelines on Corporate Governance of State-Owned Enterprises (SOEs), created in 2005, are the first international benchmark aiming at helping governments to improve and assess the functioning of publicly owned enterprises. These guidelines are oriented toward major issues related to SOE corporate governance and provide recommendations in six main areas: (i) legal and regulatory framework; (ii) ownership policy; (iii) relations with stakeholders; (iv) equitable treatment of shareholders; (v) transparency and disclosure; and (vi) responsibility of the board. Given that SOEs often represent a significant share of economies and are present in a wide range of sectors, the guidelines are intended to contribute to economic efficiency, and to improve accountability and transparency.

Despite recent developments in SOE corporate governance in Uruguay, including the adoption of compulsory external and private audits,[14] and international accounting standards,[15] Uruguay could deepen its efforts, especially in clarifying the state's function[16] and the general application of laws and regulations.[17] Concerning the latter, the OECD Guidelines recommend that SOEs should not be excluded from the adoption of general laws and regulations since commercial structures increase transparency and provide the same conditions for private and public enterprises, effectively ensuring competition. In contrast, most SOEs in Uruguay are governed by public law, including the labour relations and bankruptcy law.

Regarding the clear identification of the state's functions, the Office for Planning and Budget, the Ministry of Economy and Finance and other ministries are in charge of monitoring SOEs. Part of their decision making still depends on these entities and often involves multiple bodies, which hinders the clear identification of functions and roles. In particular, the National Administration of Fuels, Alcohol, and Portland Cement and the State Telecommunications and Energy Enterprise are under the supervision of the Ministry of Industry, Mines and Energy; the State-Owned *Banco de la República Oriental de Uruguay* (BROU) comes under the Ministry of Economy and Finance; and the State Water Utility is under the Ministry of Housing, Use of Land and Environment. Contrary to recommendations in the OECD Guidelines, there is no single government agency with authority for monitoring SOEs. Centralising these functions in a unique entity would contribute to an efficient separation of the state's functions and would improve transparency.[18]

Chile's System of Public Enterprises (SEP) offers an example of such an agency. Created in 2001, the SEP is responsible for monitoring and evaluating most Chilean SOEs, and for nominating candidates to the country's SOEs' boards of directors. In Uruguay, board members are appointed by the Executive Branch, with a three-fifths majority approval by Parliament.[19] The BROU Board of Directors is composed of five members designated by the President of the Republic. This is not different from OECD countries, where

Box 2.6. **Improving governance of state-owned enterprises in Uruguay** *(cont.)*

boards of directors are also designated by the government. However, the guidelines suggest that transparent nomination processes be established for selecting board members who are capable of independent and objective judgement.[20] They should have relevant competence and experience; appointing board members from the private sector will help to make boards more business-oriented. In contrast with several OECD countries, tenure of the board members is not fixed in Uruguay and directors are kept in office until a replacement is announced (Robano, 2014).

In relation to the regulatory function of the state, in some cases the regulatory authority governing a SOE is directly linked to the Presidency. This is the case for the Energy and Sanitation Services Regulatory Unit, which is administratively linked to the President's office. This could imply that the government acts as owner *and* regulator, with no clear separation of the state's function and leaving the door open to politically motivated interference.

The OECD Guidelines on Corporate Governance of SOE are being reviewed and revised. The revised guidelines could provide an opportunity for Uruguay to engage further in this area.

Sources: OECD (2005), "OECD guidelines on Corporate Governance of Public Enterprises", *www.oecd.org/corporate/ca/corporategovernanceofstate-ownedenterprises/34803211.pdf*; Lehuedé, H. (2013), "Colombian SOEs: A Review Against the OECD Guidelines on Corporate Governance of State-owned Enterprises", *OECD Corporate Governance Working Papers*, No. 12, *http://dx.doi.org/10.1787/5k3v1ts5s4f6-en*; World Bank (2005), "Uruguay - Report on the Observance of Standards and Codes (ROSC): Corporate Governance Country Assessment", *http://documents.worldbank.org/curated/en/2005/09/7380129/uruguay-report-observance-standards-codes-rosc-corporate-governance-country-assessment*; World Bank, (2014), "Corporate Governance of State-Owned Enterprises in Latin America: Current Trends and Country Cases", *http://documents.worldbank.org/curated/en/2014/07/20183864/corporate-governance-state-owned-enterprises-latin-america-current-trends-country-cases*; Robano, V. (2014), "The role of public financial institutions in fostering SME's access to finance", Document CFE/SME (2013)8.

RTAs should be multilaterisable

For all the opportunities that RTAs provide to deepen integration, they remain a second-best for pursuing reform. RTAs should always be designed in ways that are multilateralisable. A number of authors (e.g. Lawrence, 2012) have called for a "multilateralisable impact assessment" of RTAs as a means to monitor their building or stumbling block effects. One proposition in the recent discussions on RTAs is the so-called "multilateralising regionalism" agenda, by which deep measures that are widely incorporated into RTAs could be diffused more widely and consistently across regional negotiations, and ultimately be multilateralised.

Table 2.6 contains a checklist of multilateral-friendly practices that could be adopted in designing Uruguay's RTAs. The checklist involves five axes. The first element relates to the degree of diffusion of certain practices. If a given deep measure is endorsed by a critical mass of WTO members, including less developed countries, it is more likely to gain traction in the WTO than if it constitutes an isolated practice or one that is only endorsed in the RTAs of particular members. In this sense, knowing how widely dispersed certain standards are could be a factor for considering including it.

RTAs need to be coherent with the WTO

The consistency of deep measures in RTAs is assessed at two levels: their coherence with corresponding obligations in the WTO and the homogeneity of WTO-plus measures across RTAs. Deep measures that contravene corresponding commitments and obligations under the WTO could confuse the international trading environment for Uruguayan firms. One critical issue in this regard is the notification of all RTAs to the WTO, which needs to be

Table 2.6. **Checklist of best practices for "multilateral-friendly" RTAs**

Conditions	Questions for designing "multilateral-friendly" RTAs
How widespread are the identified WTO-plus practices?	
1. Critical mass of RTAs with WTO-plus	• Is the WTO-plus commitment endorsed by a critical mass of RTAs?
	• Is there a clear trend towards the consolidation of WTO-plus commitments in RTAs?
2. Representation of WTO Members	• How representative are parties to deep RTAs of WTO members (developing countries)?
	• Are there observer or open accession clauses for non-parties to join?
How coherent are WTO-plus practices, both with WTO agreements and across RTAs?	
3. Coherence with WTO rules	• Does the RTA incorporate present and future obligations of WTO agreements?
	• Does the RTAs endorse the recommendations of the WTO Committees?
4. Homogeneity across RTAs	• Is there a high degree of similarity across RTAs, within and across trading partners?
	• Does the RTA promote or require the use of international standards?
How discriminatory is the treatment granted under WTO-plus practices?	
5. Non-discriminatory nature of provisions	• To what extent does the application of WTO discriminate between foreign parties?
	• Does the deep measure discriminate between domestic and foreign operators?
6. Mechanisms for extending preferences	• How liberal are the rules of origin to qualify for the WTO-plus treatment?
	• Are there MFN (Most Favoured Nation) or non-party MFN clauses, or ratchet mechanisms?
How predictable –enforceable and transparent--are WTO-plus and WTO-beyond measures?	
7. Enforceability of WTO-plus obligations	• Do the WTO-plus create binding commitments enforceable by dispute settlement?
	• Are there other dispute-avoidance mechanisms?
8. Transparency of deep measures	• Does the RTA include provisions on technical assistance in the WTO?
What are the economic dividends of multilateralising WTO-plus provisions, and are there political costs?	
9. Economic impact	• What is the economic impact of WTO-plus provisions on trade flows and patterns?
	• Does the RTA represent the optimal area for co-operation on the deep measures?
10. Political economy conditions	• Do political motivations for entering into RTAs facilitate multilateralisation?
	• What is the optimal area for co-operation on the given deep measure?

Source: Lejarraga, I. (2014), "Deep Provisions in Regional Trade Agreements: How Multilateral-Friendly? An overview of OECD findings", *OECD Trade Policy Paper*, No. 168.

improved. Only three of Uruguay's RTAs are notified to the World Trade Organization, and except for Mexico-Uruguay FTA, they were notified under the Enabling Clause (and hence are outside the WTO review process and the requirements under Art. XXIV).

There is also a need to improve coherence with WTO obligations, as Mercosur for instance has had instance of WTO commitments. The clauses in Uruguay's existing agreements concerning WTO coherence relate to the standard Objectives and Affirmation of Agreements. Beyond these basic elements, there are other best practices that help reinforce coherence and resolve conflicts with the WTO (Table 2.7). The forum exclusion clause should be highlighted, given the conflicts there have been between Mercosur and WTO dispute settlement mechanisms. Finally, given the share of practical scope agreements, attention should be paid to substantially all trade (see below).

The principle of comprehensive coverage is the cornerstone of the multilateral rules on the formation of regional trade agreements. Article XXIV of the GATT requires RTAs to cover "substantially all the trade" in goods between the parties. Similarly, under Article V of the GATS, RTAs that cover services should have "substantial sectorial coverage" of sectors. Admittedly, the meaning of the term *substantial* – which is intended to define the liberalisation threshold of regional agreements – has never been explicitly defined and is subject to interpretation. This has meant that these requirements are applied in different ways. WTO members' practice indicates that a regional trade agreement liberalising

Table 2.7. **Good practices in ensuring coherence with WTO obligations**

Instrument	Description
Objectives	The stated objective in the preamble to the RTAs chapter is to enhance and operationalise the implementation of WTO agreements
Affirmation of WTO agreement	Article on affirmation of corresponding WTO agreement, by which RTA parties undertake to respect their existing rights and obligations under the WTO
Notification of RTAs to WTO	Ensure that all agreements are notified under Article XXIV of GATT (and Article V of GATS when they cover services)
International standards	Obligation that countries comply with existing international or regional standards (UN, OECD, regional such as APEC)
Periodic review and amendment	Provision that the chapter of the RTA can be amended or updated following any development in the WTO, including decisions from a relevant Committee
Dynamic incorporation	Provisions that automatically incorporate changes and new agreements at the WTO (e.g. in pre-existing RTAs) without the need for re-negotiation
Forum exclusion clause	Provision that states that once a matter is brought to an FTA or WTO panel, the same matter cannot be litigated another time in the other forum
Committees and working groups	A core function is to follow developments of WTO Committees and take necessary steps to implement their decisions
Co-operation	Co-operation under the RTA is explicitly linked to the WTO by reference to a WTO obligation on technical assistance or a committee decision

80% of goods would be the minimum to meet this requirement. In the same vein, Uruguay has been party to agreements that had very long phase-out periods, sometimes exceeding ten years. Hence, it would be good having reasonable length of time for regional agreements, leaving long phase-out periods to exceptional cases.

Rules of origin need to be harmonised

Avoiding discrimination, particularly in the sourcing of intermediate inputs, can be an important element in creating rather than diverting global value chains. To the extent that they remove tariffs and other barriers on partners' imported inputs, they encourage the expansion of value chains with the RTAs, which is beneficial. However, if they generate trade diversion in input sourcing, they will divert value chains from outside the RTA to inside the regional scheme. This is harmful at the global level. Hence, it is important to not provide preferences on intermediate goods and to liberalise these barriers on a most-favoured nation basis. Similarly, one element of global value chains is that intermediate goods cross borders multiple times before they reach the final consumer. For this reason, even a low level of tariffs on these goods can have multiplying effects.

The rapid growth in the number and variety of free trade agreements leads to a "spaghetti bowl" phenomenon, in which criss-crossing rules of origin impose higher transaction costs on industries and distort trade and investment flows. The governance of rules of origin is not covered by the WTO in a comprehensive manner, and as a result there is great fragmentation of overlapping RTAs with conflicting rules of origin. Many empirical studies have shown that rules of origin restrict trade. This is particularly important in the context of global value chains, which can involve two or more countries in the production of a single final product. There are two approaches that can help attenuate the spaghetti bowl effect. The first is to provide very open and flexible requirements of origin. A potential example in this regard is the way rules of origin are formulated for services. Table 2.8 ranks the restrictiveness of services rules of origin, from least to more, according to a review of a large sample of RTAs (OECD, 2013).

Table 2.8. Typology of rules of origin for services

	Natural persons	
I	Definition requiring at least permanent residency	NAFTA "National means a natural person who is a citizen or permanent resident of a Party and any other natural person referred to in Annex"
II	Definition requiring at least permanent residency with substantially the same treatment as nationals	EFTA-SINGAPORE "'Natural person of a Party' means a natural person who resides in the territory of that Party or elsewhere and who under the law of that Party: (i) is a national of that Party; or (ii) has the right of permanent residence in that Party and is accorded substantially the same treatment as nationals in respect of measures affecting trade in services."
III	Definition requiring nationality	EU-CHILE "A 'natural person' means a national of one of the Member States or of Chile according to their respective legislation."
	Juridical persons	
I	a. Constitution or organisation of juridical persons in the country of an RTA party or b. Ownership and control by natural or juridical persons of one of the parties	ANZCERTA Definitions Person of a Member State means: (b) a body corporate established under the law of that State; (c) an association comprising or controlled by: (i) persons described in one or both of sub-paragraphs (a) or (b); or (ii) persons described in one or both of sub-paragraphs (a) or (b) and persons so described in relation to the other Member State. Denial of benefits [...] a Member State may deny the benefits of this Protocol to persons of the other Member State providing a service if the Member State establishes that the service is indirectly provided by a person, not being a person of either Member State.
II	a. Constitution or organisation of juridical persons in the country of an RTA party + b. Substantive business operation in the country of *one of the parties* if non-party ownership and control.	NEW ZEALAND-SINGAPORE FTA Definitions "Legal person" means any legal entity duly constituted or otherwise organised under applicable law, whether for profit or otherwise, and whether privately-owned or governmentally-owned, including any corporation, trust, partnership, joint venture, sole proprietorship or association. Extension of Benefits A service supplier of a non-Party that is a legal person constituted under the laws of a Party shall be entitled to treatment granted under this Part provided that it engages in substantive business operations in the territory of one or both Parties.
III	a. Constitution or organisation of juridical persons in the country of an RTA party + b. Substantive business operation in the country of the party of presence if non-party ownership and control (commercial or local). *Note that in some cases the benefit can be denied also on the basis of lack of diplomatic relations with the non-party or for measures prohibiting transactions with the non-party but in any case, it the juridical person is not party-owned and controlled, it has to undertake the substantive business operation (this also applies to category II).*	US-BAHRAIN FTA Definitions of General Application "Enterprise of a Party" means an enterprise constituted or organized under the law of a Party. Denial of Benefits 1. A Party may deny the benefits of this Chapter to a service supplier of the other Party if the service is being supplied by an enterprise owned or controlled by persons of a non-Party, and the denying Party: (a) does not maintain diplomatic relations with the non-Party; or (b) adopts or maintains measures with respect to the non-Party or a person of the non-Party that prohibit transactions with the enterprise or that would be violated or circumvented if the benefits of this Chapter were accorded to the enterprise. 2. A Party may deny the benefits of this Chapter to a service supplier of the other Party if the service is being supplied by an enterprise that has no substantial business activities in the territory of the other Party and persons of a non Party, or of the denying Party, own or control the enterprise.

Source: Lejarraga, I. (2014), "Deep Provisions in Regional Trade Agreements: How Multilateral-Friendly? An overview of OECD findings", *OECD Trade Policy Paper*, No. 168.

The second aspect is to provide for "cumulation", which gives flexibility to the ruling that goods must be produced entirely in the country/region of exportation, or have undergone sufficient working or processing there, in order to qualify as originating goods. Cumulation makes it possible for goods from a free trade partner to be treated the same as those originating in the country of exportation. This therefore provides an incentive for a producer or exporter to use input materials originating from a free trade partner country. On the basis of this rule, input materials of this type must not fulfil the restrictive product specific list rules. Conversely, there is less incentive to use input materials from a third country, which can create distortions.

To reduce potential distortions, it is important to have diagonal rather than bilateral cumulation. Bilateral cumulation only covers the parties to that treaty (e.g. Uruguay-Mexico). On the other hand, diagonal cumulation makes it possible to use input materials originating in different free trade parties, provided that all parties taking part in the process have free trade agreements with one another using the same rules of origin. Although this is less widespread, there are good examples of where it has been integrated, such as in EuroMed and in the recent EPA-SACU agreement.

Uruguay could be more strategic in its RTAs

Uruguay is a signatory to six Mercosur Framework Agreements. Of these, three (Jordan, Morocco and Pakistan) have been ratified by Uruguayan law, while the other three (Syria, Palestine and Turkey) remain to be ratified and are not yet in force. All of these agreements form the basis for negotiations leading to the establishment of future FTAs.

In major OECD countries, there is a remarkable alignment in the network of agreements signed by the United States, Japan and Germany, and the respective global value chains in which they participate. The strong match between the Network Trade Index and the RTA Index reveals that existing international production schemes are almost perfectly covered by regional trade agreements. While it is not possible to infer from this correlation whether RTAs have driven global value chains, or whether global value chains have spurred the formation of RTAs, the strong alignment suggests that RTAs have a role to play in facilitating the operation of global value chains.

Uruguay could improve its insertion in global value chains by negotiating RTAs with key vertical partners. One of the key drawbacks of many of Uruguay's RTAs is that its trade partnerships are not well-aligned with global production networks. In particular, Uruguay does not have an agreement with those countries or regions that represent a source offshoring demand, notably the United States and Europe. Global value chains largely emanate from the activities of multinational enterprises in selected OECD and other advanced economies. In this regard, the revival of Mercosur-EU negotiations would be a promising step in building bridges with vertical trade partners.

Of course, the selection of trading partners should be broader than existing vertical relationships, given that global value chains are dynamic in nature, and it is not possible (or fruitful) to try to anticipate where a supply chain will emerge. A good practice that characterises recent RTAs, particularly in Asia, is to include clauses for open membership, which are not restricted to the region. In effect, this allowed the PP4 to grow into the Trans-Pacific Partnership and attract partners across three continents, bringing to the table countries like the US who have an interest in locating parts of their production abroad. Despite containing the word "Pacific" (or "Regional" in Regional Comprehensive Economic

Partnership), these agreements explicitly contain open accession clauses to any trading partner worldwide with commercial interests with the region. In the case of Mercosur, only members of ALADI are able to become members, which confines the trade ties to countries in South America. The requirement to become a member of ALADI, in turn, is confined to being a Latin American country. Open accession and observer clauses could facilitate trade ties with partners that have strategic interests in South America.

Recommendations

Uruguay has consistently pursued an investor-friendly regime, making remarkable progress in attracting FDI and achieving sustained productivity growth in recent decades. It has demonstrated strong growth in dynamic global services segments in recent years, and has put in place investor-friendly regulations to foster further investment and growth. Nevertheless, Uruguay could take steps to strengthen its integration patterns, notably by harnessing new opportunities in Global Value Chains (GVCs) and diversifying markets with fast-growing economies, particularly in Asia. Uruguay's regulatory profile in domestic backbone services remains relatively restrictive, effectively acting as a tax to other sectors of the economy and hampering its connectivity to world markets. Accordingly, Uruguay could make better use of international trade and investment agreements by forging modern, behind-the-border disciplines that are essential for sustaining the development of GVCs. The following section highlights concrete actions that Uruguay can take to strengthen and deepen its international integration and competitiveness.

Create the right framework conditions for international investment

Investment is central to growth and sustainable development. International investment can provide additional advantages beyond its contribution to capital accumulation. It can serve as a conduit for the local diffusion of technology and expertise, such as through the creation of local supplier linkages and by providing improved access to international markets and global value chains. The OECD's Policy Framework for Investment (PFI) is an internationally-supported tool to foster investment for sustainable development (Box 2.7). In the light of the findings of this volume of the Multidimensional Review, three of the PFI policy dimensions appear particularly important for Uruguay and may constitute the basis for enhanced co-operation with the OECD:

1. Responsible business conduct: Sustainability and responsible investment are integral parts of a good investment climate and should be factored in from the beginning and not as an after-thought. Principles related to the rule of law, if well implemented, will help to ensure that firms act responsibly, by setting out what is expected of them and by making clear the sanction in the event of a breach in these expectations. Responsibility is not just a consideration for foreign investors keen to preserve their international reputation, but affects all enterprises participating in supply chains, whether foreign or domestically-owned. Numerous non-OECD countries in Latin America, including Argentina, Brazil, Colombia, Costa Rica and Peru, have already adhered to the OECD Guidelines for Multinational Enterprises,[21] the most comprehensive set of government-backed recommendations on responsible business conduct in existence today. The governments that adhere to the Guidelines aim to encourage the positive contributions multinational enterprises can make to sustainable development and to minimise the difficulties to which their various operations may give rise.

2. Investment in infrastructure: The PFI also looks at how to channel investment into infrastructure sectors, including clean energy. As Uruguay strives to engage private enterprises in financing and developing infrastructure, it will be important to identify best practices that facilitate this effort, also in view of cross-cutting issues such as regional co-operation for promoting transport and clean energy infrastructure.
3. Competition policy: competition policy serves to enhance consumer welfare by promoting competition and controlling practices that could restrict it. More competitive markets lead to lower prices for consumers, more entry and new investment, enhanced product variety and quality, and more innovation. Overall, greater competition is expected to deliver higher levels of welfare and economic growth.

Box 2.7. **The OECD's policy framework for investment**

The OECD has been the lead global source of best practice and instruments for international investment policy, promoting the principles of openness, transparency and fairness embodied in the OECD Declaration on International Investment and Multinational Enterprises. Its work in this area is increasingly attracting the interest of major emerging markets, such as Brazil and China.

The Policy Framework for Investment (PFI) is an internationally-supported tool to foster investment for sustainable development. The PFI addresses the issue of sustainable and inclusive development through the lens of investment promotion and private sector-led development. This focus is not meant to accord primacy to the concerns of private investors; private and social returns from investment are not always congruous, and governments appropriately have a broader development agenda than corporate profitability. But it does provide a framework for understanding how policies interact and affect outcomes, while also bringing out the critical importance of public governance.

The PFI looks at all forms of investment involving all types of firms. A good investment climate is one which provides opportunities for all investors: public and private, large and small, and foreign and domestic investors. The heterogeneity of investors, the multiplicity of factors which drive investment decisions and the multiple policy objectives pursued by governments all call for a whole-of-government approach so as to increase policy coherence. This policy coherence approach applies to each component of the investment climate, whether encouraging foreign investment, promoting linkages and technology spillovers, raising the quality of the workforce, improving infrastructure or any other area.

The PFI is non-prescriptive; there is no one-size-fits-all approach to investment promotion and private sector development that will work in all countries in all sectors and at all times. It recognises the role of competition in stimulating productivity growth and the related principle of non-discrimination and national treatment, but it also acknowledges that economic efficiency is only one part of the sustainable development equation.

Public governance matters as much as policies for the investment climate. The PFI considers not just policies themselves but also how they are developed, designed, co-ordinated, implemented, evaluated and ultimately updated. Investment involves a judgment about the future. What matters for investors are all the principles embodied in the notion of the rule of law: predictability, transparency, credibility, accountability and fairness. The PFI was created in response to this complexity, fostering a flexible, whole-of-government approach which recognises that investment climate improvements require not just policy reform but also changes in the way governments go about their business.

Source: www.oecd.org/investment/pfi.htm.

Be more strategic in trade treaty terms

A strategy for expanding or deepening engagement in trade and investment agreements should not create conflicts in existing partnerships. The various modalities and vehicles for trade and investment agreements cannot be tackled in isolation. The multilateral, regional, and bilateral trade processes are highly interlinked and have significant impact on each other. Accordingly, addressing the prospects for Uruguay to leverage international trade and investment policy needs to be considered alongside its objectives to maintain coherence with its existing commitments in various fora. Thus, Uruguay cannot separate its Mercosur membership from its bilateral or multilateral strategies. At the same time, these regional strategies need to be aligned and co-ordinated with Uruguay's participation in multilateral negotiations under the World Trade Organization. It is important to avoid creating confusion and contradictions among different regimes, which complicates administrative procedures and creates transaction costs and uncertainty for businesses who no longer know which policy applies.

The best way to ensure coherence among commitments is to develop a strategy or model agreement based on Uruguay's unique situation and needs. Uruguay's treaties show a great deal of diversity in their design, and in the language used in investor-state dispute settlement (ISDS) clauses. This suggests that Uruguay lacks a model for its agreements, and simply tends to adopt the model treaty of its partners. This in turn exposes Uruguay, as MFN clauses allow investors to choose from among different treaties to benefit from the treaty that is most favourable to their own interests. Uruguay could benefit from a more strategic approach in developing BITs that advance its own economic and development goals. This will create greater coherence and harmony across BITs, and will enhance Uruguay's negotiating position in these accords.

Strengthen competitiveness through coherent regulation

Uruguay has put in place considerable investor-friendly legislation, as indicated by its relatively low FDI restrictiveness score, and demonstrating its commitment to protecting the economic interests of both domestic and foreign stakeholders. Nevertheless, Uruguay still effectively limits foreign access in certain service sectors through other behind-the-border measures as discussed above. Bearing in mind the need for effective and transparent regulations for ensuring competitive markets and ensuring consumer safety – among other valid goals – the trade restricting impacts and administrative burdens should be limited as much as possible. To this end, Uruguay could consider seeking feedback from private sector participants in key sectors. This type of regulatory impact analysis can play an important role in accurately gauging the impacts of existing regulations, particularly in sectors where regulations are more restrictive than in other countries. Furthermore, aligning regulatory profiles with those of key partners and adopting international standards whenever possible could help to minimise the regulatory complexity faced by both domestic and international companies.

Increase institutional co-ordination and efficiency

Although Uruguay has made significant efforts to improve its institutional setting for external promotion, it still needs a broad, integral vision for its trade and investment policies. An investment promotion strategy could cover:

- **Image building:** Uruguay's investment image has improved considerably thanks to efforts by Uruguay XXI. It could now consolidate this image.

- **Lead generation:** targeting specific sectors and companies with a view to creating investment leads. Although Uruguay XXI has made important steps in this direction, there is a need for a broader strategy regarding investment attraction.
- **FDI targeting:** Uruguay XXI could be more strategic and could learn from good practice in other countries (Box 2.8).
- **Investor aftercare:** several improvements in the aftercare of investors, one of the most important responsibilities of Uruguay XXI, could be made to strengthen Uruguay's integration agenda. Aftercare involves facilitating the successful start-up and development of a foreign affiliate in a host country or region. It is also critical in encouraging re-investment by established investors and in generating investors' links with local suppliers. Canada and the United Kingdom are considered two good models of aftercare in investment. *Invest in Canada's* aftercare programme follows up with investors for the duration of the project, and undertakes regular back-to-back outcalls to targeted investors. These visits promote dialogue with investing companies after the investment and encourage further reinvestments. UK Trade and Investment (UKTI) builds relationships with different branches of government in order to create a collective understanding of the operations of target companies, to establish long-term strategies *vis-à-vis* major investors (OECD, 2014c).
- **Overseas presence:** the presence of investment promotion agencies abroad is an important dimension of their reach and capacity (Gallo et al., 2010). Several Latin American investment promotion agencies have a foreign representation in ten or more countries (i.e. Colombia, Chile, Mexico). Although Uruguay XXI is expecting to open its first representation in the US and has commercial attachés in a few of Uruguay's embassies (in Argentina, Brazil and Spain), more could be done.

By various standards, the size of Uruguay XXI seems insufficient to comply with its responsibilities (Gallo, Jordana and Volpe, 2010).

Box 2.8. **Strategic approaches to FDI targeting**

Sectoral clustering is one of the activities that investment promotion agencies have strengthened in several OECD countries. In the Czech Republic, for instance, the local Investment Promotion Agency (Czechinvest) has established a cluster support programme to promote innovation and increase the competitiveness of the Czech economy through sector mapping, feasibility studies for sustainable clusters and capacity building (OECD 2014c). Other countries, such as Chile, have taken a more integrated supply-chain approach to investment promotion. For instance, in addition to seeking further investment in mining, it has also targeted fostering investment into upstream and downstream segments of the chain such as mining machinery and engineering services. This type of holistic approach could ensure greater competitiveness along the entire value chain, rather than in targeted products or sectors.

Source: OECD (2014c), "Strengthening Chile's Investment Promotion Strategy".

Do more to integrate small and medium-sized enterprises

Uruguay's current instruments for trade and investment promotion lack a proper strategy for involving small and medium enterprises. Although the focus of Uruguay's integration policy lies in supporting high-potential sectors, the SME dimension does not seem to be embedded in the design and implementation of policy instruments for economic integration. The Special Economic Zones census, for instance, suggests that small and medium-sized firms implanted in these areas are mostly subsidiaries of larger multi-nationals, and only a small share are domestic SMEs. There are multiple factors explaining the current deficit of SME participation in the instruments described above. First, information asymmetries regarding SME activities have been pointed out, and further exchange with the tax office (DGI) is needed. Second, financing instruments for export companies are mainly targeting large firms, and less traditional instruments need to be designed to include smaller firms. Third, SMEs' integration in global value chains is still limited to targeted sectors.

Create a more integrated skills-building strategy

The focus of the finishing schools and Talent Portal on training and linking human capital with opportunities in services sectors is crucial, but should be incorporated into a broader skills strategy for services. A stronger link with universities and the Ministry of Education and Labour could facilitate more comprehensive actions to ensure that fast-growing services segments will be able to meet their labour requirements and that graduates are well equipped to carry out the tasks expected of them. Another strategy could involve creating closer connections between universities or other technical training education institutions and services firms, in order to offer students opportunities to participate in internships and get valuable on-the-job training.

ANNEX 2.A1

The OECD foreign direct investment regulatory restrictiveness index

The OECD FDI Regulatory Restrictiveness Index seeks to gauge the restrictiveness of a country's FDI rules. The index measures statutory restrictions on FDI in 60 countries, including all OECD and G20 countries (Figure 2.A1.1). It assesses the restrictiveness of a country's FDI rules in four categories:

1. the level of foreign equity ownership permitted
2. the screening and approval procedures applied to inward foreign direct investment
3. restrictions on key foreign personnel
4. other restrictions such as on land ownership, corporate organisation (e.g. branching).

The FDI Index covers 22 sectors, including agriculture, mining, electricity, manufacturing and the main services (transport, construction, distribution, communications, real estate, financial and professional services). Restrictions are evaluated on a 0 (open) to 1 (closed) scale. The overall restrictiveness index is a weighted average of individual sector scores.

The discriminatory nature of measures, i.e. when they apply to foreign investors only, is the central criterion for scoring a measure. However, non-discriminatory measures are also covered when they are burdensome for foreign investors. This is the case, in particular, for rules regarding nationality of key personnel/directors which may hinder the foreign investor's control over the enterprise. The FDI Index scores overt regulatory restrictions on FDI, excluding other aspects of the regulatory framework, such as the nature of corporate governance, the extent of state ownership, and institutional or informal restrictions which may also impinge on the FDI climate. State ownership and state monopolies, to the extent they are not discriminatory towards foreigners, are not scored.

The index does not provide a full measure of a country's investment climate as it does not score the actual implementation or enforcement of formal restrictions and does not take into account other aspects of the investment regulatory framework, such as the extent of state ownership, and other institutional and informal restrictions. Nonetheless, FDI rules are a critical determinant of a country's attractiveness to foreign investors and using the FDI Index in combination with other indicators measuring various aspects of the FDI climate helps to assess countries' international investment policies and to explain variations among countries in attracting FDI. The measures taken into account by the index are limited to statutory regulatory restrictions on FDI, typically listed in countries' lists of reservations under free trade agreements or, for OECD countries, under the list of exceptions to national treatment.

Figure 2.A1.1. **OECD FDI Regulatory Restrictiveness Index, 2013**

Closed = 1; Open = 0

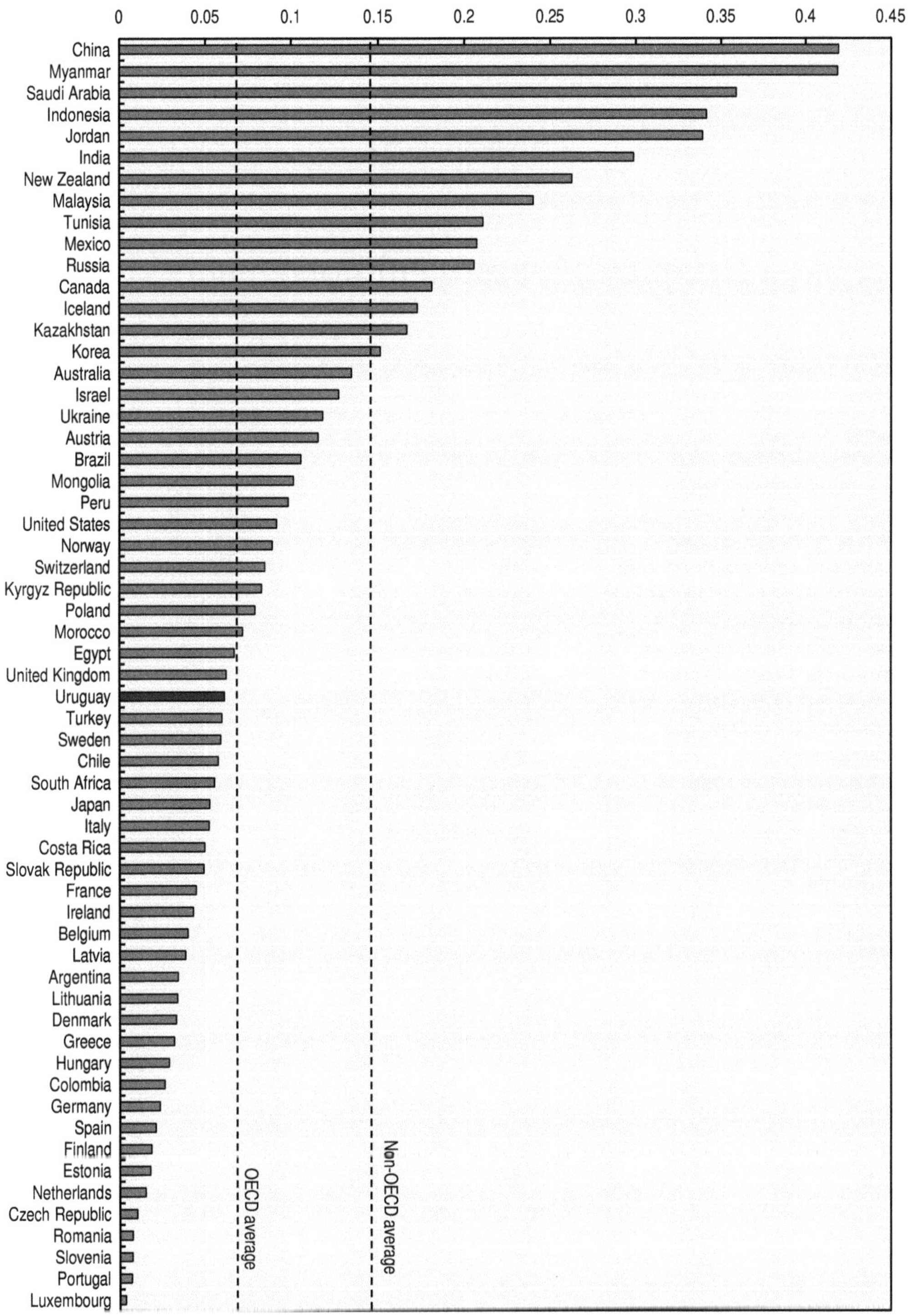

Source: OECD (2015), *FDI Regulatory Restrictiveness Index* (database), *www.oecd.org/investment/fdiindex.htm*, OECD. For the latest scores, see *www.oecd.org/investment/index*.

StatLink http://dx.doi.org/10.1787/888933330173

ANNEX 2.A2

Uruguay's investment agreements

Short title	Partner countries	Date of signature	Date of entry into force
LAIA Treaty		12/08/1980	18/03/1981
Mercosur Investment Protocol (intra)		17/01/1994	
Mercosur Investment Protocol (extra)		05/08/1994	
EC-Uruguay Co-operation Agreement	EU (European Union)	04/11/1994	01/01/1994
EC-Mercosur Co-operation Agreement	EU (European Union)	15/12/1995	01/07/1999
Chile-Mercosur Complementation Agreement	Chile	25/06/1996	01/10/1996
Bolivia-Mercosur Complementation Agreement	Bolivia, Plurinational State of	17/12/1996	28/02/1997
Mercosur Services Protocol		15/12/1997	07/12/2005
ANDEAN-Mercosur Framework Agreement	ANCOM (Andean Community)	16/04/1998	16/04/1998
Canada-Mercosur Cooperation Agreement	Canada	16/06/1998	16/06/1998
Mercosur-Mexico Complementation Agreement	Mexico	05/07/2002	05/01/2006
India-Mercosur Framework Agreement	India	17/06/2003	01/06/2009
Mexico-Uruguay FTA	Mexico	15/11/2003	15/07/2004
Egypt-Mercosur Framework Agreement	Egypt	07/07/2004	
Mercosur-Colombia-Ecuador-Venezuela complementation agreement	Colombia, Ecuador, Venezuela, Bolivarian Republic of	18/10/2004	01/04/2005
Mercosur-Peru Complementation Agreement	Peru	30/11/2005	06/02/2006
US-Uruguay TIFA	United States of America	25/01/2007	25/01/2007

Source: UNCTAD (2016), *International Investment Agreements Navigator, http://investmentpolicyhub.unctad.org/IIA.*

Notes

1. Mercosur is a sub-regional bloc comprising Argentina, Brazil, Paraguay, Uruguay and Venezuela.
2. Captured by its participation in global value chains, taking into account both foreign content of exports and the re-export of Uruguayan content by third countries.
3. Decreto No. 101/006, issued 18th March 2006.
4. Law No. 16.906, "*Interés Nacional, Promoción y Protección*".
5. Law No 18.786 (*Ley de Participación Público-Privada*) establishes the regulatory framework applicable to the Public-Private Partnership Contract regime which covers railways, roads, ports, airports, waste treatment, prisons, health centres, educational establishment, and housing.
6. Decree No. 230/997 (Article 5.1) Acuerdo sobre Transporte Internacional Terrestre (Article 22), as adopted in Resolución del Ministerio de Transporte y Obras Públicas del 10 de Mayo de 1991, and published in the Official Gazette of 8 July 1991.)
7. Decreto N° 349/001 - Transporte Terrestre Profesional de Carga. Reglamentación. Art. 17.
8. Referring to domestic vessel transportation services between the Uruguay's ports and coastal areas, including rescue operations, unloading of cargo, towing, and other vessel operations.
9. Decree-Law No. 14.650 of 12 May 1977.
10. The terms *shallow* and *deep* integration were coined in the mid-1980s to distinguish between agreements that addressed tariffs and other quantitative market access barriers from those that tackled behind-the-border barriers of a regulatory nature. While these schemes were confined to North-North agreements and specific regions in the first round of regionalism (mid-1980s to the end of the 1990s), they have now become the norm in 21st century regionalism (2001 onwards).
11. Estimates; misrepresentation possible for FDI flows channelled through third countries.
12. Based on a sample of between 1660 and 2200 treaties analysed by the OECD Secretariat.
13. Ibid.
14. OECD guideline V.C : "This guideline recommends SOEs be subject to an annual independent external audit based on international standards. The existence of specific state control procedures does not substitute an independent external audit".
15. OECD guideline V.A: "The co-ordinating or ownership entity should develop consistent and aggregate reporting on SOEs and publish annually these reports". OECD guideline on Corporate governance of SOEs.
16. OECD guideline I.A: "There should be a clear separation between the state's ownership function and other state functions that may influence the conditions for state-owned enterprises, particularly with regard to market regulation".
17. OECD guideline I.B: "Recommends that governments strive to simplify and streamline the operational practices and legal form under which SOEs operate".
18. OECD Guideline II.D: "The exercise of the ownership rights should be clearly identified within the state administration and may be facilitated by setting up a co-ordinating entity or, more appropriately, by the centralisation of the ownership function".
19. Art. 187 Constitution.
20. OECD Guideline VI.C: "The boards of SOEs should be composed so that they can exercise objective and independent judgement."
21. See *www.oecd.org/corporate/mne/oecdguidelinesformultinationalenterprises.htm*.

References

AfDB/OECD/UNDP (2014), *African Economic Outlook 2014: Global Value Chains and Africa's Industrialisation*, OECD Publishing, Paris.

Ahcar, Jaime Rafael and Jean-Marc Siroen (2014). "Deep Integration : Free trade agreements heterogeneity and its impact on bilateral trade", *Université Paris-Dauphine Working Paper* DT/2014-25.

AT Kearney (2014), *A Wealth of Choices: From Anywhere on Earth to No Location at All: The Global Services Location Index 2014*, *www.atkearney.com/fr/research-studies/global-services-location-index/full-report#sthash.G2ygB6TH.dpuf.*

Baldwin, R. (2008), "Big-Think Regionalism: A Critical Survey", *NBER Working Papers* No. 4056, National Bureau of Economic Research.

Baldwin, R. and J. Lopez-Gonzalez (2013) "Supply-Chain Trade: A Portrait of Global Patterns and Several Testable Hypotheses", *NBER Working Papers* No. 18957, National Bureau of Economic Research.

Bamber, P. et al. (2014), "Connecting Local Producers in Developing Countries to Regional and Global Value Chains: Update", *OECD Trade Policy Papers*, No. 160, OECD Publishing, Paris, *http://dx.doi.org/10.1787/5jzb95f1885l-en.*

Banco Central del Uruguay (2015), "Inversión Extranjera Directa en Uruguay", June 2015, Uruguay XXI, *www.uruguayxxi.gub.uy/informacion/wp-content/uploads/sites/9/2015/07/IED-en-Uruguay-Uruguay-XXI-Julio-2015.pdf.*

Blyde, J.S. (ed) (2014) *Synchronized Factories: Latin America and the Caribbean in the era of global value chains*, Springer, DOI 10.1007/978-3-319-09991-0_2.

Connolly, M. (2012), *UN Manual on Statistics of International Trade in Services 2010*, Department of Economic and Social Affairs, Statistics Division, United Nations publications, ISBN 978-92-1-161542-5.

Di Comite, Francesco, Antonella Nocco and Gianluca Orefice (2014). "Tariff Reductions, Trade patterns and the Wage Gap in a Monopolistic Competition Model with Vertical Linkages", CEPII Working Paper, N°2014-02, *www.cepii.fr/CEPII/en/publications/wp/abstract.asp?NoDoc=6449.*

Ferreira, N. and M. Vaillant (2014), "Uruguay's trade policy and specialisation over two decades: A gradual and permanent path to trade openness," background paper, mimeo.

Feridhanusetyawan, T. (2005), "Preferential Trade Agreements in the Asia-Pacific Region", *IMF Working Paper* No. 05/149.

Gallo, A., J. Jordana and C. Volpe (2010), "Export Promotion Organizations in Latin America and the Caribbean: An Institutional Portrait", *IDB Working Paper Series* No. IDB-WP-198.

IMF (2015), *Co-ordinated Direct Investment Survey (CDIS)* (database), *http://data.imf.org/?sk=40313609-F037-48C1-84B1-E1F1CE54D6D5&sId=1390030109571.*

Klinger, B. and D. Lederman (2006), "Diversification, Innovation, and Imitation Inside the Global Technological Frontier", *World Bank Policy Research Working Paper* No. 3872, *http://ssrn.com/abstract=923225.*

Lalanne, A. and M. Vaillant (2013), "Un caso de transformación productiva y comercial : Zonas francas en el Uruguay", *Estudios y perspectivas*, Naciones Unidas CEPAL, ISSN 1727-8686.

Lawrence, R. (2012), "How Can Trade Policy Help America Compete?", *Policy Briefs* PB12-21, Peterson Institute for International Economics, *www.piie.com/publications/pb/pb12-21.pdf.*

Lehuedé, H. (2013), "Colombian SOEs: A Review Against the OECD Guidelines on Corporate Governance of State-owned Enterprises", *OECD Corporate Governance Working Papers*, No. 12, OECD Publishing, *http://dx.doi.org/10.1787/5k3v1ts5s4f6-en.*

Lejarraga, I. (2014), "Deep Provisions in Regional Trade Agreements: How Multilateral-Friendly? An overview of OECD findings", *OECD Trade Policy Paper* No. 168, OECD, Paris.

MEF (2013), "Incentivos productivos, competitividad y cambio estructural" [Production incentives, competitiveness and structural change], presentation by Minister Fernando Lorenzo, 19 November, Ministry of Economy and Finance, Montevideo.

Miroudot, S., J. Souvage and B. Shepherd (2013), "Measuring the Cost of International Trade in Services", *World Trade Review*, Vol. 12, No. 4.

OECD (2015), *FDI Regulatory Restrictiveness Index* (database), *www.oecd.org/investment/fdiindex.htm.*

OECD (2014a), "Part 1 of a report to G20 Development Working Group on the impact of BEPS in low income countries", *http://www.oecd.org/tax/tax-global/part-1-of-report-to-g20-dwg-on-the-impact-of-beps-in-low-income-countries.pdf.*

OECD (2014b), *Perspectives on Global Development 2014: Boosting Productivity to Meet the Middle-Income Challenge*, OECD Publishing, Paris, *http://dx.doi.org/10.1787/persp_glob_dev-2014-en.*

OECD (2014c), "Strengthening Chile's Investment Promotion Strategy", Investment Committee, Directorate for Financial and Enterprise Affairs.

OECD (2013a), *Trade Facilitation Indicators*, *www.oecd.org/trade/facilitation/indicators.htm*.

OECD (2013b), *Action Plan on Base Erosion and Profit Shifting*, OECD Publishing, Paris, *http://dx.doi.org/10.1787/9789264202719-en*.

OECD (2013c), *Colombia: Implementing Good Governance*, OECD Public Governance Reviews, OECD Publishing, Paris, *http://dx.doi.org/10.1787/9789264202177-en*.

OECD (2006), *Policy Framework for Investment: A Review of Good Practices*, OECD publishing, Paris, *http://dx.doi.org/10.1787/9789264025875-en*.

OECD (2005), "OECD guidelines on Corporate Governance of Public Enterprises", OECD Publishing, Paris, *www.oecd.org/corporate/ca/corporategovernanceofstate-ownedenterprises/34803211.pdf*.

OECD/ECLAC (2014), *Multi-dimensional Review of Uruguay: Volume 1: Initial Assessment*, OECD Development Pathways, OECD Publishing, Paris, *http://dx.doi.org/10.1787/9789264209459-en*.

OECD/WTO (2015), *Trade in Value Added (TiVA)* (database), *www.oecd.org/sti/ind/measuringtradeinvalue-addedanoecd-wtojointinitiative.htm*.

OECD/WTO (2013), *Trade in Value Added (TiVA)* (database), *www.oecd.org/sti/ind/measuringtradeinvalue-addedanoecd-wtojointinitiative.htm*.

Robano, V. (2014), "The role of public financial institutions in fostering SME's access to finance", Document CFE/SME(2013)8, OECD, Paris.

Soegaard, Christian (2013). "An Oligopolistic Theory of Regional Trade Agreements", The Warwick Economic Research Paper Series (TWERPS) 1007, University of Warwick, Department of Economics, *www2.warwick.ac.uk/fac/soc/economics/research/workingpapers/2013/twerp_1007.pdf*.

Tholons Top 100 Outsourcing Cities 2015. December 2014. New York. Available at: *www.tholons.com/TholonsTop100/*.

UNCTAD (2016), *International Investment Agreements Navigator*, *http://investmentpolicyhub.unctad.org/IIA*.

UNCTAD-EORA GVC database (2015), *The Eora Multi-Region Input-Output Database*, *http://worldmrio.com*.

UNCTAD (2014), *World Investment Report - Investing in the SDGs: An Action Plan*, United Nations Publications, Switzerland, ISBN 978-92-1-112873-4.

UNCTAD (2013), *World Investment Report - Global Value Chains: Investment and Trade for Development*, United Nations Conference on Trade and Development, United Nations Publications, Switzerland *http://unctad.org/en/publicationslibrary/wir2013_en.pdf*.

United Nations (2015a), *United Nations Commodity Trade Statistics (Comtrade)* (database), *http://comtrade.un.org/*.

United Nations (2015b), *Service Trade Statistics* (database), *http://unstats.un.org/unsd/servicetrade/default.aspx*.

Uruguay XXI (2014), *Informe de comercio exterior de Uruguay*, Año 2013, Instituto de promoción de inversiones of exportaciones, Montevideo.

Uruguay XXI (2013), *Planes estratégicos de promoción servicios de procesos y profesionales* (BPO-KPO), República Oriental del Uruguay.

The World Trade Organization (WTO) (2012), *Trade Policy Review of Uruguay*, World Trade Organization, *www.wto.org/english/tratop_e/tpr_e/tp363_e.htm*.

World Bank (2015), *Services Trade Restrictiveness* (database), *http://data.worldbank.org/data-catalog/services-trade-restrictions*

World Bank (2014), "Corporate Governance of State-Owned Enterprises in Latin America: Current Trends and Country Cases", Washington D.C., *http://documents.worldbank.org/curated/en/2014/07/20183864/corporate-governance-state-owned-enterprises-latin-america-current-trends-country-cases*.

World Bank (2005), "Uruguay - Report on the Observance of Standards and Codes (ROSC): Corporate Governance Country Assessment", Washington D.C., *http://documents.worldbank.org/curated/en/2005/09/7380129/uruguay-report-observance-standards-codes-rosc-corporate-governance-country-assessment*.

Zhang, Y. and M. Shen (2011), "The Status of East Asian Free Trade Agreements", *ADBI Working Paper* 282, Asian Development Bank Institute, Tokyo, *www.waseda.jp/gsaps/eaui/educational_program/PDF_2/TU_PRASIRTSUK,%20Kitti_Reading2_The%20Status%20of%20East%20Asian%20Free%20Trade%20Agreements.pdf*.

Multi-dimensional Review of Uruguay
Volume 2. In-depth Analysis and Recommendations

Chapter 3

Transport infrastructure for development in Uruguay

Uruguay has an infrastructure gap in the condition and management of its transport sector. In terms of planning, the country lacks a clear strategy, such as a National Transport Plan. Accordingly, project programming is difficult as there is no clear agreement on prioritisation. In terms of infrastructure delivery and operations, the country appears to be focusing on PPPs to close the gap. Due to prudential constraints, Uruguay needs first to adopt a holistic view on how its infrastructure sector should be planned and organised before considering private participation. Infrastructure projects developed as PPPs need to be aligned with a National Transport Plan. Also, the prioritisation and procurement decisions should be carried out by separate entities to avoid potential bias. Uruguay should enforce and strengthen the current regulations, avoiding off balance sheet PPP execution. Clearer regulations should be set for PPPs' contract renegotiation. At present, PPPs should only be considered where there is a critical and clear present need.

The statistical data for Israel are supplied by and under the responsibility of the relevant Israeli authorities. The use of such data by the OECD is without prejudice to the status of the Golan Heights, East Jerusalem and Israeli settlements in the West Bank under the terms of international law.

Adequate infrastructure is an essential ingredient for growth and for boosting productivity, playing a key role in reducing income inequality and fighting poverty (Balmaseda et al., 2010). In Latin America, however, evidence shows that an infrastructure gap *vis-à-vis* other industrial and developing regions opened up in the 1980s and 1990s (Calderón and Servén, 2010), as governments sought fiscal balance by cutting back on public investment. While the region experienced high rates of economic growth in the 1990s, poor infrastructure stock and quality has been holding back the region's full potential for growth and poverty reduction.

Uruguay's infrastructure gap is significant and its poor quality seems to be putting an important brake on economic growth. Even though improvements have been made, major challenges remain, especially in the transport sector. This chapter outlines Uruguay's main challenges, including an overview of its transport infrastructure planning and governance processes. It assesses the pros and cons of public-private partnerships and other models for infrastructure investment, before making some detailed recommendations for the country's next steps.

Poor transport infrastructure is undermining growth

Uruguay needs to improve the quality of its existing infrastructure to boost its productivity and to increase its citizens' quality of life. Since the 1980s, retrenchment in overall investment in Latin America has seen the infrastructure gap grow between this region and other middle-income and more developed economies. Although Uruguay had a reasonable infrastructure stock in the 1980s, the reduction in investment has undermined government capacity to maintain it. Infrastructure is considered among the top five most problematic factors for private sector development in Uruguay. While major investment in the electricity and telecommunications sectors over the past decade has boosted the quality of these sectors compared to other economies in the region (Figure 3.1), Uruguay's transport challenges may be limiting its successful insertion in global value chains.

Uruguay's electricity supply is among the most efficient in Latin America. This sector has received most private investment in the last decade, allowing for significant improvements in the provision and quality of the service. Hence, the percentage of firms that consider electricity to be a major constraint is below the regional average and its quality ranks as medium-high (WEF, 2014). Uruguay's telecommunication infrastructure has surpassed the OECD average in less than a decade. The number of mobile and fixed line subscriptions – a general measure of telecommunications infrastructure – tripled between 2005 and 2013 (WEF, 2014). This radical improvement in coverage may be the result of a significant increase in private investment in the sector, involving more than 20 projects in the last decade.

Figure 3.1. **Overall infrastructure quality**

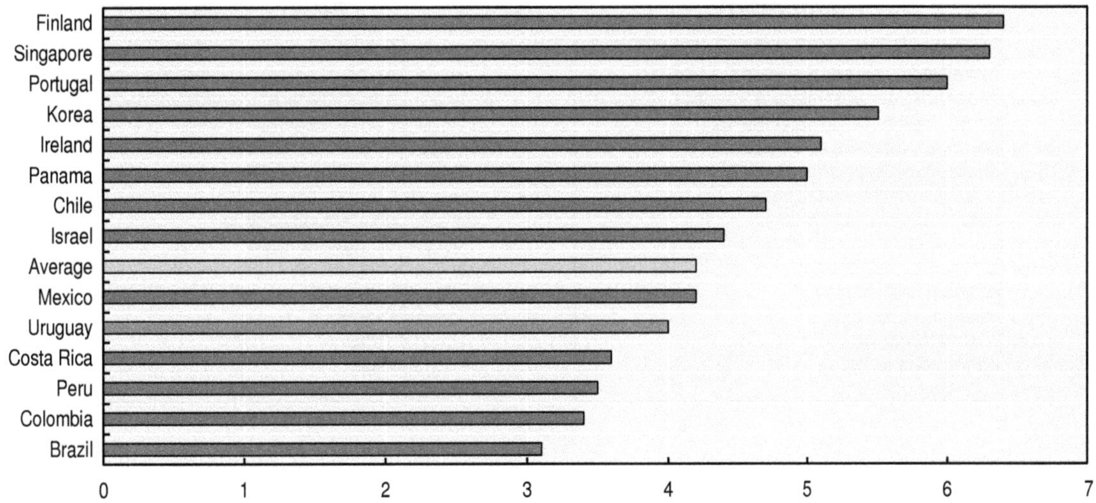

Note: Index includes telecommunications, electricity and transport. The index is interpreted as: 1=extremely undeveloped - among the worst in the world-; 7=extensive and efficient - among the best of the world

Source: WEF (2014), *World Competitiveness Report 2014-2015*, World Economic Forum.

StatLink http://dx.doi.org/10.1787/888933330185

Uruguay's port infrastructure is also considered to be above international standards; nevertheless, the country will face challenges in meeting demand in the medium term, given the strong growth of logistics-related sectors such as mining and pulp mill. The improvements in port infrastructure are the result of a clear national policy to develop the export sector and logistics services. This began in 1992 with the approval of the Port Law (*Ley de Puertos*) and since then government national policy has concentrated on creating a regulatory framework that will attract foreign investment, promote market diversification, update operational procedures to international standards and reduce costs (Olazabal, 2013). The use of integrated technology services such as "Sistema Lucia", which allow for electronic and real time processing of various operations such as freight forwarding and clearing, has seen Uruguayan ports become the reference for the region in terms of efficiency. Nevertheless, more investment is required in multimodal infrastructure to foster long-term economic growth.

The main restrictions for business development in Uruguay are therefore the poor condition of its road and rail networks. The length of the railway in Uruguay is 2 961 km, equivalent to 1.7% of the total surface of the country; only 57% of the railway is operational, accounting for 6.5% of total national load, including passengers and freight (Tettamanti, 2013). Infrastructure capacity is quite low and railways are not in good enough condition to operate efficiently. This situation not only increases accidents, but also puts up transportation costs due to poor reliability.

Inefficiencies in the railway services have increased the demand for road transportation. Uruguay has a road density of 0.44 km of road per square km of surface, which is close to the OECD average. The total road network is 8 570 km long, equivalent to 4.9% of the country's total surface. In terms of quality, 46% of the network is in good condition, 27% in average condition and the remaining 27% in poor condition. However, only 10% of roads are paved (Figure 3.2) and since 2008, road infrastructure quality has declined, mainly because of reduced maintenance capacity (Cáceres and Farinasso, 2014).

Figure 3.2. **Quality of transport infrastructure in Uruguay, 2014**

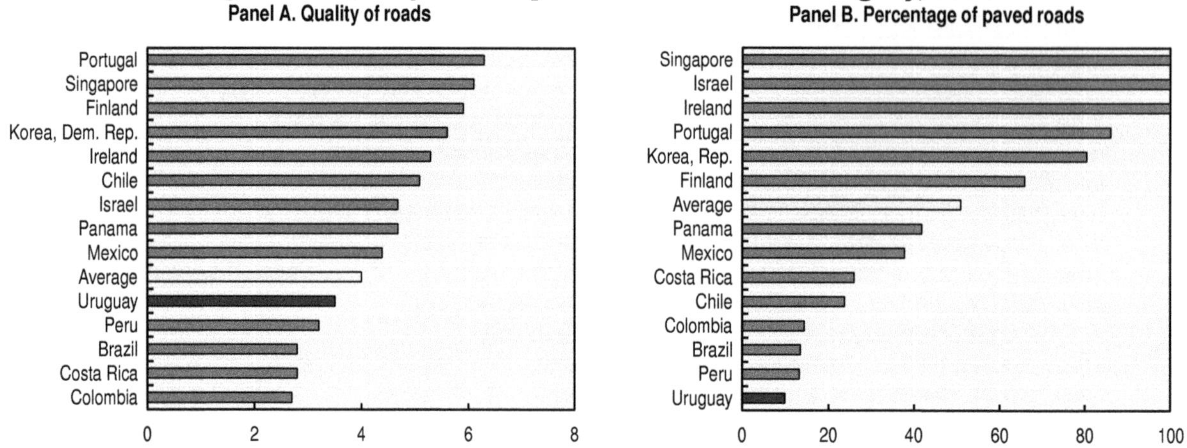

Note: The index goes from 1 (extremely undeveloped, among the worst in the world) to 7 (extensive and efficient, among the best in the world).

Source: WEF (2014), *World Competitiveness Report 2014-2015*, World Economic Forum.

StatLink http://dx.doi.org/10.1787/888933330198

The poor quality of Uruguay's road and rail networks is reducing the country's ability to locate itself as a logistics hub for the area. Figure 3.3 compares Uruguay's performance with the OECD's best performer (Germany) on the World Bank's Logistics Performance Index (LPI).[1] Uruguay's performance on logistics is only 30% that of Germany, and is largely held back by the quality of its infrastructure and customs procedures (Figure 3.3). The OECD notes that if countries were to improve their score by one in the LPI, labour productivity could improve by up to 35% (OECD/CAF/ECLAC, 2013).

Considering the high coverage of road and railroad networks, rehabilitation should be concentrated on maintenance and upgrading to increase their quality. However, the share of maintenance in overall expenditure has been falling recently, reaching half a percentage point of GDP in the allocation for 2014. At the same time the demand for transportation services has surged and the geographic direction of traffic has changed due to development in new regions (Cáceres and Farinasso, 2014). An increase in maintenance expenditure will be key to meeting the challenges arising from the increases in production and in cargo tonnage and the emergence of new destinations for cargo outside Montevideo.

Significant increases in economic growth could result from improvements to the quality of the country's infrastructure services (Calderón and Servén 2010). Despite the great heterogeneity across the region, good quality transport infrastructure is a shared challenge (Balmaseda et al., 2010). Analysis shows that Latin America's best performer in transport infrastructure is consistently below emerging Asia. Given the reduction in public investment in the past decade, the region should undertake policy measures to foster private investment in infrastructure in order to close the infrastructure gap. However, without measures to address low quality institutions, opaque procurement and concession processes, periodic re-negotiations of contracts, and inadequate regulatory frameworks for public-private partnerships, private investment in infrastructure will make little headway. The region should also increase the quality of public services and avoid future fiscal consolidation based solely on a reduction of public investment. The rest of this chapter discusses how some of these challenges can be met in Uruguay.

Figure 3.3. **Logistics performance gap to the best-performing OECD country, 2014**

Latin American and Caribbean countries

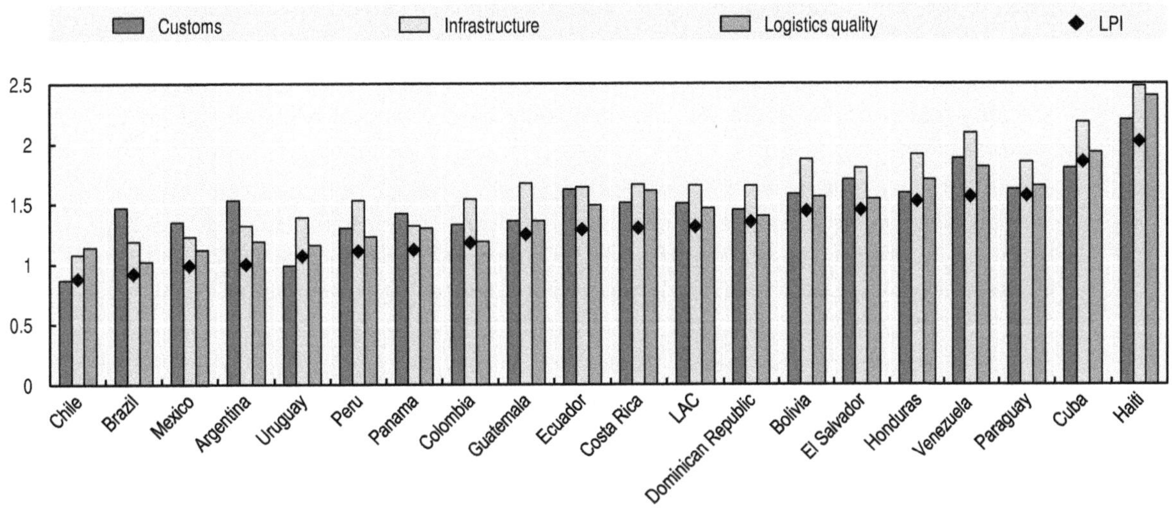

Note: The Logistics Performance Index (LPI) has a scale of 1 to 5, where 5 represents the best logistics performance. The gap refers to the difference for each logistics component with the best-performing OECD country, which is Finland for the LPI and for customs, logistics quality, and tracking and tracing; Germany for infrastructure and timeliness; the Netherlands for international shipments. Latin America and the Caribbean (LAC) consists of 19 countries.

Source: Authors' estimations based on OECD/UN-ECLAC/CAF (2013), *Latin American Economic Outlook 2014: Logistics and Competitiveness for Development*, *http://dx.doi.org/10.1787/leo-2014-en*.

StatLink *http://dx.doi.org/10.1787/888933330208*

Infrastructure development needs to start with a national plan

Without a clear sense of direction, infrastructure prioritisation will remain a challenge for Uruguay. The country currently lacks a comprehensive national or sectoral transport master plan which summarises objectives, deadlines, measures and the means for their execution and resourcing.[2] This results in an unclear project pipeline, a problem confirmed during the OECD interviews with the relevant authorities. Agreement needs to be reached not just on a general direction, but in sufficient detail to allow for clear project programming.

Uruguay has invested considerable resources in developing a national strategy[3] for the development of transport and logistics to 2030. Guided workshops were used with the help of external experts to elicit the objectives and principles for this national strategy. Numerous objectives have been proposed for individual sectors, as well as for the institutional setup of the transport sector. The strategic objectives set out in the document "Policy and Social Dialogue for Logistics in Uruguay 2030" have been appropriately agreed in a broad public consultation process. However, the document is rather abstract (Box 3.1), and with the exception of a few specific projects, only mentions the potential need to create master plans. The information includes partial analysis, opinions, and lists of projects from official and non-official sources. These projects appear to have been considered but have not been officially approved. In short, neither the existing document nor its supporting documentation include the important elements outlined in Box 3.2.

Box 3.1. **Uruguay's strategic plan for logistics, transport and infrastructure 2030: An excerpt**

The plan lists the priorities to be implemented in the short run. These include:

- Short-term feasibility study for the construction of a deep-water port, analysing the potential demand, location, jurisdiction, regional hinterlands, and the potential externalities.
- Encouraging the use of rail for inland freight transportation in a safe and efficient way; adopting modern information and communication technology in railway management; enabling and restoring some rail networks may be economically sustainable in the medium term.
- Fostering the use of the river network for transporting goods, for tourism and for other services; promoting sustainable projects in the Uruguay River and in the Hidrovia Uruguay-Brazil (Laguna Merim - Lagoa dos Patos); optimising the outlet to the sea for freight ships by deepening Canal Martín García; improving and increasing the port infrastructure in Nueva Palmira and Fray Bentos and connecting these ports to the railways.
- Improving the competitiveness of the Port of Montevideo (increasing the port area, deepening the dredging, improving its connectivity with the hinterland and using the Uruguay River as a waterway).
- Implementing a Unified Information System, including a register of drivers, traffic accidents, and traffic offenders, to achieve efficient and safe road transportation of goods and passengers.
- Developing and promoting a high-quality collective urban transport system.

Source: Uruguay Infrastructura 2030.

Box 3.2. **An overview of the main components of a national transport plan**

A proper transport plan should:

1. Provide a basis for sustainable sector development over the medium-long term;
2. Cover the whole sector development and maintenance requirements, independent of funding sources;
3. Include operations, organisation and infrastructure development;
4. Include considerations of systemic reform where necessary (e.g. the planning process);
5. Address issues of/guarantee sustainability of both construction and operation and maintenance;
6. Require robust strategic analysis of demand / functionality of the network;
7. Require clear demonstration of need/concept of particular solutions based on an analysis of underlying issues;
8. Be inter-modal;
9. Be based on the relevant economic, social and environmental developments and objectives;
10. Provide the link between the relevant (national) policies and the projects to be implemented;
11. Provide the basis for further project development;
12. Be suitable for the future incorporation of new information and developments and allow for further development of the plan.

Source: JASPERS (2014a), *Jaspers Appraisal Guidance (Transport): The Use of Transport Models in Transport Planning and Project Appraisal.*

A more comprehensive and actionable national transport plan for Uruguay could be developed by drawing on the experience of OECD countries (Box 3.3). The creation of a comprehensive national transport plan is an iterative process involving three main steps:

- Step 1: Information/data collection (including wishes of stakeholders) and checking for data quality.
- Step 2: Analysing the information/data collected (e.g. the current conditions and needs).
- Step 3: Establishing objectives and developing monitoring measures.

Box 3.3. Some OECD examples of national infrastructure plans

United Kingdom

The UK National Infrastructure Plan articulates a vision for UK infrastructure and sets out the government's plan for meeting the UK's infrastructure needs to 2020 and beyond. It identifies "Top 40" priority investments that contribute to meeting strategic objectives in different sectors and will therefore benefit from increased government attention. The criteria used to select the Top 40 priority investments are:

- Potential contribution to economic growth – investment that enhances productivity and enables innovation.
- Nationally significant investment that delivers substantial new, replacement or enhanced quality, sustainability and capacity of infrastructure.
- Projects that attract or unlock significant private investment.

Australia

Infrastructure Australia has enunciated the following targets to guide infrastructure investment and reforms. Investment proposals need to make a positive contribution to these priorities and be aligned with national, state or regional strategic plans.

- Enhance national productivity by more than 2% a year.
- Increase economic growth by more than 3% a year.
- Increase the scale and distribution of private infrastructure investment across the economy.
- Eliminate the avoidable cost of congestion in our cities.

Step 2 can involve transport modelling

An essential part of Step 2 (analysis) is to develop a national transport model (Box 3.4), which is currently lacking in Uruguay's national strategy. This provides an idea of how transport needs could change over time and informs decision makers on the impacts of alternative solutions. It can also be used to analyse the impact of a proposed measure/ infrastructure project. The model can be used in different ways to inform the decision-making process (JASPERS, 2014a):[4]

- Understanding the function of existing infrastructure in terms of passenger groups, freight types, trip types and origins and destinations.
- Identifying bottlenecks in the network and understanding the need for additional capacity.
- Providing demand data for appropriate options analysis, design and dimensioning of new infrastructure and operational services (e.g. public transport timetables) responding to traffic forecasts and functional requirements.

- Understanding how transport conditions will change in the future in response to changes in population, employment, economic activity, car ownership and development patterns.
- Implicitly, the outputs above provide quantitative information that informs scheme design, cost benefit analysis, financial analysis, and environmental assessment.

Simulations for the movement of passengers and goods may also be linked to other models (e.g. the national macroeconomic model).

Box 3.4. **What is a national transport model?**

A traffic model is a fundamental tool for understanding the current traffic system, also allowing for realistic traffic forecasting, taking into account the socio-economic and land-use developments of the study area, and how these affect transport demand and its interaction with the transport supply. Analyses of the interventions can be both qualitative and quantitative. For informing a National Transport Plan the model must be multi-modal, in order to capture the complexity of users' behaviour, and should cover the entire national territory and transport network, plus the main access/exit corridors beyond the national borders. The model should also involve more detailed modelling for each region, from which relevant data can be extracted for nationwide analyses. Furthermore, the model should also permit to assess not only the different interventions on the transport infrastructure, but also on the organisation and operation of entire transport system. The model can be provided by an external consultant, but its conceptual management and maintenance (of data on transport demand and supply, of the types of analyses to be carried out, etc.) must always be in the hands of public stakeholders (ministries of transport, regional/local authorities and operators, etc.).

Source: JASPERS (2014a), *Jaspers Appraisal Guidance (Transport): The Use of Transport Models in Transport Planning and Project Appraisal.*

If a transport model is developed, to remain up to date and useful it must also be maintained. In practice, it is often difficult to maintain complex transport planning models as an up-to-date planning tool. They require specialised knowledge, and the data requirements can be very large and expensive to collect. While it could be recommended that Uruguay develops such a model to support more informed decisions, a more serious priority is to develop and agree on an operational master plan for each mode of transportation. These plans should have a greater level of detail than the current strategy and summarise objectives, deadlines, measures and the (realistic) means for their execution and affordability.

Several OECD countries have developed guidance for transport modelling, which is used in the terms of reference for procuring the model from a private supplier. Where such guidance is not available, external experts could be sought to adapt existing documentation.[5]

Step 3. Setting objectives and developing monitoring measures

The comprehensive transport plan should be drafted on the basis of sectoral analyses, complemented by functional regional concepts[6] as appropriate (JASPERS, 2014a). Figure 3.4 below presents one example. Although it has some EU specific elements (i.e. in part it relates to concepts and policies, such as TEN-T,[7] which were adopted on a supra-national level), the approach is generic.

Figure 3.4. **Integration of sub-sectoral and functional regional documents to the EU's Transport Plan**

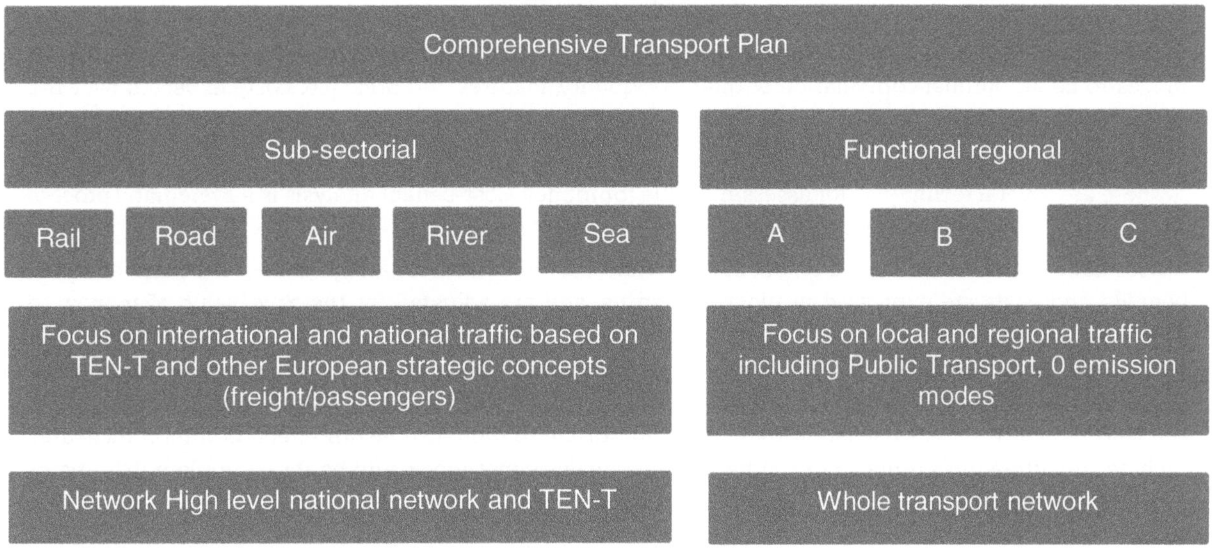

Source: JASPERS (2014a), *Jaspers Appraisal Guidance (Transport): The Use of Transport Models in Transport Planning and Project Appraisal.*

In the EU the entire process is subject to Strategic Environmental Assessment (to ensure preservation of natural habitats, and address trans-boundary effects and climate change issues). The final part of the process involves a public consultation, making the draft document available to the public and allowing the finalisation and adoption of the document at an appropriate government level. Adequate mechanisms for monitoring operational and capital expenditures should also be introduced at this stage.

Infrastructure investment prioritisation can be considerably improved

Once a comprehensive national transport strategy has been agreed and adopted, all investment projects should be prioritised according to government goals and a social evaluation. The decision to invest should be based on a whole-of-government perspective and be separate from considerations of how to procure and finance the project. Those projects that survive the needs analysis and preliminary feasibility study, as well as the initial prioritisation and affordability tests, should then be subjected to a proper feasibility study and ex-ante value-for-money assessment. This includes the full development of the project idea. In countries where ex-ante value-for-money assessments are done, they often constitute the key component of the planning and prioritisation phase of the procurement cycle. Once the ex-ante value-for-money assessment is done, the government should also revisit its initial prioritisation of projects to ensure that the results of the proper feasibility study and ex-ante value-for-money assessment coincide with those of the preliminary feasibility study. If there are deviations affecting the value for money of the project, they may also affect the initial project prioritisation.

Although the OECD understands that value for money should be the only test as to whether a particular project is procured by PPP or through conventional procurement routes, not all OECD countries perform value-for-money analysis for PPP projects (see Box 3.5). The decision to invest should also be based on a holistic cost-benefit analysis (CBA) addressing the project's interaction with other government policy tools and objectives. In OECD countries,

Box 3.5. **Value for money in OECD countries**

Any project, whether it is a PPP or a traditionally procured project, should only be undertaken if it creates value for money (Burger and Hawkesworth, 2011). Value for money can be defined as what a government judges to be an optimal combination of quantity, quality, features and price (i.e. cost), expected over the project's lifetime. Thus, the value-for-money concept attempts to encapsulate the interests of citizens, both as taxpayers and recipients of public services.

There are several techniques for assessing value for money. Cost-benefit analysis is a systematic process for calculating and comparing benefits and costs of a government policy.

Cost-benefit analysis is related to, but distinct from cost-effectiveness analysis. In cost benefit analysis, benefits and costs are expressed in monetary terms, and are adjusted for the time value of money, so that all flows of benefits and costs over time are expressed on a common basis in terms of their "net present value". Cost-effectiveness analysis is a form of economic analysis that compares the relative costs and outcomes (effects) of two or more courses of action. Cost-effectiveness analysis is often used in the field of health services, where it may be inappropriate to monetise health effect. Common measures include "quality-adjusted life years". Other relative analysis methods could be for example public sector comparators (Figure 3.5).

Figure 3.5. **Value for money in OECD countries: Specific tools used in VfM analysis**

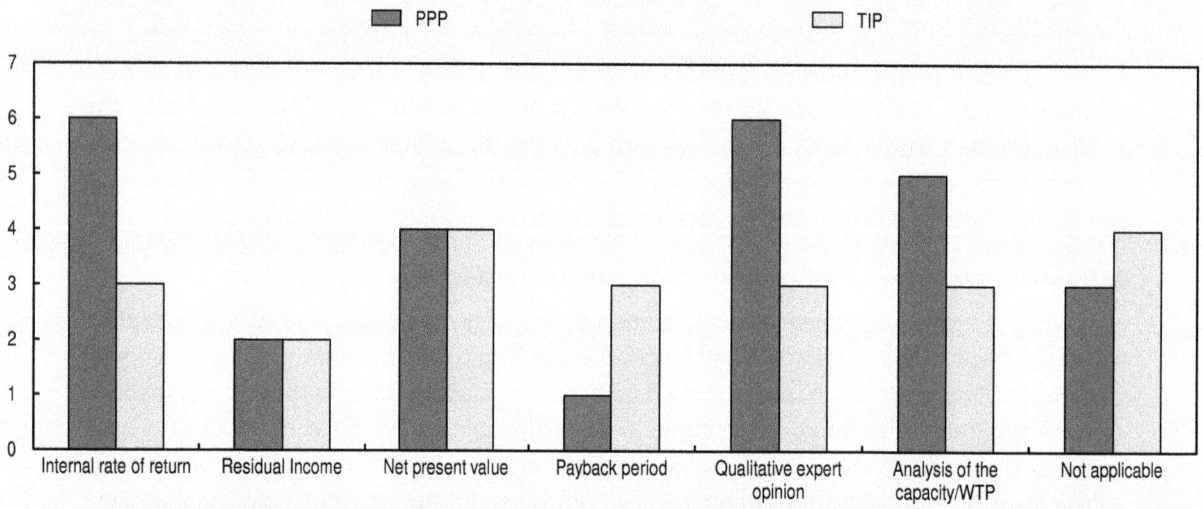

Source: OECD (2014), *Budgeting Practices and Procedures in OECD Countries*, OECD Publishing, *http://dx.doi.org/10.1787/9789264059696-en.*

StatLink http://dx.doi.org/10.1787/888933330214

About half of the OECD countries do an absolute value-for-money analysis such as cost-benefit analysis for all PPP projects. Two-thirds of the countries do such analysis either for all PPP projects or projects above a certain threshold. This is the case for 56% of traditional infrastructure projects. Most of the rest do such analysis on an ad hoc basis. Only one country (Slovak Republic) reports that they do not perform absolute value-for-money analysis on TIP projects. Five countries report that an absolute value-for-money analysis is not applicable for PPP projects while two more countries report that an absolute value-for-money analysis is not applicable for TIP projects, of which Switzerland reports not applicable for both types of projects.

The net present value methodology is used by almost two-thirds of the OECD countries followed by the internal rate of return methodology (48% on PPPs and 39% on TIPs) and qualitative expert opinion (42% on PPPs and 33% on TIPs). Between 15% and 18% of the countries do not use such specific tools.

Source: OECD (2014), *Budgeting Practices and Procedures in OECD Countries*, OECD Publishing, *http://dx.doi.org/10.1787/9789264059696-en.*

the CBA is more frequently required to approve PPP projects than traditional infrastructure projects; while 42% of OECD countries require that CBA approves all PPP projects, this is the case for only 18% of traditional infrastructure procurement projects (OECD 2014).

Although Uruguay has the methodologies to implement a value-for-money analysis, it does not possess enough detailed historical information for comparing a proposed procurement option with other procurement methods. Instead the country has to rely on international agencies with the expertise to perform the analysis based on regional or international benchmarks. Uruguay needs systems in place that allow for the compilation of detailed information on project execution. Some measures to foster this process have been set in place with the implementation of a programme budget and the National Public Investment System (SNIP; see Box 3.8), but more needs to be done. Uruguay should aim for budget detail at project level and to establish reliable data collection systems that will allow for the construction of a significant database for value-for-money analysis.

Chile's National Public Investment System is a good example of a structured and coherent framework for identifying, co-ordinating, evaluating and implementing public investments (Box 3.6).

Box 3.6. **Chile's National Public Investment System (SNI)**

In Chile, all central and regional (even local) public bodies wishing to undertake an investment project or programme must apply to the National Public Investment System (SNIP) for funding. Chile's system gives a major role to the social appraisal of publicly funded projects and programmes. The Planning Ministry (Mideplan) applies a system of checks aimed to verify, first, the formal admissibility of the project and, second, its contribution to a positive welfare change.

A key feature of the project appraisal procedure is the institutional separation between the entity promoting the project and Mideplan, the institution in charge of taking the funding decision, as well as of both ex-ante and ex-post project evaluation. This institution is responsible for regulating the procedures for appraising projects that seek public funding, developing and managing an information system for investment initiatives, developing project preparation and appraisal methodologies and training public officials. Project appraisal is carried out according to a multistage assessment with different filters depending on the phase of the project implementation as well as the complexity of the project. Finally, a strong emphasis is put on standardisation of criteria and formats for the information presented, facilitating project comparison and ranking. The methodology, standards and norms are widely disseminated and systematically taught to public officials at all levels of government, which has contributed to an appraisal culture permeating the Chilean public sector.

Source: Gomez-Lobo (2012), "The ups and downs of a public transport reform: the case of Transantiago", *Working Papers* WP 354.

What are Uruguay's infrastructure governance challenges?

Developing a national transport plan is the first step; it then has to be implemented, maintained and funded. Together this is referred to as infrastructure governance (Figure 3.6). There are several approaches or models of infrastructure governance, including state-owned enterprise (SOEs), public-private partnership (PPPs) and regulatory asset base (RAB) models, described below. Uruguay's current approach shares elements of both SOEs and PPPs.

Figure 3.6. **The transport infrastructure planning and governance process (an investment perspective)**

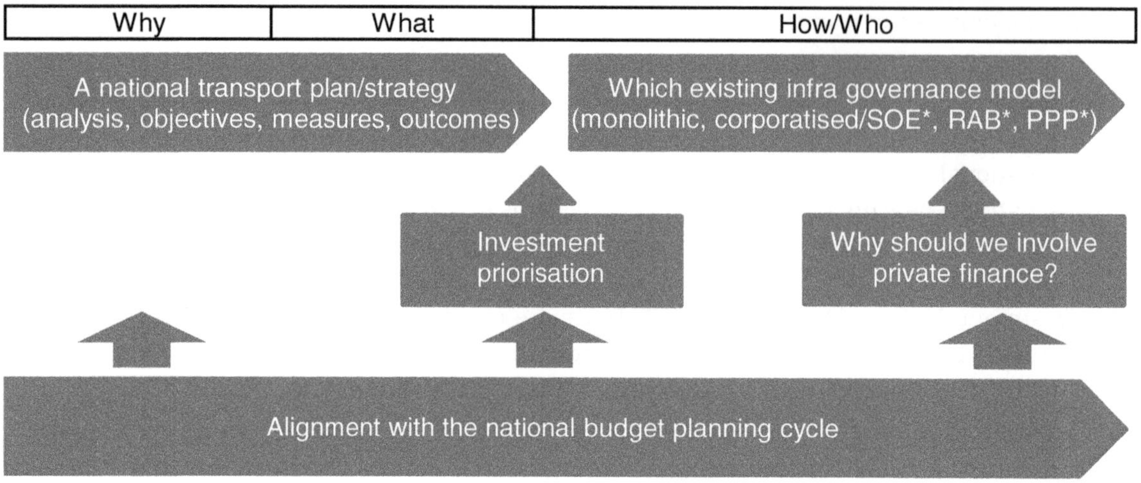

Notes: SOE: State-owned enterprise; PPP: public-private partnership; RAB: regulatory asset base model.

This section first describes Uruguay's current approach to infrastructure governance, before reviewing the pros and cons for the country of new approaches (e.g. PPPs or RAB) and of improvements to the existing approach.

Uruguay's existing infrastructure governance needs to be strengthened

The traditional and dominant model of infrastructure governance in OECD countries involves transport infrastructure being exclusively managed through a state agency (e.g. a highway agency) or a corporatised entity (e.g. a highway company, a railway company). The agencies are distinct and separate organisational units from the ministries, but they are considered to be a part of the public sector (i.e. subject to the same rules and obligations in terms of financial reporting, worker pay systems, etc.). The infrastructure companies are subject to corporate law and are generally state-owned. The financial reporting in a company is a clear advantage, when compared to an agency. Companies are subject to accrual-based accounting, which is a more complete way of reporting than the cash flow-based accounting used in the public sector (e.g. there is no depreciation in the cash flow system). These infrastructure managers answer to the line ministry and execute the relevant strategic policy documents, using direct provision, traditional public procurement (with simple or multi-year performance contracts)[8] or outsourcing.[9] The infrastructure managers are directly in charge of all or the majority of the sectoral infrastructure (e.g. the road or rail network). Annex 3.A1 contains a detailed discussion of the challenges of the traditional infrastructure governance model.

In Uruguay, SOEs and PPPs have been preponderant for the governance of infrastructure projects. Uruguay has not yet fully established a corporatised structure in its transport sector. The National Road Directorate (DNV) at the Ministry of Transport is in charge of the core road network, with less than 20% being managed by a corporatised highway company – CVU. The works on the CVU's network are however undertaken by the DNV (under the terms of a contract signed with CVU to provide technical support to ensure that these roads are maintained according to prevailing standards in the Uruguayan road network). Uruguay uses multi-annual maintenance performance contracts (known as CREMA) in the road sector. The maintenance management types on the road network are outlined in Table 3.1 below.

To improve its performance, Uruguay needs to corporatise its infrastructure management function. This will mean creating an institution in charge of managing infrastructure, which will need to prepare financial statements in line with private sector rules. This company should have a performance and a multi-year financing contract in place. It should also publicly report on its fulfilment of performance objectives and the condition of the infrastructure. An important part of this process – beyond the scope of this paper – then becomes the state corporate governance (the procedures for setting a competent management, supervisory boards etc.).

Table 3.1. **Road condition in Uruguay by management type**

Management type	Road condition (Km)			
	Good and very good	Acceptable	Bad	Total
Concession with tolls	119	0	0	119
DNV	2 338	1 628	1 392	5 358
Contracted maintenance (CREMA)	183	89	40	312
Routine maintenance (microempresas)	815	375	256	1 446
Concession MTOP-CND	1 375	87	0	1 462
Total	**4 830**	**2 179**	**1 688**	**8 697**

Source: CAF (2010), *Análisis del sector transporte.*

In the rail sector Uruguay has already embarked on a model that is closer to OECD practice. Recent restructuring involved the corporatisation of the railway functions and vertical separation between the infrastructure management company – AFE (*Administración de los Ferrocarriles del Estado*) and the operator – SELF (*Servicios Logísticos Ferroviarios*). The general idea is to enable competition between operators in terms of infrastructure management. The restructuring process also involves the establishment of a regulator (DNTF - *Dirección Nacional de Transporte Ferroviario*, part of the Ministry of Transportation and Public Works - MTOP), to ensure fair access to investment on the part of the infrastructure manager. Uruguay has also decided to introduce a government regulator, with external experts providing capacity-building advice (World Bank, 2014). However, Uruguay might want to consider establishing an independent regulator rather than a government regulator in the future.[10] This may not only be desirable from the perspective of regulating fair access to infrastructure – it would also allow for a more transparent approach to financing and efficiency incentives which are not possible under government regulation.

The restructuring of the sector is a positive development, but should be more than a formal change. A multi-annual performance contract needs to be established between MTOP and AFE, to ensure budget predictability and efficiency. Table 3.2 summarises the benefits of multi-annual contracts[11] according to European rail infrastructure managers.

Table 3.2. **Reported influence of multi-annual contracts for rail infrastructure management**

Reduction in maintenance cost due to:	Estimated efficiency gains
More efficient use of resources	2-5%
Increased efficiency in outsourcing maintenance	5-10%
More advanced personnel reduction policies	0.1- 3%

Source: Tzanakakis (2013), *The railway track and its long term behaviour: a handbook for a railway.*

Does Uruguay's current system achieve cost recovery?

Cost recovery and life-cycle optimisation are two key challenges inherent in the traditional model. Any investment should recover the cost of the initial investment, depreciation (to allow for the replacement/renewal of the infrastructure), operations (management and current maintenance), and the cost of financing (including an adequate return). In short, the entity that is managing the infrastructure should have enough resources to pay for its operational expenditures (OPEX), capital expenditures (CAPEX) and the cost of sustainably maintaining the condition of the infrastructure. Uruguay has not yet managed to achieve full cost recovery.

Life-cycle optimisation, on the other hand, involves taking decisions which optimise costs over the whole life-cycle. It also requires predictable funding. If an infrastructure manager's funding is not predictable or is insufficient, the efficiency of infrastructure governance will be severely impaired (see Table 3.2 above).

In theory, full cost recovery should be easy to achieve. Investment appraisal deals with the question of what investments should have priority. Priority investments should have the highest expected social and economic welfare outcomes. In the absence of economic crises, if a country has chosen the right infrastructure investments, economic growth will generate the additional public finance, which can then be used for new welfare-generating investments and to maintain existing infrastructure for future generations. In practice, however, both cost recovery and life-cycle optimisation are influenced by political cycles. The short political cycles of individual governments lead to short-termism and are driven by voters' expectations. Voters appreciate the lowest possible prices, which can mean insufficient spending on maintenance because this does not immediately affect the quality of the service they receive, and instead defers these costs to the next generation. The costs of deferred maintenance are however thought to be much higher than bank interest rates (see Annex 3.A1).

An important part of the process towards full cost recovery in transport is to develop a national, multi-sector infrastructure balance sheet. This would record the value of the infrastructure in line with the current cost accounting principles[12] and include the cost of deferred maintenance so as to reflect the true value of infrastructure in a transparent way. Some OECD countries have achieved this in some sectors (e.g. the Netherlands for its railway infrastructure), but there is a need to expand this to all network industries.

Despite rapid growth in road traffic, Uruguay is starting from a relatively low base. The annual average daily traffic on many major inter-urban roads is between only 1 000 and 3 000 vehicles. As a comparison, the traffic volume on New Zealand's motorways and expressways is above 8 000 vehicles a day, and 12 000 in arterial roads. This suggests that Uruguay's initial core road network has been over-provided, raising questions about affordability and what parts of the network should be recovered and to what extent.

For rail, the situation is more serious, with about 50% of nearly 3 000 km of lines in disuse due to poor condition (Tettamanti, 2013). Table 3.3 also suggests that the use of the operational part of the network is minimal, which is again related to the poor technical condition of the infrastructure.

Table 3.3. **Freight traffic in Uruguay, 1999-2007 (in thousand tons and millions of ton kilometers)**

	1999		2007		Variation in ton-km 2007-1999 (in %)	Average distance 2008 (km)
	Tons (1000s)	Ton-km (in millions)	Tons (1000s)	Ton-km (in millions)		
Uruguay	1 321	239	1 393	304	27	218

Source: CAF (2010).

The traditional model of infrastructure governance described above has developed to different levels of sophistication in different countries and will likely evolve further. Nevertheless, the traditional model around the world to date has had difficulty establishing an efficient and transparent incentive framework that is resistant to the myopic perspective of individual governments or individual interest groups (see Annex 3.A1). Moreover, it is also lacking in transparency in terms of full cost recovery (to what extent the current generation is deferring the cost of existing infrastructure to the next). The next section explores other options.

Can private sector participation close the infrastructure gap?

The United Nations *Economic Commission for Latin America and the Caribbean estimates that* to close the region's infrastructure gap, Latin American countries will need to invest 6.2% of GDP annually (ECLAC, 2014). This is a much greater investment than Uruguay has made over the last decade (less than 2% on average – below the region average of 2.7%). Nonetheless, investment in infrastructure has risen significantly in Uruguay in the last five years due to a major expansion in private sector participation (Figure 3.7).

Public sector expenditure on infrastructure has remained constant over the last decade (at around 1.5% of GDP), concentrating on greenfield road projects. While most resources have been allocated to capital investment, recent years have seen some increases in human resources investment as a consequence of the implementation of the Public Private Partnership Law (detailed below) and the new railroad regulatory framework, which demands greater technical expertise.

There are several options for private sector participation in infrastructure delivery and operation. In principle, however, these boil down to two main generic models, distinguished as competition with the economic regulator and competition for the contract.

The regulated asset base model (RAB) involves competition with the economic regulator. It normally (but not necessarily) involves the privatisation of an existing infrastructure management company. The company is granted a license from an independent institution – the economic regulator. This approach is otherwise known as (economic) regulation by contract. The license is in effect a contract with the regulator, which entails rights and obligations for both parties. The incentives in this case come from the economic regulator, mimicking competition.

Figure 3.7. **Total infrastructure investment in Uruguay 2011-13**

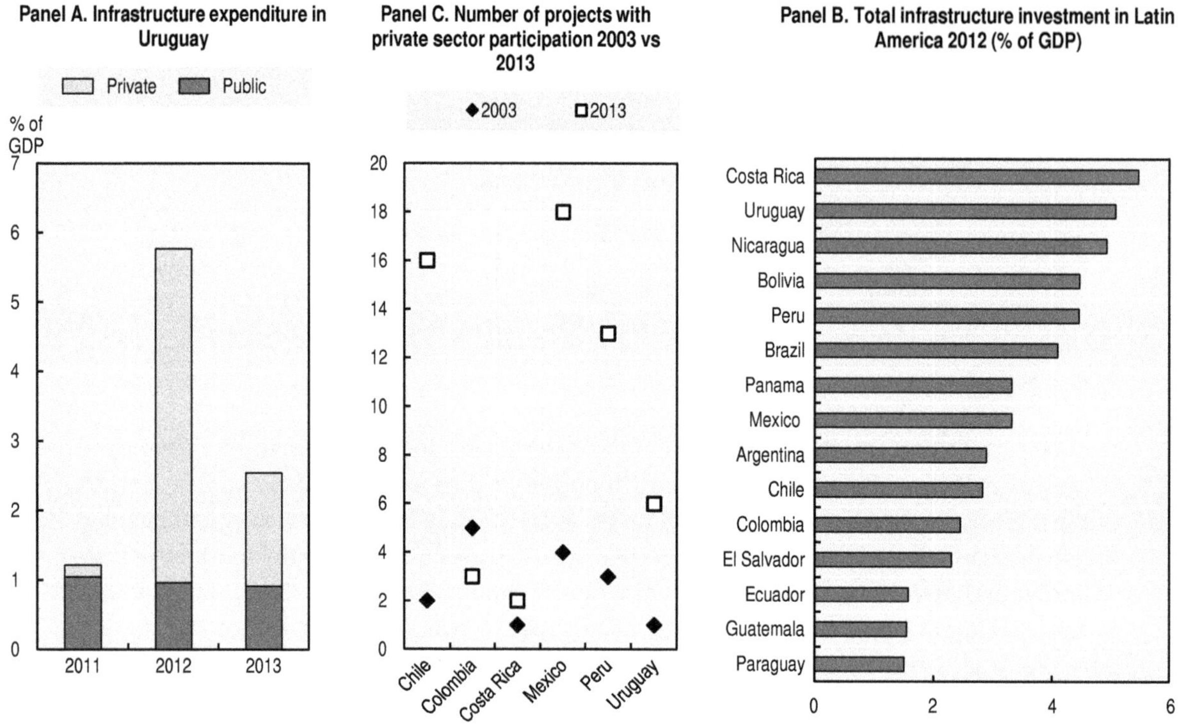

Source: Public sector data: Authors' calculations based on data from *Observatorio de Políticas Públicas de Uruguay*. Private sector data: World Bank (2014), *Private Participation in Infrastructure* (database), accessed March 2014, *http://ppi.worldbank.org/*.

StatLink http://dx.doi.org/10.1787/888933330220

The public-private partnership (PPP) model involves competition for the contract and the use of a concession. It can apply to the operation of existing infrastructure or the creation and operation of new infrastructure in terms of project finance. Both approaches are generally included under the term of PPP. The concession length is limited, usually to the expected life of the infrastructure in question (e.g. 20 years in the case of roads). In this case, ensuring competition is crucial in maximising the social welfare benefits of the project/concession.

Both approaches encourage efficiency and create a contractual "bubble" aimed at protecting the infrastructure manager from the time-inconsistent behaviour of policy makers. However, they both vary in their characteristics and challenges. Annex 3.A1 summarises their general characteristics more fully, while below we outline what they have to offer Uruguay.

PPPs may offer efficiency benefits

There are good reasons why Uruguay (or any country) should consider private sector participation. However, these are primarily related to efficiency rather than new sources of financing (Box 3.7). In developing countries, the introduction of economic regulation and private sector participation through PPPs has had a substantial impact on the performance of network industries. Estache and Rossi (2010) explored a representative sample of 220 electricity utilities from 51 development and transition countries between 1985 and 2005 to show that privatised firms were more efficient than regulated, state-owned enterprises, and that the establishment of a regulatory agency was essential for greater efficiency.[13]

There is little difference in the scope of investment undertaken by state-owned and privately held enterprises, however (Gassner et al., 2009). Furthermore, private sector participation (henceforth PSP) in developing and transition economies does not go hand in hand with the achievement of full cost recovery. As many examples of PSP in these cases are fixed duration concessions, if they fail to sufficiently invest in and maintain infrastructure, the assets will be hard put to maintain their service levels (if at all possible), but residual value at the end of the concession will be reduced.

The way in which PSP can outperform traditional infrastructure governance is in its efficiency in constructing and operating infrastructure. This is explained by the incentives inherent in such approaches (see Annex 2.A1 for more detail). The private sector does not necessarily have superior technical knowledge in the management of infrastructure, but public governance is generally not sufficiently developed to match the performance of the PSP.

Box 3.7. **The myth of PPPs and new money for infrastructure**

The motive for the increased introduction of private sector participation (PSP) in infrastructure was strongly influenced by budget constraints. In the case of privatisation of utilities and other companies, sales proceeds were generated. And in the case of PPPs off balance-sheet treatment appeared to extend the borrowing constraint, allowing new investment. The gains are more apparent than real, however. In the absence of changes in efficiency, the sale of a company is a one-off measure. The money "earned" will have to be repaid by future generations. Off balance-sheet treatment in the context of PPPs also does not create new funding possibilities. By now it has become accepted by OECD countries that the use of PPPs for achieving an artificial extension of the public sector's borrowing constraint is inadequate as it draws on a "pool" of affordability which is limited. Funding projects with the same tax base, regardless of whether the funds are collected as taxes or user charges, reduces the ability of the tax base to fund other projects. In this context, it is crucial to choose the best procurement route, which generates greatest social welfare, PPP or another). Recognising this point, UK has for example adopted the IFRS (International Financial Reporting Standards) for public accounting purposes, which basically requires that almost all the PFI projects are accounted for on the balance sheet. In simpler words, PPPs do not generate "new" or "free" money.

Source: OECD, 2012, *Recommendations of the Council on Principles for Public Governance of Public-Private Partnerships*.

Uruguay established a regulatory framework for PPPs in 2011. But for more than 15 years prior to this, private sector participation in public works lacked a clear and transparent framework, even though major investments were made in the telecommunication and electricity sectors. Private participation in Uruguay was covered by a variety of different legislation, such as the Accounting and Financial Administration Text (TOCAF) and the Law Governing the Concession of Public Works.

The public-private partnership regulatory framework approved in 2011, Law No. 18 786, was based on regulations already in place in OECD countries,[14] especially Spain. The law aims to create a clear, predictable and legitimate institutional structure for PPP implementation, including information on project oversight, sanctions and means of appeal, and general provisions for contract renegotiation, contract extinction and dispute settlement.

The law allows projects to be funded through PPPs to be introduced to the government by a public entity and the private sector. This process is co-ordinated through the *Corporación Nacional de Desarrollo* or CND, a non-state entity created by Law No. 15 785.

Submitted projects are validated by the CND and then submitted to the corresponding public sector entity. For transport infrastructure, most proposals will be directed to the Ministry of Transportation and Public Works (MTOP), which should determine if the project fits into the National Development Plan or a National Transport Plan (which Uruguay does not yet have in place). Public entities direct their proposals to the Planning and Budget Office (OPP) as part of the public investment process, and to the Ministry of Economy and Finance (MEF).

The CND has important responsibilities for productive development, projects and services, and fiduciary administration. It is mandated to promote the implementation of projects through PPP procurement, develop the guidelines and methodologies required by the PPP law, advise the public sector at all stages of the PPP process through an agreement with the entity responsible for implementation, promote inter-institutional co-ordination and acquire any private company as a financial instrument to foster PPP development.

The law envisions the line ministry or entity pursuing the PPP as being ultimately responsible for PPP implementation, from project proposal to supervision and reporting. This includes preparing the pre-feasibility, feasibility and impact studies to submit to OPP and MEF. This process is similar to the one established in the National Public Investment System (SNIP; see Box 3.8), according to Law No. 18 996, which is co-ordinated by the OPP. After the project has been approved through SNIP's procedures and by MEF, the line ministry has to hire a financial advisor and/or the CND to perform the value-for-money analysis and prepare other documentation required by the PPP law.

Box 3.8. **Uruguay's National Public Investment System**

The National Public Investment System (SNIP) is the set of standards, tools and procedures to manage and guide the process of public investment in the country. It aims to optimise the allocation of public resources through the implementation of the most suitable investment options from an economic and social point of view. The framework includes priorities and strategic guidelines established by the government to achieve sustainable development.

The SNIP is composed of the OPP in its capacity as governing body, and by other government institutions that must propose and implement their projects through the SNIP. These institutions include:

a) all the institutions covered by the national budget

b) the autonomous entities and decentralised services of industrial and commercial state domain

c) local governments

d) private and public capital companies

e) private entities with 100% public-sector ownership, independent of their legal status.

Source: Planning and Budget Office (OPP).

However, there are some imperfections in Uruguay's PPP set-up. These include:

- Contract renegotiation
- Bottlenecks and biases
- Effective competition

Unclear contract renegotiation terms leave the government vulnerable to cost increases

One aspect which needs careful handling is the topic of contract renegotiation, whereby the private partner in a PPP demands new contract terms in response to a change in circumstances. There are numerous triggers for renegotiations, from exogenous shocks (such as the global economic downturn, which affected traffic/demand levels).[15] Most evidence indicates that the incidence of renegotiations is large (especially in Latin America) and most undermine the economic purpose of the PPP contract. This is a result of the strategic behaviour of one or both parties to the contract and endangers the political viability of the approach. Renegotiations may be inherently necessary to the PPP approach, but can be managed by establishing a distance between the government agency responsible for the PPP and the private partner. An obvious mechanism would be the creation of a PPP regulator, which would bring us closer to the RAB approach – see the next section.

Contract modification is not clearly delimited in Uruguay's regulations. As experience in some countries may show, contract renegotiation may imply additional costs for government (Bitran, et al., 2013). The legislation in place in Uruguay establishes that contract modifications and renegotiations cannot increase the cost of the project by more than 50% of the original cost, or the operational expenditure, depending on the original contract signed. Modifications requested during the construction phase of the project cannot exceed 30% of the original cost or operational expenditure. Furthermore, the law (Law No. 18 786) states that renegotiations can only occur under the following circumstances, leaving the door wide open for all kinds of renegotiations that would jeopardise the economic purpose of the competition for the PPP:

- The public administration modifies the cost and benefits established by the contract when all the following conditions apply:
  - The modification occurs after the contract was signed, and there was no means of foreseeing it.
  - The adjustment significantly modified the economic-financial estimates.
  - The modifications are significant for the contract and are not due to measures implemented that will yield a general economic and financial improvement.
  - Events of force majeure have significantly modified the economic-financial estimations.
  - Any of the events established in the contract regarding the modification of the contract happen and the parties do not reach an agreement.

Procedural bottlenecks and biases exist

In Uruguay projects subject to the PPP law are meant to be funded by PPP prior to any feasibility study or value-for-money analysis. The fact that these projects already have a funding vehicle in place can create some bias in the project structuring and evaluation process. For example, the public administration may be tempted to propose larger projects as they do not have to be financed with their own resources. Similarly, evaluation may be biased towards the selection of projects to be funded through a PPP without considering any social welfare impacts. In contrast, in OECD countries, projects must be evaluated and prioritised *before* any funding vehicle is chosen.

Private sector project proposals may involve higher costs for the entities involved than to any government entity proposing the same project. Although the provision for private sector project proposals aims for the government to receive a proposal with minimum compliance with the regulations, it could make the project proposal stage a bit costly, as private entities will have to perform a prefeasibility study of a project that the line ministry may not agree upon pursuing.

Moreover, the many and varied roles of the CND may undermine the implementation of a transparent and clear framework. The general guideline dictates that two separate institutions should develop the methodologies and carry out the evaluation; yet the CND performs both roles during the PPP process. Government should foster market competition between CND and other financial advisors. Even though in-house provision is an established form in OECD countries, governments should avoid any policy measures that may generate unfair competition between the private sector and the CND. Additionally, government institutions should not receive preferential treatment pricewise when soliciting CND expertise for project and value-for-money evaluations.

The decision to invest should be taken from a whole-of-government perspective and be separate from the decision on how to procure and finance the project; there should not be any institutional, procedural or accounting bias either in favour of or against PPPs (OECD, 2012). The approval or prioritisation of a project should not only occur at different stages of the investment cycle – they should also be performed by different institutions. The PPP law mandates both OPP and MEF with the roles of project approval and procurement. This may reflect the roles of these institutions in the budgetary and investment processes – even though OPP has the constitutional and legal mandate to co-ordinate and advise the presidency in both processes, actual practice requires approval of any decision by MEF.

According to the OECD (2012), the roles of each actor can exist in a number of institutional set-ups, but it is important that they be kept separate so as not to confuse the key tasks of each actor and to ensure clear lines of accountability. The Central Budget Authority in Uruguay is split among three institutions: MEF, OPP and the National Comptroller Office. The PPP law fosters this institutional overlap. Although almost all OECD countries have localised the central budget authority with the Ministry of Finance and/or Economy, it can also be split among two or more institutions, as is the case for Australia, Canada and Ireland. As long as roles are clearly established and there are no overlaps in decision-making processes, having a split central budget authority may not be a major restriction to the efficient implementation of the budget, investment or PPP process.

Once prioritisation has been established and the procurement mechanism approved, the line ministry is responsible for preparing the bidding documentation and opening the competitive dialogue process with potential applicants to discuss technical and financial aspects of the project. The bids are submitted to the PPP Unit (Box 3.9), which evaluates them against the original feasibility and value-for-money documentation provided by the line ministry. In the meantime, the project is provisionally awarded to one of the bidders, pending the report from the PPP Unit.

Before the contract is signed the company needs to secure the financing and warranties required to start project operation. At this stage some issues may arise, specifically in the capital markets where regulations require a signed contract as part of the documentation to request a bond issue approval. If the company overcomes any restrictions that may exist the contract is signed and the construction of the project should begin, otherwise it will go to the bidder at second place in the bidding process.

The oversight and reporting of implementation are the responsibility of the line ministry, who needs to audit the company and report progress to the PPP unit. The line ministry also has the obligation to register all the expenditures related to the PPP project as a budget line within their reporting to the central budget authority, which responsibilities in this case are represented by OPP. The payment stream from government under the PPP contract should be highlighted; the information should be disclosed at the same time as the results of the long-term fiscal analysis that shows the long-term effects of the stock and new flow of PPP contracts.

Box 3.9. **The role of a PPP Unit**

Given the complexity of PPPs and their infrequent use, the OECD recommends that the critical skills to ensure value for money may need to be concentrated in a unit that services all relevant authorities (OECD 2012). The law established a PPP unit within the Ministry of Economy and Finance. In a survey of budgetary practices, 18 out of the 33 participating OECD countries have established one or more PPP units within their central government. Most of these countries have established the PPP unit in the Ministry of Finance or a subordinate unit of this ministry. Seven countries have more than one PPP unit, meaning PPP units are present in line ministries in addition to the unit in the Ministry of Finance. Four countries (Chile, Denmark, Hungary and Japan) have PPP units only in line ministries and one country (Greece) has a PPP unit in another body.

Figure 3.8. **OECD countries with one or more PPP units in central government**

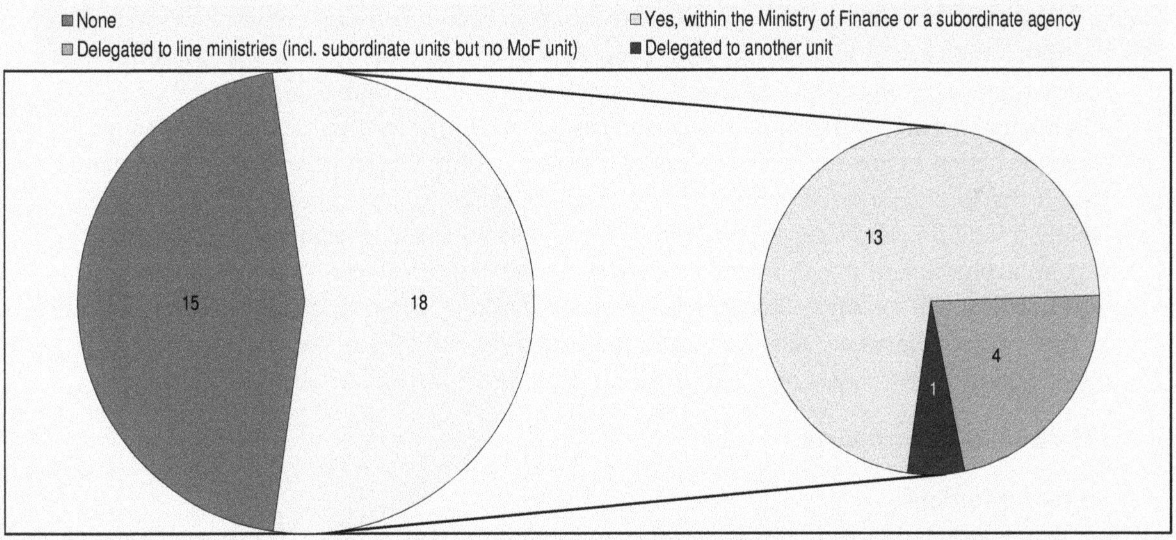

Source: OECD (2014), *Budgeting Practices and Procedures in OECD Countries*, *http://dx.doi.org/10.1787/9789264059696-en.*

StatLink *http://dx.doi.org/10.1787/888933330231*

According to the law, the PPP Unit has to follow up on the financial and economic aspects, as well as budget requirements, risk assessment and perform the analysis and registry of PPP projects that the law mandates to the MEF. The unit's responsibilities shall be limited to the assessments and registry task which should align with the current National Public Investment System. As recommended by the OECD, the PPP unit should help the relevant authorities prepare and negotiate the PPP contract, but it should not decide on whether the PPP should move forward; this green-light process should be anchored in the Central Budget Authority.

Source: OECD (2014).

Competition

Achieving strong competition for the PPP is of crucial importance. Without it, the projects will not deliver the desired social welfare outcomes. Uruguay's current PPP law and corporate legislation could be hindering the development of competition in the context of PPPs. As pointed out in the chapter on FDI (Chapter 2) only Uruguayan nationals or enterprises may be granted concessions in the transport sector. Uruguayan enterprises are those that are managed, controlled, and in which more than 50% of the capital is owned by Uruguayan nationals domiciled in Uruguay. This effectively means that foreign private sector participation is only possible by establishing a subsidiary in Uruguay, while direct cross-border competition is unlikely (becoming a minority partner in a PPP/concession).

In principle, protectionist policies in this context would not be a bad idea if the country was sufficiently large to generate strong competition in its internal market. This, however, is rarely the case. Indeed, one of the main concerns in the protection of national interest and protectionist behaviour is the fear that private competition in construction from abroad might lead to the transfer of infrastructure capital expenditures to that country. At the same time, several OECD economies have been subject to collusion between bidders in construction.[16] Large projects and/or large risk transfer requirements also reduce potential competition, leading to few potential bidders and an increased risk of collusion, especially if the same three bidders are present on multiple projects (Zitron, 2006).

However, direct cross-border competition is not the preferred mode of competition in construction in general. This is primarily because each country has some local specifics in construction standards and requirements. It is also advantageous to have a local partner, familiar with other local market specifics. The dominant approach in cross-border competition is through joint ventures and establishment of local subsidiaries, but this is also an area where current rules and regulations in Uruguay may be obstructive. Other aspects of construction involve sourcing materials, where in most cases the economics dictate that if the local market is competitive, it is also best to procure construction materials locally. In addition some types of materials have to be within a specific range of the project (e.g. an asphalt plant needs a source of gravel etc.). These local specificities could explain why in the EU, for example, despite the "common market", direct cross border competition in construction between 2008 and 2012 accounted for only 3% of all tendered works in construction (above public notice thresholds) (Kutlina-Dimitrova and Lakatos, 2014).

PPPs and RABs compared

Sector limitations

The RAB is generally applied in utilities (electricity transmission, water supply, railways infrastructure), whereas PPPs are predominantly present in transport, health, social and other projects. In principle, both approaches can be applied on individual projects (buildings/sections of a network) or on an entire network, but in the case of RAB there is no practice yet for standalone greenfield projects. For transport, RAB is used in railway infrastructure management, although there is no OECD evidence of a country applying the model to the road sector. This would be considered an innovation.

Financing and costs

In principle in both PPP and RAB the financing for the functions of the infrastructure company can come from the user charges or from the government budget (i.e. the availability-based PPP model; see Box 3.A1.1 in the annex). In terms of the cost of financing it is generally accepted that PPPs are substantially more expensive to finance than RABs (see also PPP issues with risk and uncertainty). The decision and political responsibility to ensure full cost recovery (through the budget or through user charges) remains with the policy makers in both cases.

Ownership

In the case of the RAB there is also the question of the ownership of the infrastructure company. The company can be public or private. Given the research on privatisation in regulated network industries, it is generally understood that in the network industries, which have characteristics of a natural monopoly and require economic regulation, ownership is important.[17] The results in the literature cited suggest that in terms of cost efficiency the public ownership without regulation performs least well, public ownership with regulation follows, and private ownership with regulation is on average expected to perform best.

The challenge of the state-owned regulated company is that it can still be subject to following political objectives (incl. political appointments of the management) or that the efforts of the regulator might be reduced, because of insufficient tension if both entities are state owned. An example of such an outcome can be found in Slovenia in Europe (Makovšek and Logožar, 2014). There the text book application of efficiency incentives in electricity and gas distribution networks, combined with lax regulation of the regulator failed to produce any efficiency improvement in the first five-year period.

Government credibility

The ability of the government to uphold its contractual commitments, pipelines etc. is a crucial element for the success of either approach. RAB or PPP contractual framework should shield the infrastructure manager from political short termism. Clearly this will not be the case if the government decides to renege on its contractual commitments. In the case of the RAB this may involve government interference with the economic regulation. For PPPs, opportunistic renegotiations of the initial contract by either side or both can reduce or destroy the social welfare outcomes that PPPs are supposed to deliver. A more serious setback to private participation in infrastructure would be expropriation.

Capacity

In both cases (RAB or PPP) a capacity building period is necessary. In the case of the PPPs, the capacity building involves the creation of a dedicated PPP unit, promotion of the concept and its understanding, the maturing of the PPP market etc. Similarly, in the case of RAB, a newly created regulator will not have the same capacity as an established institution with a decade of track record. Nevertheless, it may be easier, with the help of private consultants, for a government to deploy a PPP faster than a RAB model. The reason is that in the latter model, a legislative framework would first have to be set up, then the economic regulator. Once that is achieved, the regulator would have to require from the regulated firm to introduce a range of tools, that are necessary for the regulator to properly execute its function and which any company in the sector should have anyway to properly manage its business. Among other things, an essential part of this is a modern accounting and (physical) asset management system (see section: The dominant approach to infrastructure governance in the OECD and Uruguay).

Recommendations

Overall our review finds that in principle, there are no immediate restrictions to the application of either PPP or RAB to infrastructure delivery. The main difference is in the speed of deployment. Implementing an RAB model is a longer-term option as it would first require some preconditions to be fulfilled (see below). However, given the long-term nature of infrastructure investment, the potentially longer introduction of RAB is relative. It has to be viewed as a long-term policy direction - a system of infrastructure governance for the country for decades to come. PPPs appear to be a more costly option, but would enable projects to get done and may yield improvements to the practice of the traditional model, as was acknowledged in the UK.

One of the main motives for introducing PPPs in Uruguay seems to be to alleviate the government's borrowing constraint. During the OECD interviews this position was stated several times. This overlooks the fact that with Uruguay's availability-based model, all such PPPs will have to be disbursed from the government's budget, requiring an increase in line ministries' budgets to pay the unitary charges. Even if there were cases of PPPs in Uruguay which could fund themselves (through user charges, tax increments or other means), the ultimate borrowing constraint is the affordability of infrastructure for the tax base or its users.

Even if Uruguay was successful in deploying the PPP model, in the short and medium term it will still only apply to a small share of the total infrastructure stock. PPPs cannot hope to fully replace the existing approach to infrastructure governance in Uruguay, and this is also true for all OECD economies. This is because most PPP applications in Uruguay will be availability-based and will count against a prudential fiscal exposure limit. This limit is currently set by Uruguayan PPP law, which states that the net present value of PPP commitments should not exceed 5% of GDP. Uruguay's GDP in January 2014 was UYU 55.71 billion, so 5% is about UYU 2.7 billion. As a rough illustration, this amount is perhaps sufficient to rehabilitate the major road corridors using PPPs, but not the entire main road network (according to interviews). Moreover, if the entire PPP commitment was spent on the road sector, little room would remain for other sectors. According to recent technical reports (World Bank 2014), the density of Uruguay's rail and road traffic is insufficient to merit commercially viable PPPs, thus the only possible model is the availability-based PPP, in which projects are funded from the government budget or in combination with user charges/tolls. The same applies for an RAB.

The steps involved in implementing an RAB approach in Uruguay's road sector, given that it has already embarked on a PPP path, can be illustrated as follows:

1. The country continues on its existing path, setting up and executing a road PPP pipeline.
2. In parallel, a regulatory framework would have to be set up, following the establishment of a new independent institution – the economic (road) regulator.
3. CVU which is state-owned, would be placed in an RAB and an incentive framework.
4. Following several years of capacity building of the regulator (with the help of external international institutions/experts), CVU would be privatised.
5. New projects next to CVU's territory could be delivered by CVU using traditional procurement or project finance, where after the construction phase the new/refurbished asset is introduced/bought into CVU's RAB.
6. Other existing PPPs at that time could be either left as they are to run their course or be "bought" into the RAB framework.

7. Other RABs aside from CVN could be established, if economically feasible (to make benchmarking/yardstick competition easier; but subject to critical minimal size of the company) or there could just be a single national highway company.

- **Create a national transport plan.** Private sector involvement and healthy competition require a clear and credible project pipeline. Our review finds that Uruguay's existing transport strategy is not sufficiently detailed to allow credible project programming. We recommend that Uruguay creates a national transport plan. Uruguay should strive to define details in the national transport plan for each mode (or more detailed master plans if necessary). Such a document should summarise objectives, deadlines, measures and the (realistic) means for their execution and affordability.
- **Conduct a detailed review of the public investment management system** (including the investment evaluation/budgeting process).
- **Postpone the value-for-money test until the country has sufficient compiled data to perform it.** Instead Uruguay should assume that PPP represents value for money. The country should set a time in the future (in the medium term), when this assumption will be tested and revised if needed. Such a requirement, its execution and funding, should by binding by law (possibly the PPP law). The current process should only assess the feasibility/eligibility of projects for PPP (e.g. is the project of sufficient size to justify transaction costs, can a good output specification be defined etc.). When the data conditions are met, the country can reintroduce the VfM test.
- **Conduct an ex-post analysis of a sample of traditionally procured projects.** This would not only serve as a comparison for PPP performance, but would also improve existing project appraisal and delivery practices.
- **Create a clear budget and procurement framework.** The institution responsible for the decision of procurement in the budget and investment process is not clearly established. To ensure the efficacy of the PPP process, it is imperative for Uruguay to develop a budgetary framework which entrusts clear mandates and an efficient budgetary and procurement procedure. As a suggestion, project approval should remain in OPP within the SNIP framework, while the procurement method determination should be the responsibility of MEF, since it possesses more accurate information on the country's overall macroeconomic and fiscal situation.
- **Do more to maximise competition for PPP and other construction projects.** An independent intergovernmental/international institution should be asked to assess the potential economic impact of foreign competition in the construction sector in general. That being said, should foreign direct cross-border competition prove to be a problem, the country should instead resort to sourcing requirements,[18] rather than hindering foreign competition. Sufficient attention (notably funding) should also be given to the competition authority and its operational capacity. The OECD did not address this aspect in this review, but it is nevertheless important to stress its importance.
- **Establish clear guidelines for contract re-negotiation and private sector compensation for unforeseen circumstances.** Despite the fact that Uruguay is just setting out on the PPP path, it should have a view on contract renegotiations. The OECD recommends that Uruguay adopt a mandatory guidance document which contains detailed descriptions of when renegotiations of PPP contracts are allowed and to what extent. Only if conditions change due to discretionary public policy actions should the government consider compensating the private sector. Any other compensation for changes in commercial

conditions should be explicitly negotiated in the contract. Otherwise, the risks to re-negotiations of PPP contracts due to changes in international conditions not foreseen at the moment of the contract award could significantly increase fiscal costs of PPPs for the government (OECD 2012). Clear, predictable and transparent rules for dispute resolution should be in place to resolve disagreement on the above between the public and private parties. Furthermore, any re-negotiation that substantially alters the original agreement should be made public and be subject to approval by the authority responsible for approving PPPs. Such an agreement should be as competitively done as possible. The responsibility for the supervision/administration of renegotiations should be devolved to a body which is considered to be independent (e.g. the competition authority, or supreme audit institution). The substance and economic impact of renegotiations should be publicly available.

ANNEX 3.A1

Infrastructure governance: Three models compared

The traditional model: Infrastructure governance by the state

In the traditional model, infrastructure is generally delivered through government procurement. This involves the tendering of works through simple contractual schemes, which at most, bundle the phases of design and construction (the Design-Build contract). The dominant reliance is still on the traditional DBB contract (Design-Bid-Build), where each phase is procured separately. This approach has some general characteristics:

1. In traditional procurement the public sector retains most of the risks.
2. The public sector retains the possibility of changing the scope of the project during construction, but that option is often abused. There is a well recorded tendency of public project sponsors to misrepresent the true expected costs and benefits of projects, to make them more attractive to the decision makers (Flyvbjerg et al 2002). Although changes to scope in this mode of procurement are generally less costly than in a PPP arrangement, they are still very expensive.[19]
3. A lack of risk transfer translates into higher competition between the bidders and potentially lower prices. In such projects capital requirements for the construction companies are much less demanding than in contracts, where substantial risk is transferred.
4. In traditional procurement, the operations phase is normally not bundled to the design and construction. This greatly reduces the incentives of considering future consequences of decisions in each of the phases. The short government voting cycles also introduce short-termism into decisions (Helm, 2010). Politicians tend to favour the red ribbon cutting for as many projects as possible, without considering the future costs of this infrastructure. As a consequence, cheaper infrastructure may be built, which is later more expensive to operate and maintain. This means there are fewer incentives for project life cycle cost optimisation to be achieved.

In recent years, OECD countries have paid much attention to on-time and on-budget performance issues of traditional public delivery. It is generally accepted that PPPs have a better performance in terms of on-time and on-budget delivery. Box 3.A1.1 provides some empirical detail on the topic.

After the construction phase, the infrastructure in the traditional model in most OECD countries is operated by a government agency or a state-owned corporatised entity. This raises two major challenges, for: i) performance incentives; and ii) cost recovery and life-cycle cost optimisation.

Performance incentives are limited:

- Infrastructure management companies (or agencies) share several characteristics with natural monopolies (entry barriers in terms of sunk cost, economies of scale and scope etc.). Accordingly, they are not subject to adequate competitive pressures. The main efficiency thus comes from the management of the entity. In this model, it can be common, despite safeguards, for the management to not be selected according to competence. The model may pursue other objectives as well, which may be in conflict with the tenets of performance and efficiency.
- It is also not uncommon for large and powerful unions to develop in such entities, with considerable involvement not only in workers' rights, but also business decisions and overall strategy. And because governments tend to make quick savings in infrastructure expenditures in times of need, publicly-owned companies often pursue strategies to protect their cash flow. These can translate into low efficiency and quality levels (e.g. hiring too many employees, granting excessive benefits). Decision makers usually avoid social unrest or confrontation with the unions. The "budgeting" of the government then provides enough funding for the wages of the infrastructure manager, but not enough to fully recover the cost of the infrastructure. The "savings" of this process are then manifested in a slowly deteriorating condition of the infrastructure. From an engineering perspective, the cost curve for catching up deferred maintenance is exponential. The cost of catching-up very quickly becomes far greater than what are considered to be the normal ranges of government borrowing cost in industrialised countries. The limit of the process is, of course, when a complete reconstruction of the infrastructure is required. Indeed, such a policy transfers the cost of catching-up with the maintenance backlog to the next generation of taxpayers and makes optimisation of the infrastructure lifecycle cost impossible.
- When the infrastructure manager does not have a modern asset management system in place, lack of maintenance eventually leads into a process where infrastructure on the network "randomly" starts to fail, creating the need for many interventions within a short period of time (i.e. putting out "fires" on the network). The consequences of this are many unexpected expenditures, which make future planning (or cash-flow optimisation) impossible.

The main challenges of infrastructure delivery and management are thus two-fold. Firstly, they involve the creation of a framework or a "bubble", which will protect the infrastructure manager from the time-inconsistent behaviour of decision makers. Secondly, they require the creation of a framework or an instrument to introduce efficiency incentives in the system, and which are more robust than the traditional model. Both aspects are a matter of government credibility or institutional maturity. While there are examples of the traditional model performing well in some sectors and countries,[20] in many instances, this will not be the case.

In summary, the traditional model of infrastructure delivery and management does not entail sufficiently robust incentives to ensure adequate efficiency and can be outperformed by other governance models. The efficiency concerns were however not necessarily the primary motive for the expansion of private capital participation in infrastructure that started in the 1980s, as illustrated in the box below.

Public-private partnership model

The PPP (concession or the project finance model) approach is well known (Box 3.A1.1), so this annex does not go into great detail of its general characteristics. The focus is rather on some characteristics of this approach which are less well known and the challenge of renegotiations in PPP contracts.

Box 3.A1.1. **Defining a PPP**

Public-private partnerships (PPPs) are long-term contractual arrangements between the government and a private partner whereby the latter delivers and funds public services using a capital asset, sharing the associated risks. In a PPP agreement the service delivery objectives of the government are intended to be aligned with the profit objectives of the private partner. The effectiveness of the alignment depends on a sufficient and appropriate transfer of risk to the private partners.

In a PPP contract, the government specifies the quality and quantity of the service it requires from the private partner. The private partner may be tasked with the design, construction, financing, operation and management of a capital asset required for service delivery as well as the delivery of a service to the government, or to the public, using that asset. A key element is the bundling of the construction and operation and maintenance of the underlying asset over the life of the contract. The private partner will receive either: a stream of payments from the government (an **availability-based PPP**) for services provided or at least made available; user charges levied directly on the end users (a **commercially-viable PPP**); or a combination of both.

This definition excludes a wider array of arrangements in which non-governmental organisations such as non-profit civil society groups, trusts, church groups etc. are involved in the development and delivery of public or semi-public services. It includes concession type arrangements where the concession is designed to deliver a public service but excludes concessions such as licenses to use government assets such as mining which are another way for government to raise revenue. It also excludes traditional public works contracts. The government may also establish service standards as a representative of the public interest when PPPs are financed from tolls or user charges. Public-private partnerships are often undertaken by a special purpose vehicle acting as the government's private sector counterparty. A special-purpose vehicle is often (but not always) a consortium of companies responsible for the main activities of the public-private partnership.

Source: OECD (2012), *Recommendations of the Council on Principles for Public Governance of Public-Private Partnerships.*

In a typical example of a project finance structure, the developer is a parent company, which is the equity investor in the project company (The Special Purpose Entity- SPE). The SPE normally transfers the construction risk to a construction contractor. The SPE sells the services of the infrastructure built to the users and is remunerated, either with a user charge or through an availability payment.

In the OECD countries financiers in PPP/project finance generally use turnkey fixed price/fixed date contracts (full transfer of endogenous construction risk), resulting in a very good on time/on budget performance. In Latin America this is generally not the case. Instead the lenders/investors or the SPVs in question include a larger contingency in the project's budget for potential cost overruns, due to insufficient capital strength of the developers/construction companies.

Regardless of this technical difference, risk is not shifted outside of the PPPs contractual scheme (to the procuring entity) and must be paid for – either through the higher base CAPEX cost (the cost of the construction) or through the higher expected rate of return.

The cost of construction risk transfer is considerable. Evidence in the roads sector shows a higher ex-ante cost for a large share of traditional and PPP procured projects *vis-à-vis* the cost of traditional procurement (Blanc-Brude et al., 2006). The costs are actually also substantially above the expected cost overruns in traditional procurement for road projects (Makovšek, 2013).

There are several dimensions of the risk transfer premium. For the construction risk one potential explanation is the construction of a higher quality infrastructure to achieve lower cost of maintenance of operation later – the optimisation of life-cycle cost. In general, however, there is little evidence to support such an assumption. In addition, there is evidence available, that the IRRs (IRR-Internal Rate of Return) are ex-post consistently higher, than envisaged in the IRR of the winning bid. It would appear that, at least in terms of construction performance, the limited existing evidence suggests that PPPs do not outperform the traditional model.

The risk transfer premium has some potential explanations, but is still a matter for research. The risk premium is substantial and some evidence indicates that even in developed economies competition is insufficient or cannot reduce this risk premium. The size and complexity of the projects also leads to self-selection, as not every firm can bid. This may be an inherent characteristic of the PPP approach and remedies to this challenge are not straightforward. In that context, there is currently no mechanism in a PPP to share potentially excessive gains (apart from sharing refinancing gains, which is common in PPP contracts in developed countries), but one could be introduced. It is not clear though, whether the market would accept such a mechanism.

Another potential challenge in a PPP is the assumed efficiency throughout the contract's lifetime. It is accepted that PPPs are not subject to the same excess employment issues as the traditional model, i.e. perform better. As circumstances change in the long life of the project, further efficiency gains might be possible. The PPP approach assumes that the ex-ante competition for the PPP contract ensures maximal efficiency incentives throughout the contract's lifetime. With regard to the core services in a PPP contract there is no mechanism to provide additional incentives for efficiency during the long operational life of the infrastructure. There is no research available on the evolution of operational performance in a PPP.

The regulated asset base model

The RAB model is one of two approaches towards the calculation of efficient service provision in economic regulation literature. It is generally seen as an alternative to the PPP (project finance) model. The approach is normally applied to existing infrastructure assets, not to standalone greenfield projects (such a practice has not yet developed). Nevertheless, an existing infrastructure manager in a RAB scheme can deliver new projects, using traditional procurement or project finance. After the completion of the construction phase, the infrastructure can be absorbed into the RAB regime.

The model as such is generic and does not preclude a source of finance. The figure below presents an illustration of a RAB model in which the economic regulator has a "duty to finance" the functions of the regulated company, while the money to sustain this can come from a dedicated budgetary source (e.g. fuel tax for the road users) or user charges (e.g. tolls). If the source of finance is budgetary, it should be sufficiently protected (ring fenced or dedicated) from spurious government intervention.

An illustration of the RAB model

The RAB model has several characteristics. Some of the main ones are:

- The model adheres to the principle of financial capital maintenance (maintaining monetary or market value of the assets through time).
- It provides incentives for efficiency where for example the regulator tries to determine what is the efficiency target (through benchmarking, cost modelling or other techniques) and aims to provide rewards (or penalties) for achieving (or not) the efficiency gains within a pre specified time frame and procedure.
- Full cost recovery should be ensured, including the provision of an adequate return (on the value of the regulatory asset base), provided the efficiency gains are met.

An example of a well-known incentive mechanism associated with RAB is the RPI-X mechanism. The "X" reflects a measure of inefficiency, which the regulator determines and applies on the annual allowed price growth (RPI – Retail Price Index). The inefficiency adjustment is reset in regular price review periods, which typically last five years. This gives the regulated company a sufficient amount of time to adjust, with the efficiency targets or gains being jointly negotiated.

The RAB approach is not without challenges. One is the difficulty of the regulator to assess and incentivise the efficiency of capital expenditures (Makovšek et al., 2015). This involves the appropriate management of infrastructure delivery without cost overruns. It can also involve an inadequate preference for expensive infrastructure solutions. The other challenge for the regulator is the establishment of what an "adequate[21, 22]" rate of return is. It is thought that because the investors' return depends on the value of the asset base, the management of the regulated company might have an incentive to excessively increase the asset base beyond what is optimal. This problem is called the "CAPEX bias" and involves decisions that favour CAPEX over OPEX solutions (e.g. building a water treatment plant instead of financing a responsible water use campaign).

Notes

1. The LPI is an interactive benchmarking tool created to help countries identify the challenges and opportunities they face in their performance on trade logistics and what they can do to improve their performance. The LPI 2014 allows for comparisons across 160 countries. The LPI is based on a worldwide survey of operators on the ground (global freight forwarders and express carriers), providing feedback on the logistics "friendliness" of the countries in which they operate and those with which they trade. See *lpi.worldbank.org*.
2. In many cases the national transport plan also defines the future strategy of infrastructure governance.
3. As can be determined for example through the overview of Uruguay 2030 documents on the homepage of Ministerio de Transporte y Obras Públicas/Dirección Nacional de Planificación y Logística (*http://www.mtop.gub.uy/*).
4. JASPERS (Joint Assistance in Supporting Projects in European Regions) is a special technical assistance unit set up by the EU to help countries in the technical execution of projects and policies. This includes assistance to countries which do not yet have a national transport plan or model. See *http://ec.europa.eu/regional_policy/en/funding/special-support-instruments/jaspers*.
5. Such as, "JASPERS Appraisal Guidance (Transport): The Use of Transport Models in Transport Planning and Project Appraisal" (JASPERS 2014b).
6. Functional regions are not necessarily the same as administrative regions – they reflect areas with a high level of transport interactions, such as a city and its hinterlands. They may also be defined on a transnational level (i.e. a functional region that covers more than one state).
7. The European Union (EU) aims to develop Trans-European Networks (TEN). In the context of transport these refer to the creation of international corridors within the EU, which are expected to foster the economic development in the EU as a whole. EU co-funding is available to support the deployment of the infrastructure projects on these corridors.
8. In many cases in the OECD the relationship between the infrastructure manager and the ministry is defined by a multi-annual contract and/or a performance statement. The performance statement can follow the principle of "management by objectives". It defines the desired outcomes (in terms of performance of the infrastructure/quality, investment etc.) and is directly linked to financing, which must be agreed with the state (when user-charging policy is in question) or provided by the state budget.
9. This is more present in the road sector with the performance contracts. In the rail sector, which is thought to be more complex, the Dutch rail infrastructure manager, which is vertically separated from the operators, is the only company in Europe (no other national infrastructure manager in the World is known to the OECD), who has successfully outsourced railway maintenance and attempts to create competition between the maintenance companies. The UK also made the attempt but was unsuccessful.
10. In all regulation models, a high level of professional skills is required of the regulator. The differences between them are primarily the "distance" from political intervention. In the government regulation approach a state entity assumes directly a regulatory role in the markets, subject to market failures. Independent regulation involves an independent agency. A high degree of political commitment and functional and economic independence of the regulatory agency are necessary. When an independent regulator is also responsible for supervising the performance contract and providing economic incentives to a public service infrastructure provider, this is generally known as regulation by contract. The OECD has developed guidelines on the governance of the regulators (OECD, 2014).
11. In the EU, substantial energy has been devoted to achieving the principles of multiannual contracts, but this remains a challenge, even though the EU directives require their application (*http://ec.europa.eu/transport/modes/rail/infrastructures/contracts_en.htm*).
12. Infrastructure is long-lived, and so in the elementary accounting approach assets are depreciated against their historical purchasing value. Even though historical cost accounting accommodates the price growth over time, the money "put aside from the depreciation" may not suffice to replace the historical asset with the new asset. One tool to determine the current cost of replacement is the modern equivalent value or MEV. This involves an audit of the network and the establishment of the cost of the modern replacement asset. This technique is especially important in sectors which rely on technology that substantially changes over time (i.e. railways, telecommunications etc.).
13. Gassner et al. (2009) studied a dataset of 1 200 utilities (water distribution, waste water collection and treatment, electricity distribution) in 71 development and transition economies, including

301 utilities with PSP and 926 state-owned enterprises. This study found significant efficiency gains of private over public management.

14. The countries used as benchmark to develop the regulatory framework for PPPs were: Australia, Canada, Chile, Spain and United Kingdom.

15. The subject has been abundantly covered by World Bank experts (e.g. Guasch 2004; Guasch et al 2014) and the OECD (Bitran et al. 2013).

16. Historically, collusion in the UK in the construction industry was also possible on smaller scale projects than PFI schemes, as evidenced by past OFT investigations: *http://webarchive.nationalarchives.gov.uk/20140402142426/http:/www.oft.gov.uk/OFTwork/competition-act-and-cartels/ca98/decisions/bid_rigging_construction*.

17. See section: Closing the gap - private sector participation in infrastructure.

18. Alternatively the government could introduce a requirement on local sourcing of materials and personnel in the tendering procedure (e.g. award 5% of the selection points to the bidder with higher reliance on local sourcing of material and personnel).

19. Bajari et al (2014) show, that in small sized road construction works (in their sample the largest contract is USD 15 m), adaptation costs during the project construction account for 7.5-14.1% of the total project cost (without accounting for legal and other fees).

20. A recent ITF roundtable on railway efficiency (*www.internationaltransportforum.org/jtrc/RoundTables/2014-Railway-Efficiency/index.html*) revealed a glimpse into the complexity of ownership and incentives in the railway sector. It was noted that the performance of the SBB (the Swiss infrastructure manager and operator) and the Dutch ProRail are comparable, although they are differently organised state owned companies, responding directly to the state (decision makers/politicians). Both appear to outperform Network Rail in the UK, which was at one point private and is now subject to efficiency incentives from an economic regulator – the Office of Rail Regulation.

21. The "adequate" return is determined through WACC (weighted average cost of capital).

22. A well-known theoretical problem with regard to excessive investment in physical assets is the Averch-Johnson-Welisz effect. In simple terms, it suggested that if the regulator would choose the rate of return above the company's true rate of return, the regulated company would excessively invest into physical assets to increase its return. Despite the fact that the regulators normally probably do set the rate of return of regulated companies above the company's "true" rate of return, because they cannot precisely determine the "true" rate, there is no or very little evidence (Law 2014) that this effect is actually material.

References

Bajari, P., D. Nekipelov, P. R. Stephen and Y. Miaoyu (2014), "Demand Estimation with Machine Learning and Model Combination", University of Texas at Austin.

Balmaseda, M., C. Daude, A. Melguizo and L. Taft (2010), "Infrastructure patterns in emerging markets: an empirical analysis with a focus on Latin America", *Global Economic and Construction Outlook*, June, pp. 25-31, CEMEX Economic Analysis.

Bitran, E., S. Nieto-Parra and J. Robledo (2013), "Opening the Black Box of Contract Renegotiations: An Analysis of Road Concessions in Chile, Colombia and Peru", *OECD Development Centre Working Papers*, No. 317, OECD Publishing, Paris, *http://dx.doi.org/10.1787/5k46n3wwxxq3-en*.

Blanc-Brude F., H. Goldsmith and T. Välilä (2006) "Ex ante construction costs in the European road sector: A comparison of public private partnerships and traditional public procurement", European Investment Bank, Economic & Financial Report 2006/01, Economic and Financial Studies, Luxembourg.

Burger, P, and Hawkesworth, I. 2011. How To Attain Value for Money: Comparing PPP and Traditional Infrastructure Public Procurement, *OECD Journal on Budgeting*, Volume 2011/1, pp OECD, Paris.

Cáceres, L. and F. Farinasso (2013), "Infraestructura vial del Uruguay: 2015-2030" [Uruguay road infrastructure: 2015-2030], *www.infraestructurauruguay.org*, accessed 1 March 2014.

CAF (2010), *Análisis del sector transporte*, Serie informes sectoriales, Infraestructura, *http://publicaciones.caf.com/media/1131/IS_URUGUAY.pdf*.

Calderon, C. and L. Serven (2010), "Infrastructure in Latin America", *Policy Research Working Paper Series* 5317, World Bank. Available at: *https://openknowledge.worldbank.org/bitstream/handle/10986/3801/WPS5317.pdf*.

Daito, N. and J. Gifford (2014), "US highway public private partnerships: Are they more expensive or efficient than the traditional model?", *Managerial Finance*, 40(11), 1131-1151.

ECLAC (2014), La Brecha de Infraestructura Económica y las Inversiones en América Latina. Boletín FAL, Edición No. 332, Número 4, *http://repositorio.cepal.org/bitstream/handle/11362/37286/Boletín+FAL+332_es.pdf?sequence=4*.

Estache, A. and M.A. Rossi (2010), "Regulatory Agencies: Impact on Firm Performance and Social Welfare", *Working Papers* ECARES 2009_010, ULB — Universite Libre de Bruxelles.

Flyvbjerg B., M.K. Skamris and S. Buhl (2002), "What causes cost overrun in transport infrastructure projects?", *Transport Reviews*, Vol. 24, No. 1, 3-18, January 2004, *http://flyvbjerg.plan.aau.dk/COSTCAUSESASPUBLISHED.pdf*.

Flyvbjerg, B., M.S. Holm and S. Buhl (2002), "Underestimating costs in public works projects: Error or lie?", *Journal of the American Planning Association*, 68(3), pp. 279-295.

Gassner, K., A. Popov and N. Pushak (2009), "Does Private Sector Participation Improve Performance in Electricity and Water Distribution?", *Trends and Policy Options*, 6, World Bank.

Gómez-Lobo, A. (2012), "The ups and downs of a public transport reform: the case of Transantiago", *Working Papers* wp354, University of Chile, Department of Economics.

Guasch, J. L. et al. (2014), "The Renegotiation of PPP Contracts: An Overview of its Recent Evolution in Latin America", *International Transport Forum Discussion Papers*, 2014/18, OECD Publishing, Paris, *http://dx.doi.org/10.1787/5jrw2xxlks8v-en*.

Guasch, J.L. (2004), *Granting and Renegotiating Concession Contracts: Doing it right*, World Bank Publications.

Helm, D. (2010), Infrastructure and infrastructure finance: The role of the government and the private sector in the current world, *EIB papers*, 15(2), 8-27.

Hill, A. (2011) Foreign Infrastructure Investment in Chile: The Success of Public–Private Partnerships through Concessions Contracts, *Northwestern Journal of International Law & Business*, Vol. 32 Issue 1.

HM Treasury (2013), Annual report and accounts 2013 to 2014. Available online: *https://www.gov.uk/government/publications/hm-treasury-annual-report-and-accounts-2013-to-2014*.

JASPERS (2014a), "Jaspers Appraisal Guidance (Transport): The Use of Transport Models in Transport Planning and Project Appraisal", Joint Assistance in Supporting Projects in European Regions.

Joskow, P. L. (2007), Regulation of natural monopoly. Handbook of law and economics, 2, 1227-1348.

Kutlina-Dimitrova, Z. and C. Lakatos (2014), "Determinants of direct cross-border public procurement in EU Member States", DG TRADE Chief Economist Notes 2014-2, Directorate General for Trade, European Commission.

Law, S. M. (2014), "Assessing the Averch-Johnson-Wellisz Effect for Regulated Utilities", *International Journal of Economics and Finance*, 6(8), p41.

Makovšek, D. (2013), "Public Private Partnerships, Traditionally Financed Projects, And Their Price", *Journal of Transport Economics and Policy* (JTEP), Vol. 47(1): pp 143-155.

Makovšek, D. and K. Logožar (2014), "A vision of the policy concerning the financing, and management of physical infrastructure in network industries in Slovenia", *International Public Administration Review*, Vol. XII, No.1.

Makovšek, D., B. Hasselgren and S. Perkins (2015), "Public Private Partnerships for Transport Infrastructure: Renegotiations, How to Approach them and Economic Outcomes", *Discussion Paper* No. 2014-25, International Transport Forum at the OECD, Paris.

Megginson, W. L. and J.M. Netter (2001), "From State to Market: A Survey of Empirical Studies on Privatization", *Journal of Economic Literature*, 39(2), 321–389. Retrieved from *www.jstor.org/stable/2698243*.

Odgaard, T., C. Kelly and J. Laird (2005), Current Practice in project Appraisal in Europe, Association for Transport and Contributors.

OECD (2014), *Budgeting Practices and Procedures in OECD Countries*, OECD Publishing. *http://dx.doi.org/10.1787/9789264059696-en*.

OECD (2012) *Recommendations of the Council on Principles for Public Governance of Public-Private Partnerships*, *www.oecd.org/governance/budgeting/PPP-Recommendation.pdf*.

OECD/UN-ECLAC/CAF (2013), *Latin American Economic Outlook 2014: Logistics and Competitiveness for Development*, OECD Publishing, Paris, United Nations Economic Commission for Latin America and the Caribbean, Corporacion Andina de Fomento, *http://dx.doi.org/10.1787/leo-2014-en*.

Olazábal, A.G. (2013), "Segunda parte: Propuesta para el sistema portuario" [Part 2: Proposal for portsystem], *www.infraestructurauruguay.org* (accessed 1 March 2014).

P. Burger and I. Hawkesworth (2011), "How to attain value for money: Comparing PPP and traditional infrastructure public procurement", *OECD Journal on Budgeting*, No. 1.

Tettamanti G. (2013), *Análisis del Ferrocarril del Uruguay 2015-2030*, Proyecto Infraestructura Uruguay 2030, Montevideo.

Tzanakakis, K. (2013) *The railway track and its long term behaviour: a handbook for a railway*, Springer Tracts Transp, Traffic.

Infraestructura Uruguay 2030 (2013), "Resumen Ejecutivo", Montevideo, Available at: *www.infraestructurauruguay2030.org/*.

Vecchi, V., M. Hellowell and S. Gatti (2013), "Does the private sector receive an excessive return from investments in health care infrastructure projects? Evidence from the UK", *Health Policy*, 110.2: 243-270.

WEF (2014), *The Global Competitiveness Report 2014-2015*, World Economic Forum, Geneva. Available at: *www3.weforum.org/docs/WEF_GlobalCompetitivenessReport_2014-15.pdf*.

World Bank (2014), *Private Participation in Infrastructure* (database) accessed March 2014. *http://ppi.worldbank.org/*.

Worsley, T. (2015), "Summary and conclusions of the roundtable: Ex-post assessment of transport investments and policy interventions: Prerequisites for ex-post assessments and methodological challenges", *International Transport Forum/OECD Discussion paper* 19, Paris.

Zitron, J. (2006), "Public-private Partnership Projects: Towards a Model of Contractor Bidding Decision-making", *Journal of Purchasing and Supply Management*, 12, 53-62.

Multi-dimensional Review of Uruguay
Volume 2. In-depth Analysis and Recommendations

Chapter 4

Towards greater equity in education in Uruguay[1]

Although Uruguay's provision of basic education is strong, inequalities in the access to and quality of education, particularly within secondary schooling, remain a critical challenge. Currently, the insufficient provision of human capital and skills in Uruguay is considered one of the country's main obstacles to growth and social inclusion. This chapter discusses these challenges and suggests measures to improve support both for the students, such as mechanisms to identify students in need of support and standardised examinations to allow for a better understanding of students' needs, and also for the teaching profession, including measures to improve work-time flexibility, school leadership, autonomy and job-safety. Public higher education in Uruguay faces similar equity challenges, with access rates being in stark contrast to success rates. To improve overall performance, Uruguay should introduce greater autonomy to and mobility between higher education institutions, increase support for students and involve the private sector to provide students with a more technical, labour market-oriented training.

The statistical data for Israel are supplied by and under the responsibility of the relevant Israeli authorities. The use of such data by the OECD is without prejudice to the status of the Golan Heights, East Jerusalem and Israeli settlements in the West Bank under the terms of international law.

What does Uruguay's education system look like?

Education in Uruguay is a fundamental human right, as enshrined in the General Education Law of 2008. This law stipulates 14 years of compulsory schooling, made up of two years of pre-school, six of primary education (starting at the age of six), three years of lower secondary education, and (currently) two years for upper secondary education.

The management of the education sector is highly centralised, although responsibilities are shared by several independent councils. The Ministry of Education and Culture is responsible for setting the general direction of national educational policies, but does not have a strong operational mandate. The agency in charge of managing the public system is the National Administration of Public Education (*Administración Nacional de Educación Pública* or ANEP). ANEP enjoys full autonomy and comprises several bodies of central importance for the education system: the Central Board Council (*Consejo Directivo Central* -CODICEN); the Council of Early and Primary Education; the Council of Secondary Education; the Council of Technical-Professional Education; and the Council of Educational Training. CODICEN is the highest administrative authority in the education sector. Its five members are appointed directly by the President and confirmed by the Senate, and are in charge of appointing the directors of the other councils. Although the other councils are subordinate to CODICEN, in practice they function autonomously. Their main task is to administer and supervise the provision of education in the country. In addition to that, the ministry co-operates with three more councils outside the CODICEN structure: the National Council for non-formal Education, the Coordination Council for Early Childhood Education and the Advisory Council for Tertiary Education. The main institution in charge of public education provision at tertiary level is the University of the Republic (*Universidad de la República* – UdelaR).

Public education is provided free of charge and there are no requirements for accessing any levels (including tertiary) other than graduation from the preceding level. Pre-school coverage in 2011 was close to 92%, which is higher than the international average and partly explained by considerable enrollment in privately managed institutions (27%; Table 4.1). In contrast, the secondary school network had the lowest share of private enrolment in the education system, only 16%. In 2011, the higher education institutions accommodated over 100 000 students (12% of total enrolment in education), 81% of whom attended UdelaR, the only public university in the country. That same year, public expenditure on education reached 4.4% of gross domestic product (GDP); higher than in previous years, but still lower than average education expenditure across OECD countries (6.3%). Uruguay's share of its national wealth spent on primary and secondary education was also lower than the OECD average: at 2.7% compared to 3.9%.

Table 4.1. **Basic data on education in Uruguay, 2011**

	Notes	Number of institutions	Students enrolled	Enrolment by type of institution (public/private)	Net enrolment rate	Teacher-student ratio	Public expenditure per level as share of GDP	Public expenditure per level as share of GDP - OECD average (5)
		1	2	3	4	5	6	7
All institutions, of which	1	3 777	864 749		n.a	n.a	4.40%	6.30%
public		2 789	685 015	79.20%				
private		651	127 257	14.70%				
Pre-school institutions, of which	2	252	108 244		91.9.%	29	0.50%	0.60%
public		189	79 405	73.40%	m	27		
private		63	28 839	26.60%	m	35		
Primary schools, of which	3	2477	325 509		95.20%	13	1.30%	3.90%
public		2074	273 440	84%	m	15		
private		403	52 069	16%	m	7		
Secondary schools, of which	4	930	272 535		74.40%	7	1.40%	m
public		588	230 153	84.40%	m	m		
private		342	42 382	15.60%	m	m		
Initial VET schools (lower and upper secondary)		118	57 158					
Tertiary institutions, of which		m	101 303		m	n.a	1.10%	1.60%
public		m	81 774	80.70%	m	n.a		
private		m	19 529	19.30%	m	n.a		n.a

Notes: 1. Column 1: excluding post-secondary and tertiary institutions. 2. Excluding early childhood institutions.3. Excluding institutions for children with special educational needs. Column 7: primary and secondary education combined. 4. Excluding *Ciclo Básico Rural.* 5. Data from 2010.

Sources: MEC (2012, 2013), *Anuario Estadístico de Educación*; OECD (2013a), *Education at a Glance: OECD Indicators, http://dx.doi.org/10.1787/eag-2013-en.*

Schools need a greater focus on equity

What do the PISA results tell us?

Uruguay's regionally good performance in the OECD's Programme for International Student Assessment (PISA) was a recurrent theme both during the desk research for this chapter on education, and during the site visits that followed. The most recent PISA results (2012), however, deliver a mixed message (OECD, 2014e). In 2012, Uruguay's 15-year-olds achieved a mean score of 409 points in mathematics, 411 points in reading, and 416 points in science. This positions Uruguay among the top three countries in the Latin America and Caribbean (LAC) region (along with Chile and Mexico).[2] Yet, it is still below the OECD average scores in all three subjects (OECD averages: 494 in mathematics, 496 in reading and 501 in science). Student achievement in reading and mathematics in 2012 had also fallen from 2009, when Uruguay achieved the highest score in mathematics of all the LAC countries participating in OECD's assessment.

While performance matters, so too does the price that has to be paid for it. Uruguay's disparities in performance among students are greater than in any other country in the LAC region and are, for the most part, associated with the socio-economic background of schools and their students. The strength of the relationship between student background and performance seems to go hand in hand with the large disparities in income distribution that are common in Uruguay (Figure 4.1). The graph distributes national school systems according to their countries' levels of income inequality (measured as the Gini coefficient) and their relationship between student performance and socio-economic background. Countries with high levels of income inequality and a strong link between student performance and socio-economic background are in the upper-right corner. In Uruguay in 2012, this relationship was the third-strongest of all economies that participated in PISA; 74% of the difference in student achievement between schools was associated with differences in the socio-economic background of their students.

Figure 4.1. **High income inequality and the strong link between socio-economic background and performance**

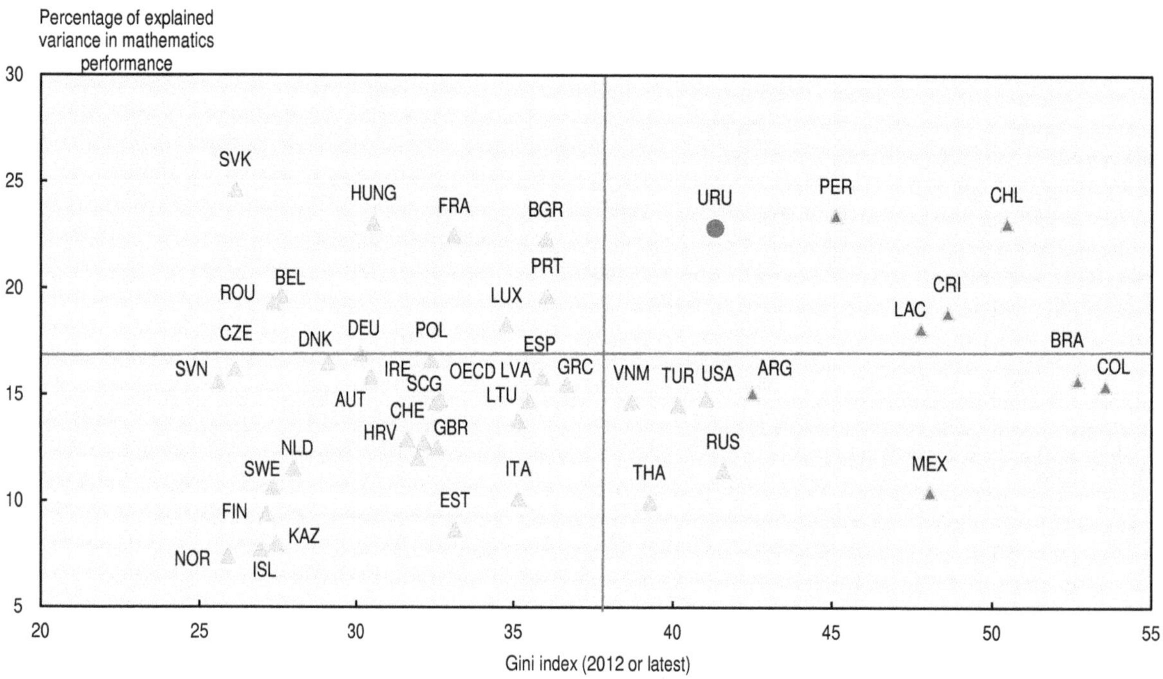

Note: According to World Bank definition the Gini index of 0 represents perfect equality, while an index of 100 implies perfect inequality. Arithmetic mean for Latin American average.

Source: OECD calculations based on PISA 2012 database *www.oecd.org/pisa/*, and World Bank (2015), *World Development Indicators, http://data.worldbank.org/data-catalog/world-development-indicators.*

StatLink http://dx.doi.org/10.1787/888933330244

There is a great deal of awareness of this challenge; all education reforms in Uruguay since the 1990s have attempted to target inequities in education. This is a commendable choice of priority – not only for reasons of fairness, but also because education quality cannot be improved without simultaneous improvements in equity (OECD, 2010a) (see Box 4.1). Efforts included directing services and compensation to underprivileged children, for example by extending pre-school coverage; financing school outreach programmes to increase enrolment in secondary education; providing more hours of instruction for students from weak economic backgrounds; and introducing Full Time Schools – these initiatives are discussed in more detail later in the section (Benveniste, 2000).

Despite these efforts, it seems that the socio-economic disparities of Uruguayan society continue to be replicated in the classrooms to the detriment of a worryingly high share of students. In 2012, almost 56% of the secondary school population performed below proficiency Level 2 in PISA (OECD, 2014a). Level 2 could be judged the baseline level at which students begin to demonstrate the competencies in mathematics that will enable them to participate effectively and productively in education and employment.[3] Results from longitudinal studies in Australia, Canada, Denmark and Switzerland show that students who perform below Level 2 often face severe disadvantages in their transition into employment and higher levels of education in subsequent years (OECD, 2012a). Students who perform below this baseline proficiency level can thus be considered a critical group with a limited learning and employment outlook later in life.

Box 4.1. **What is equity in education?**

Equity in education has two dimensions. The first is fairness, which implies ensuring that personal and social circumstances – for example gender, socio-economic status or ethnic origin – are not an obstacle to an individual achieving their educational potential. The second is inclusion, which implies ensuring a basic minimum standard of education for all – for example that everyone should be able to read, write and do simple arithmetic. The two dimensions are closely intertwined: tackling school failure helps to overcome the effects of social deprivation which often causes school failure.

Source: Field, S., M. Kuczera and B. Pont (2007), *No More Failures: Ten Steps to Equity in Education*, Education and Training Policy, *http://dx.doi.org/10.1787/9789264032606-en.*

Why do schools in Uruguay persistently fail to provide equal opportunities to all their students, despite the good intentions?

Attitudes of education professionals towards the potential for success of their students can have a powerful effect (OECD, 2010b). In education systems where teachers and schools are required to embrace the diversity of their student population and adopt more personalised approaches to student learning, outcomes[4] tend to be better and distributed more equitably (OECD, 2010a) than in countries where lower achieving students are believed to have a predetermined path and receive limited support. The site visits for the education chapter of this report included interviews with a broad selection of counterparts involved in (or with a stake in) education in Uruguay. While caution is needed in generalising, a recurring theme in these interviews was that success (and failure) in public education is considered to be the responsibility of the individual student, rather than of his or her school. Schools and teachers on the other hand are in charge of communicating knowledge and are less responsible for preventing academic failure.

While in practice the public education system guarantees access to education at all levels, in fact educational success seems to be left entirely to the students and their families. Consequently, those households that can afford to do so invest in individualised support and more conducive learning environments for their children. This largely involves enrolling them in private schools: socio-economically advantaged students in Uruguay are 2.5 times more likely to attend privately managed education institutions than students from backgrounds that are similar to the national average. They are also more likely to have tutoring activities or other forms of student support (Avendano et al. 2016). Of all 74 economies that participated in PISA in 2009,[5] only Panama had a higher likelihood that students would be educated privately (3.2 times more likely than the average) (OECD, 2012b).

This additional household investment pays off. Table 4.2 compares the gap in reading performance for students in the top (90th) percentiles of the performance distribution in PISA in 2012 with the median score[6] for each country. It suggests that Uruguay's achievement gap between students at the top of the PISA scale and those that are only average is the 13th largest of all economies participating in PISA in 2012.

Table 4.2. **Difference in reading performance between the top (90th) percentile and the median for each PISA participating economy, 2012**

	All students				
	Mean score		90th percentile		Score points difference to mean
	Mean	S.E.	Score	S.E.	Score
OECD					
Australia	512	(1.6)	634	(2.3)	122
Austria	490	(2.8)	603	(2.5)	114
Belgium	509	(2.3)	633	(2.3)	124
Canada	523	(1.9)	638	(2.6)	115
Chile	441	(2.9)	541	(3.3)	100
Czech Republic	493	(2.9)	604	(3.8)	111
Denmark	496	(2.6)	602	(2.8)	106
Estonia	516	(2.0)	618	(2.8)	102
Finland	524	(2.4)	639	(2.5)	115
France	505	(2.8)	639	(3.9)	133
Germany	508	(2.8)	621	(3.2)	113
Greece	477	(3.3)	597	(3.9)	120
Hungary	488	(3.2)	603	(3.9)	115
Iceland	483	(1,8)	602	(2,4)	119
Ireland	523	(2,6)	631	(3,2)	108
Israel	486	(5,0)	624	(4,5)	138
Italy	490	(2,0)	609	(2,2)	119
Japan	538	(3,7)	658	(4,4)	120
Korea	536	(3,9)	640	(4,0)	104
Luxembourg	488	(1,5)	620	(2,3)	132
Mexico	424	(1,5)	525	(1,9)	102
Netherlands	511	(3,5)	625	(3.6)	114
New Zealand	512	(2.4)	645	(4.0)	133
Norway	504	(3.2)	627	(3.9)	123
Poland	518	(3.1)	626	(4.8)	108
Portugal	488	(3.8)	604	(3.5)	116
Slovak Republic	463	(4.2)	591	(5.2)	128
Slovenia	481	(1.2)	598	(2.5)	117
Spain	488	(1.9)	601	(2.3)	113
Sweden	483	(3.0)	614	(4.2)	131
Switzerland	509	(2.6)	622	(3.2)	113
Turkey	475	(4.2)	588	(6.8)	112
United Kingdom	499	(3.5)	619	(3.8)	120
United States	498	(3.7)	614	(4.0)	116
OECD total	495	(1.1)	618	(1.2)	123
OECD average	496	(0.5)	613	(0.6)	117
Partners					
Albania	394	(3.2)	536	(3.4)	142
Argentina	396	(3.7)	516	(4.4)	120
Brazil	410	(2.1)	520	(3.0)	110
Bulgaria	436	(6.0)	585	(6.1)	149
Colombia	403	(3.4)	509	(4.5)	106
Costa Rica	441	(3.5)	536	(5.0)	95
Croatia	485	(3.3)	593	(4.9)	108
Hong Kong-China	545	(2.8)	648	(3.4)	103
Indonesia	396	(4.2)	492	(6.1)	96
Jordan	399	(3.6)	510	(4.6)	111
Kazakhstan	393	(2.7)	487	(3.5)	94

Table 4.2. **Difference in reading performance between the top (90th) percentile and the median for each PISA participating economy, 2012** *(cont.)*

Latvia	489	(2.4)	593	(2.8)	105
Liechtenstein	516	(4.1)	630	(10.6)	114
Lithuania	477	(2.5)	585	(3.1)	108
Macao-China	509	(0.9)	611	(1.6)	102
Malaysia	398	(3.3)	503	(4.3)	105
Montenegro	422	(1.2)	540	(3.4)	118
Peru	384	(4.3)	504	(6.4)	120
Qatar	388	(0.8)	535	(2.3)	147
Romania	438	(4.0)	555	(5.3)	117
Russian Federation	475	(3.0)	592	(4.2)	117
Serbia	446	(3.4)	566	(4.6)	120
Shanghai-China	570	(2.9)	667	(3.5)	97
Singapore	542	(1.4)	668	(3.2)	126
Chinese Taipei	523	(3.0)	633	(3.6)	110
Thailand	441	(3.1)	541	(4.4)	100
Tunisia	404	(4.5)	515	(5.6)	111
United Arab Emirates	442	(2.5)	562	(3.1)	120
Uruguay	***411***	***(3.2)***	***534***	***(4.1)***	***122***
Viet Nam	508	(4.4)	599	(5.0)	91

Note: S.E. stands for Standard Error, which is the standard deviation of the mean's estimate.

Source: OECD PISA 2012 database, Table I.4.3a, *http://pisa2012.acer.edu.au/*.

The children of those families who cannot afford to invest in remedies and support are most likely to repeat school years. The self-reported repetition rate among students in Uruguay in 2012 was close to 25% in lower secondary education, the fifth-highest in the PISA world after Spain and Macao-China, Tunisia, Colombia and Argentina (Figure 4.2). Across OECD countries, on average, 5% of students who participated in PISA in 2012 reported they had repeated a lower secondary grade, although in some countries grade repetition was non-existent, for example in Japan, Malaysia, Norway and Turkey. Over 95% of students in 21 other OECD countries reported they had never repeated a grade in lower secondary education (OECD, 2014b).

Those students who do not have the means or the resilience to cope with the motivational and financial shock of repetition, drop out. Household surveys suggest that by the end of secondary school this would be the fate of almost 70% of the repeating students: in 2011 only 34% of the population aged 18 to 23 had completed secondary schooling (see also Filardo and Mancebo, 2013).

What makes academic survival in secondary education a challenge for such a large share of the student population? This question is commonly tackled through a discussion of out-of-school factors such as poverty or family background, and their influence on student achievement. The following sections offer a complementary, more systemic view by taking a closer look at the schools instead, in particular at their capacity to identify students who struggle academically and provide them with individualised attention and support. The focus of analysis is on how student achievement is assessed and on the conditions in which secondary schooling (teaching and learning) takes place. Shortcomings in these two areas are likely to be among the main factors preventing public education in Uruguay from fulfilling the full potential of all students.

Figure 4.2. **Repetition rate in lower secondary education, selected PISA economies, 2012**

Results based on students' own responses

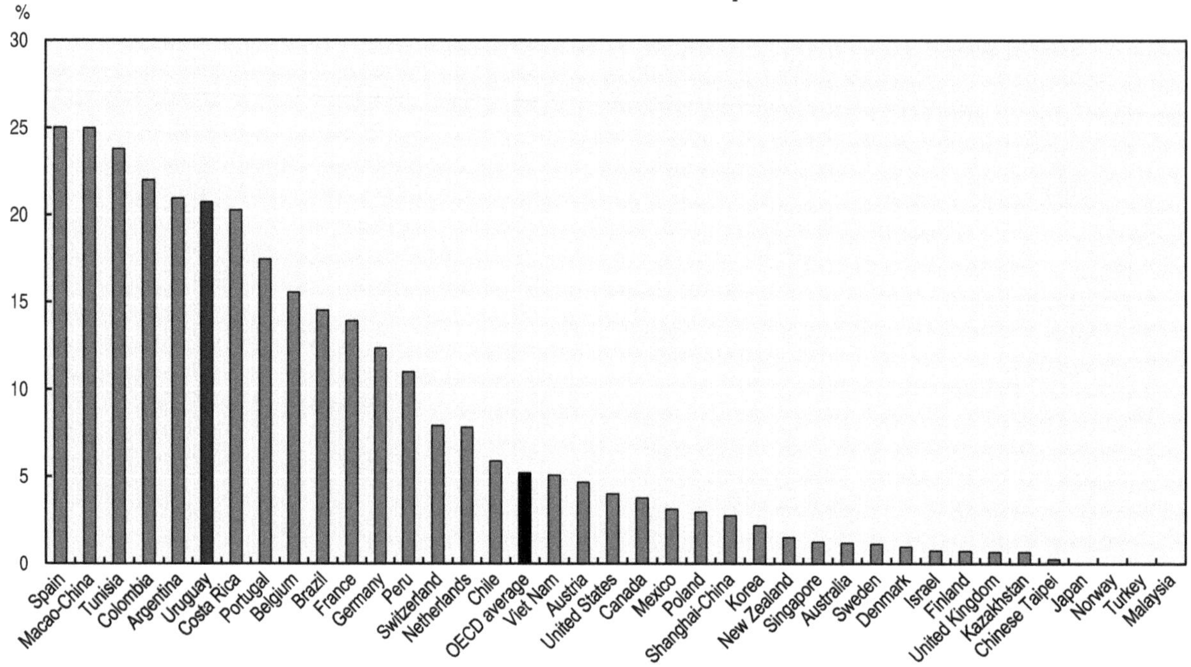

Note: Percentage of students reporting that they have repeated a grade once in lower secondary school.

Source: OECD calculations based on PISA 2012 database, Table IV.2.18, *http://pisa2012.acer.edu.au/*.

StatLink *http://dx.doi.org/10.1787/888933330255*

Student assessment approaches are variable

Student assessment involves the planned and systematic collection of evidence of learning (EPPI, 2002). It may be designed and implemented internally by the school or externally through standardised assessments, either to record and certify achievements (assessment of learning or "summative assessment"), or to identify aspects of learning in order to better shape subsequent instruction (assessment for learning or "formative assessment") (OECD, 2013b). Student achievement in Uruguay is currently assessed both externally and internally, but the type, reliability and purpose of assessments in primary education are different to those in secondary level.

Assessment in primary education

Assessment in primary education combines summative and formative elements, and standardised external assessments (both census and sample-based[7]) are quite common. The latest external assessment – the 6th National Learning Assessment of Grade 6 (the last year of primary school) – was carried out in November 2013. This assessment has been conducted regularly since 1996. The tests usually include multiple choice and open-ended questions in mathematics, science and reading, complemented by questionnaires on the socio-economic background that are completed by teachers, principals, students and families. The questionnaires focus on both in-school variables (such as infrastructure and facilities, human resources, etc.) and out-of-school factors (such as housing conditions, material and cultural goods, parents' levels of education, etc.) (Ferrer, 2006).

All assessments deliver information on learning outcomes and factors that influence performance, but in primary education in Uruguay their architecture and results are also meant to help and inspire teachers to develop their own tests, to work with peers in analysing and learning from test results, and to draw from a rich pool of test items that are accessible online.[8] ANEP's assessment platform (SEA – *Sistema de Evaluación de Aprendizaje*) suggests that the online database can be used to develop customised tests, diagnostic evaluations and, importantly, for formative assessment purposes in which students' responses are used to identify problems with learning and determine corresponding adjustments in teaching, rather than to mark success or failure (Box 4.2).

Box 4.2. **Promoting formative assessment in primary education in Uruguay**

"Uruguay has always recognised the use of assessment as a process to improve teaching. For the past four years, Uruguay has been developing an education system based on an online learning assessment system for students in the 3rd, 4th, 5th and 6th grades, in the subject areas of reading, mathematics and sciences, leveraging the Ceibal Plan (which provides a computer for each child and teacher in the public education system, for their personal use, connected to the Internet).

It is an education-based assessment, which provides teachers with a different perspective to complement their own assessments to analyse students' progress. This online assessment system works with portals: one for teachers and another one for students. The teachers' platform permits access to applicable tests for the grade that the teacher covers, and then applies these tests. Each test activity has accompanying theoretical materials that underpin the logic behind the assessments in each area. For each activity, these describe what is being assessed, and what hypotheses may be behind each of the incorrect answers that students could give. These materials serve to shed light on bases of and principles behind the test. Immediately after the assessment is conducted, the teacher can access the test and the results for use as tools in the classroom.

The platform permits both multiple choice questions and longer, constructed answer questions, which the teacher then marks in accordance with a marking scheme. There are plans to implement adaptive tests to replace single, monolithic assessments in 2013, whereby the system uses each student's answers to suggest activities in line with their skills; innovation is a vital aspect in making progress towards personalising teaching.

This allows online assessments to become a permanent support resource to allow teachers to enhance continuing improvement in learning achievement…".

Source: Interview with Andrés Peri, National Co-ordinator in Uruguay of the UNESCO Regional Bureau for Education in Latin America and the Caribbean, 2013.

A new cycle of formative assessments was carried out in June 2013 with this in mind; it mobilised the participation of over 100 000 students who took around 226 000 tests: 71 577 in science, 78 157 in mathematics, and 76 074 in reading (SEA, 2013). The results have been processed and made available to the participating teachers and schools in time to support their individual guidance planning for students at the beginning of the new school year. While the use of this information is not obligatory and the way it is used can vary from school to school, from teacher to teacher, and from year to year, it nevertheless provides reliable, externally validated data that can help determine early on how individual students are faring academically so that appropriate teaching and learning strategies can be devised.

This practice is consistent with assessment practices that are linked to better student performance across OECD countries. According to PISA, those OECD countries that use standards-based external examinations tend to perform better, even after accounting for national income (OECD, 2010b). In OECD countries there is a growing interest in particular in using evaluation results for formative purposes, and school leaders, teachers and policy makers are increasingly using results to identify areas where students and schools are performing well, and where they may need to improve (OECD, 2013b).

Assessment in secondary education

The assessment practices in secondary schools in Uruguay are, unfortunately, quite different from those used in primary. The only student assessment applied at secondary level is developed and administered by classroom teachers. PISA data for 2009 suggested that 96% of students in Uruguay attend schools where teachers' own judgemental ratings are the predominant form of assessment, followed by teacher-developed tests (85%) and homework (75%) (OECD, 2010b). The principals of schools attended by 98% of these students noted that the main aim of this assessment was to support decisions about retention or promotion; for 96% of them it was also to inform parents about the child's progress (OECD, 2010b).

Countries across the OECD have long-standing traditions of teacher-developed assessment and historically attribute high importance to their professional judgement. These assessments are frequently guided by national or sub-national assessment policy frameworks that specify classroom assessment procedures and objective criteria (OECD, 2013b). In the absence of such frameworks and criteria, however, teachers have to resort to more subjective, classroom and school-specific norms, for example comparisons of each student's achievements with those of other students in the same class or in an otherwise defined group. Such "norm-referenced" assessments are common practice in Uruguay and, as elsewhere, have many disadvantages. "Norms" depend on individual factors (i.e. on the teacher and on the quality of the student intake) and can vary from year to year, between teachers in the same subject and even between classes in the same year of the same school. Hence, even when teachers are highly experienced and try to be as fair as possible in their assessments, there can be no assurance that the same mark indicates the same level of student performance between different students, classes and schools and that it provides a clear enough picture of the knowledge and skills acquired by students. Without objective criteria as a reference, such marks are not suitable for tracking students' successes or failures over time, identifying knowledge and skills gaps (Melguizo and Perea, 2016), or communicating reliable information on success and failure (including decisions about repeating a year) to parents or students (OECD, 2013b; OECD, 2014c).

Uruguay is not alone in this. OECD analysis of PISA data and responses to additional questionnaires found that schools and teachers in other countries systematically reward certain student characteristics that are unrelated to learning. For example, after accounting for students' reading proficiency and attitudes to learning in all countries and economies that participated in PISA in 2009, girls and socio-economically advantaged students were receiving higher marks than their peers (OECD, 2012c).

To compensate for the shortcomings of norm-referenced classroom assessments, OECD countries complement them with external standardised examinations. In most countries these exams are more common at higher levels of education, where the stakes of success and failure are also higher (OECD, 2013b). Another common remedy is the introduction of appropriate methods of "criteria-based assessment" in which students' achievements are assessed against clearly defined, collectively developed criteria that are known in advance to all participants of the process (teachers, students, their parents, school administrators) and are likely to be more transparent and fair to students (OECD, 2014c). This is in line with lessons learned from experiences with marking practices in OECD countries, which suggest that those that include "communication of clear and useful information with the purpose of promoting learning" and resort to marks based on "clear and specific criteria measuring achievement against pre-established goals" are very effective (OECD, 2012c). Teachers at all levels of education are also increasingly expected to take responsibility not only for summative, but also for other forms of assessment (i.e. formative) (OECD, 2013b; Box 4.3).

Box 4.3. **Internal formative assessment in OECD countries**

Given the widely reported benefits of formative assessment for the improvement of teaching and learning, many OECD education systems have developed policy frameworks (national or state laws or regulations) to promote and support formative assessment practice in the classroom.

The frameworks generally include a requirement for schools to implement formative assessment in the classroom. In Australia (ISCED 2 and 3 only), Korea and Mexico, they also include a requirement for formative assessment to be part of initial teacher education programmes. In Korea, there is also a requirement for teachers to undertake professional development in this area. In Estonia, it is mandatory for schools to report on their strategies to promote formative assessment. In Spain, the regulations are most extensive including a requirement for schools to implement student formative assessment and to report on their strategies to promote it, as well as for student formative assessment to be part of initial teacher education programmes and for teachers to undertake professional development in this area.

In some education systems, while formative assessment is not inscribed in national or state education law, it is promoted through other documents. In the Flemish Community of Belgium, primary schools are required to monitor the progress of every student and report observations to parents, but there are no specific regulations regarding the procedures for doing so. In Hungary, elements of formative assessment, such as verbal assessment and differentiated assessment methods, are included in legal regulations and the national core curriculum.

Sources: OECD (2013b), *Synergies for Better Learning. An International Perspective on Evaluation and Assessment*, OECD Reviews of Evaluation and Assessment in Education, *http://dx.doi.org/10.1787/9789264190658-en*; OECD (2014d), *PISA 2012 Results: Excellence through Equity (Volume II): Giving Every Student the Chance to Succeed*, PISA, *http://dx.doi.org/10.1787/9789264201132-en*.

In Uruguay, the information gaps caused by the limitations in teacher classroom assessment are filled by information collected through regular and rigorous school inspections. The inspections are carried out by experienced staff (former school principals) of the School Inspectorate – a powerful institution which acts as intermediary between the public schools and the ANEP National Administration of Public Education and which is in charge of assessing the work of teachers, principals and schools (Bogliaccini, 2006). Schools are required to design and administer initial, mid-year and final exams in mathematics and languages at all grade levels, and inspectors must report on student test scores and specify the percentage of students that can master specific academic requirements (Benveniste, 2000). In addition, inspectors carry out their own institutional assessments which look beyond academic achievement to various aspects of school operation. They use this information to develop a detailed school profile and plan for institutional improvements. Since these evaluations differ from inspector to inspector and from school to school, their results are not comparable, however.

Reports and our site visits suggest that the work of the school inspectors is highly respected for its quality and importance, and that schools' development outlook depends on it to a large extent. It is very concerning, however, to note that schools and teachers also rely on these evaluations for decisions related to academic performance and – in some cases – the academic survival of students. No matter how good they might be, these evaluations of schools and their staff are carried out from an institutional perspective; they are not a substitute for a proper, "day-to-day" evaluation of student progress and needs. Considering what is at stake, this and the broader policy area of student assessment in secondary education, need urgent attention. Their shortcomings are crippling the capacity of secondary schools to identify students in need of support and to communicate reliable information about this need for designing appropriate interventions.

Schooling conditions could be improved

Teaching status and remuneration are low

Identifying and supporting struggling students is not only a matter of adequate assessment; it also requires that schools have the capacity to react to assessment findings, for example by improving responsiveness to the learning needs of an increasingly diverse student population. The socio-economic diversity of students in public education in Uruguay is particularly large. In 2012 the range between the most advantaged and disadvantaged students was the 8th largest of all the countries participating in PISA (Figure 4.3) (OECD, 2014d).

Figure 4.3. **Diversity in students' socio-economic background**

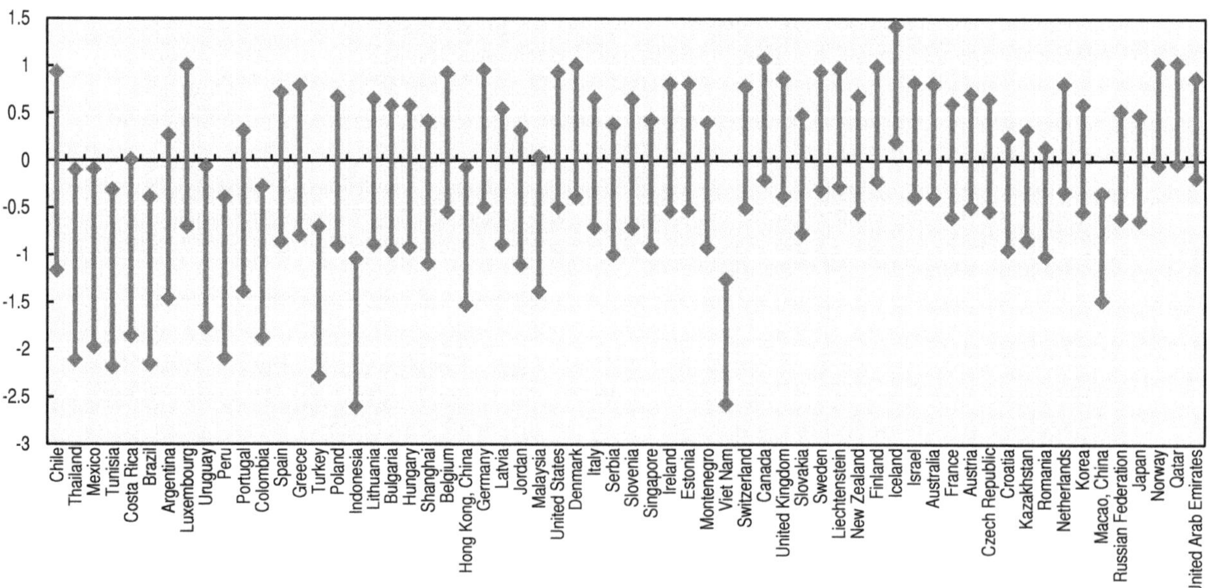

Note: Diversity denotes the relationship between a school's socio-economic intake and student performance, according to the decomposition of the gradient of the PISA Index of economic, social and cultural status (ESCS).

Source: OECD calculations based on PISA 2012 database, *http://pisa2012.acer.edu.au/*.

StatLink *http://dx.doi.org/10.1787/888933330260*

In countries like Uruguay where this gap is wide, schools are confronted with the double challenge of accommodating such a diverse student body, whilst also addressing the needs of the numerous students that are at the bottom end in terms of status and achievement (OECD, 2010a). The organisation of teaching and learning in Uruguay does not seem to be favourable in this respect and prevents schools from giving many of these students the amount of attention they require.[9]

The first and most striking limitation is the low status of the teaching profession (in terms of attractiveness and recognition) in Uruguay. This is despite the internationally acknowledged link between the status of the profession, education quality and student learning.[10] The average salaries of secondary school teachers in Uruguay are 17% lower than those of professionals and technicians with comparable qualifications in other sectors of the economy. This is lower than in all other countries in Latin America (apart from Nicaragua: Table 4.3).

Table 4.3. **How secondary school teachers' salaries compare with other professionals and technicians**

Country	Relative earnings (%)	Year of reference
Mexico	23.1	2008
Honduras	21.6	2007
Ecuador	10.2	2006
Panama	4.1	2007
Chile	-5.3	2009
El Salvador	-7.0	2009
Brazil	-10.1	2008
Uruguay	**-16.9**	**2007**
Nicaragua	-59.1	2005

Notes: Data for latest year available. Data for all countries except Uruguay are based on household surveys with national coverage. Survey coverage in Uruguay was limited to urban areas.

Source: Mizala, A. and H. Ñopo (2011), *Teachers' Salaries in Latin America: How Much Are They (Under or Over) Paid?*.

Of all the resources that countries spend on education, the only stand-alone area of investment found to be significantly and positively correlated with student performance (as measured by PISA) is the level of teachers' salaries relative to national income (OECD, 2010b). In Uruguay, even after 15 years in the profession, teachers in public secondary schools only earn around half of the national average per capita income – the lowest share of earnings in proportion to GDP per capita of all countries for which data exist, and the lowest of countries at the same level of economic development as Uruguay (Figure 4.4).

This OECD review does not intend to make statements on the appropriateness of teacher wages in Uruguay (or elsewhere). Neither will it argue in favour of or against unconditional wage increases – a very sensitive and difficult issue in OECD and non-OECD countries alike. Instead, it places the wage debate within a broader discussion of the package of measures that can ensure better quality education for all students, rather than as an isolated issue distinct from other education policy challenges. A key question in this context is: how does the current level of pay influence the teaching profession and the practices of professionals working in the public education system?

Figure 4.4. **How mid-career teacher salaries in secondary education compare with GDP per capita, 2012**

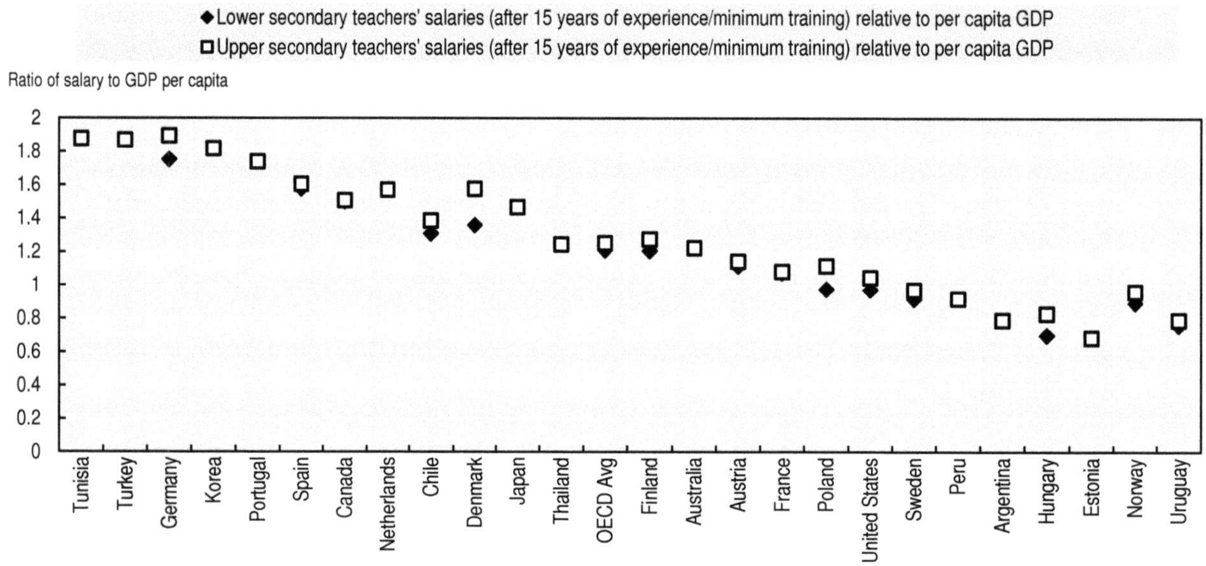

Source: OECD calculations based on PISA 2012 database, *http://pisa2012.acer.edu.au/*.

StatLink http://dx.doi.org/10.1787/888933330276

Clearly, the attractiveness of teaching in Uruguay seems modest compared to other professional alternatives (at least in terms of pay). Discussions with authorities during the site visits revealed that the country's positive employment climate makes it easy for university graduates, including those from the teacher training colleges, to find better paid jobs outside the education sector. In fact, for years now the share of university graduates teaching in Uruguay's secondary schools has been strikingly low. According to figures communicated by the Council of Educational Training (*Consejo de Formación en Educación*) during the site visits, in 2012 up to 70% of secondary school teachers were senior year students with no graduate degree. Some of them were not even enrolled in pre-service teacher training. Upon finishing their studies, the vast majority of these teachers commonly leave the schools in pursuit of better job offers. In turn, the teaching engagement delays many of them from completing their studies. Those who continue teaching for longer are likely to be those experiencing difficulties (or who are lacking time) in completing their studies.

While the better-off schools (private schools) also recognise this problem, they have the means to address it. According to PISA, advantaged schools are significantly more likely to have a higher share of certified teachers in their full-time teaching staff than other schools (OECD, 2014b). This is the case of Austria, Belgium, Chile, the Netherlands and Slovenia.

Research findings confirm that in times of stronger economic development and low graduate unemployment, fewer graduates choose to become and remain teachers (OECD, 2005) – although not as few as in Uruguay. Indeed, the higher salaries offered in other sectors can have a significant influence on graduates' decision to become a teacher (see Santiago, 2004). However, non-income related factors in some countries – such as the desire to teach, the enjoyment of working with children, and the satisfaction of seeing students achieve – can play a more important role than salaries or career prospects in decisions to join the profession (OECD, 2005); for example, see Figure 4.5.

Figure 4.5. **Most important motivations for becoming a teacher in Australia, 2002**

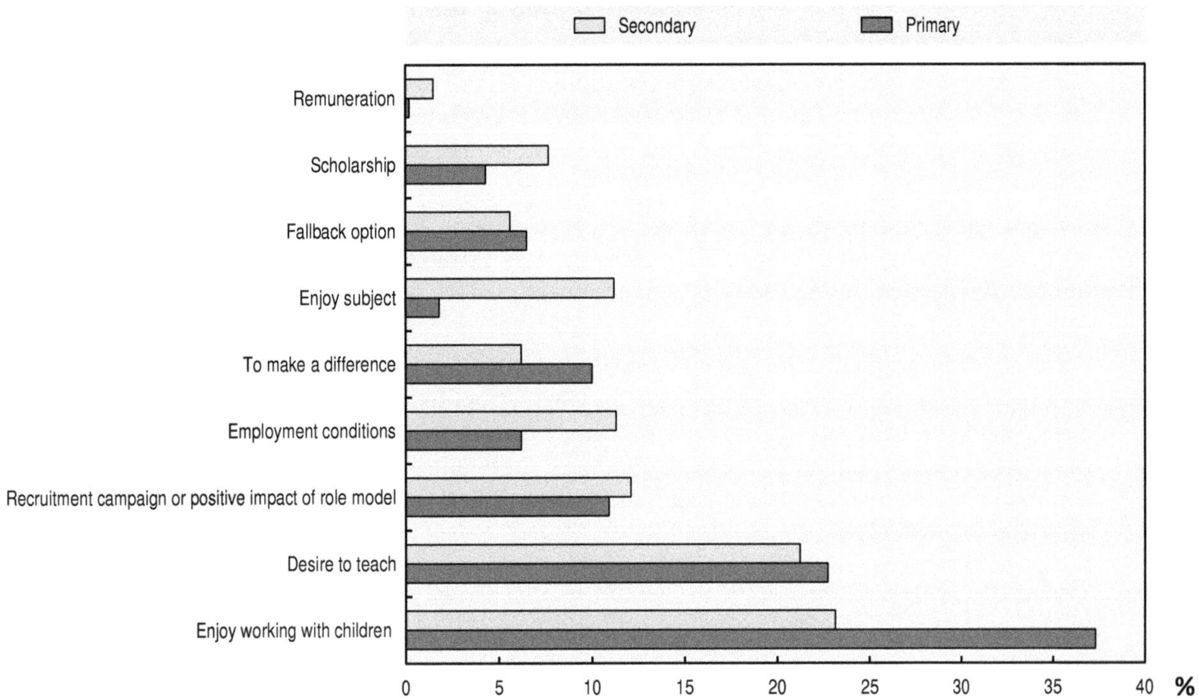

Note: Figures are based on a survey of 2 500 teachers from government and non-government schools, in metropolitan and non-metropolitan Australia, and from primary and secondary schools.

Source: OECD calculations based on Ministerial Council on Education of Australia (2003), *Demand and Supply of Primary and Secondary School Teachers in Australia*.

StatLink http://dx.doi.org/10.1787/888933330280

These findings are a reminder that teaching is not only a profession, but also a vocation. The committed teachers in some of the public secondary schools visited by the OECD (all of them operating in highly disadvantaged areas), offer daily proof of this statement. These schools had impressive rates of teacher and student retention despite their difficult working conditions. Such examples are, however, an exception. Elsewhere, teaching is downgraded to a sideline job for university students, marked by high turn-over rates and shortages of experienced, certified teachers who could act as mentors and sources of inspiration and peer guidance.

Another limitation linked to the current level of teacher compensation is the widespread practice of teaching more than one shift, in some cases up to three shifts a day, six times a week. In addition, these shifts take place often in different schools. It is understandable that the absence of sufficient financial rewards and recognition provides teachers with a strong incentive to work more hours. The current regulations also permit them to do so. Yet, this extraordinary workload has concerning side effects. Firstly, it leaves the teaching staff with very little time (if any) to prepare lessons. Secondly, it limits teachers' opportunities to exchange and reflect on their work, which undermines staff improvement (Box 4.4). Thirdly, the multiple teaching assignments (over)expose the teachers to very high student numbers, which can easily reach several hundred a day. In circumstances like these it is unrealistic to expect individualised or even basic attention to students' needs. This overload also renders impossible the introduction of fairer or state-of-the-art assessments, let alone the constructive use of their results.

Box 4.4. **Peer learning among teachers**

Studies of high-performance organisations indicate that most learning occurs informally. Such organisations seek to maximise opportunities for staff to interact and learn from one another, as well as with external sources of research and information, and try to develop ways for learning to be cumulative and more readily accessible to all members of the organisation.

There are examples of how professional development activities are being used to encourage ongoing informal learning in schools. A key strategy is to encourage teachers to become more inquiring, reflective practitioners, and to do so in collaboration with colleagues.

The peer collaboration, joint reflection and learning among teachers (including from the same school) has emerged as a valuable, affordable, school-based resource of professional development and support. Across the OECD study teams, peer reflective groups and peer coaching are becoming more and more common. These allow teachers to work together, continuously examine their assumptions and practices, and jointly develop strategies and solutions to problems.

Sources: OECD (2005), *Teachers Matter: Attracting, Developing and Retaining Effective Teachers*, Education and Training Policy, p. 130, *http://dx.doi.org/10.1787/9789264018044-en*; Guiney, E. (2001), "Coaching Isn't Just For Athletes: The Role of Teacher Leaders", *Phi Delta Kappan, 82(10)*, 740-743.

Inequality in learning conditions affects performance

It would be unfair and only partially correct to blame student failure only on problems associated with the teaching profession. Another set of important factors within the remit of the education authorities are the conditions in which teaching (and learning) takes place. Countries can influence learning outcomes by shaping these conditions to make them more conducive to learning, for example by providing organisational arrangements that promote better teacher-student relations, better disciplinary climates and better working environments for teachers (OECD, 2010b).

According to the PISA index of quality of school resources, 34% of the variation in student performance in Uruguay is attributable to the combined impact of better-off students in schools with more favourable arrangements[11] in terms of class size and/or instruction time, participation in after-school lessons, availability of extracurricular activities, teachers and material resources. Among the factors that mattered most[12] for better results was the time that the better-off schools in Uruguay allocate to additional instruction (enrichment lessons) (OECD 2010b, Table IV.2.12b).

Discussions during the site visits with teachers and students attending private education institutions suggested that the added value of more time for in-depth learning is not limited to better understanding, assimilation and handling of curriculum content, but also includes the benefits of students' longer exposure to the same teachers, which allows for a more personal approach to each student.

Another factor with a positive impact in the better-off (private) schools is their greater autonomy to adjust curricula and assessments to their and their students' needs. After socio-economic background is accounted for, curriculum and assessment autonomy as well as the form of management of the school (private) are the only two governance domains[13] that remain positively associated with learning outcomes.

Systemic failures need to be addressed

Even so, the better and/or private schools are not entirely problem-free. While more socio-economic advantaged education institutions tend to have a better learning environment and access to better educational resources, no matter how favourable their learning conditions, all schools in Uruguay, public and private, count on the same teachers trained in the same teacher training institutions, follow the same curricula, use the same learning materials and usually apply similar teaching methods. While more resources and a better learning environment do make a difference, their impact on the quality of learning outcomes remains more modest in comparison to better-off schools in other countries. The slope of the socio-economic gradient between schools (how much better an average student would fare if he/she were in a better school) suggest that a "better" school in an OECD average has a higher positive impact on the performance of a hypothetical average student than a "better" school in Uruguay (OECD, 2010a). This suggests that some of the current limitations in Uruguay's secondary school system cannot be remedied by throwing more resources at individual schools – instead they might require system level solutions.

Existing initiatives show promise

The authorities are aware of those factors and conditions favourable to student success and retention, and are investing in projects to replicate these conditions throughout the public education system. Some of these projects are recent and in the process of being introduced (such as the *Tránsito* programme to support the transition from the sixth grade of basic education into the first grade of secondary education). Others, such as the Full Time School model *(Escuela de Tiempo Completo)* and the *Compromiso Educativo* (see the next section on higher education) are well established pilots that are waiting to be scaled up nationwide. The usefulness of all of these important activities will depend on the mobilisation of political will to handle the considerable cost (monetary and time-related) of introducing them in all public schools in the country.

Probably the most promising, but also most expensive, of these initiatives is the Full Time School pilot (*Escuela de Tiempo Completo*, launched in 1998 as part of a multiannual reform effort to improve quality, equity and efficiency in public education. Initially all of these schools were located in socio-economically disadvantaged areas with the aim of providing an educational and socialisation context for children at risk and allowing teachers to devote time to them beyond the duration of a standard, one-shift school day. The initiative is driven by the motto "All children can learn" and the schools are supplied with additional material resources, technical and teacher support. These schools soon began to out-perform other schools in national assessments and established themselves as the "flagships of reform". In the first six years of the pilot their numbers almost doubled to around 200 (Bogliaccini, 2006). The key to student success in these pilot institutions is considered to be the availability and flexibility of teachers' time to devote to working with students and the fact that they can spend their working day in one school instead of several.

Another promising initiative is the Community Classroom Programme (PAC), launched in 2007 by the Secondary Education Council in co-operation with the *Infamilia* Programme of the Ministry of Social Development. The aim of PAC is to help young people aged 12-16 who have dropped out of school to get back into formal education. The programme is built around six subjects in the first semester and five in the following semester, instead of the 11 subjects taught throughout the entire year in the traditional secondary school system.

PAC also offers workshops in areas like music and art. The success of the programme is attributed to the more personalised attention received by the students, as well as the efforts to involve their families in order to gain their support (Bianchi, 2013). If the efforts to improve survival and success rates in regular secondary schooling start to show positive results, however, this programme will eventually become unnecessary.

Last but not least, Uruguay has recently established the National Institute of Educational Assessment *(Instituto Nacional de Evaluación Educativa – INEED)* to assess early, primary and secondary education. INEED is an autonomous, public, non-state organisation that may have the potential to overcome the fragmentation in the governance of the education system by supplying evidence and analysis on the functioning of the system as a whole. INEED acts as an analytical centre, but also as an entity that can prepare policy blueprints. Its first report, for example, published in 2014, was not built around data analysis, but rather a compilation of the knowledge on and insights into education accumulated in the country over the past 20 years. The report aims to build agreement on a national agenda for educational change. INEED's other goals include introducing a national assessment of learning outcomes across all levels of the education system (except tertiary), assessment training for teachers, and also consolidating national education indicators to overcome the current fragmentation of data on the sector.

Low completion rates are a major challenge in higher education

Higher education in Uruguay is offered in both university and non-university tertiary institutions. The laws and regulations do not detail the type of institutions that belong to the latter group, but as far as university institutions are concerned, between 1833 and 1985 university-type higher education[14] was only offered by the public University of the Republic (*Universidad de la República* - UdelaR) – a politically autonomous, national macro-university (Orellana, 2011).

The long-standing dominance of only one university has ingrained in the public mindset the idea that tertiary education is synonymous with university education (Pebé, 2013). This perception is proving hard to shift despite the diversification of the university sector since 1985 and the emergence of private institutions (such as the Universidad Católica del Uruguay (UCU), the Universidad ORT, the Universidad de Montevideo (UM), the Universidad de la Empresa (UDE), as well as over ten private university institutes.[15] Consequently, UdelaR still accounts for over 80% of all tertiary enrolment in the country.

Public higher education is free of charge but is contingent on completing secondary education: the three-year *ciclo basico* (basic cycle) and the two-year *ciclo diversificado* (specialised cycle). The *ciclo diversificado* is intended to prepare secondary school graduates for the field that they will pursue at university level. In 2011 the three most popular subjects of study in this cycle were social and behavioural sciences (20.9% of total enrolment), followed by medicine (18%) and business and administration (14.2%). The subjects with least enrolment (below 1%) were social services, mathematics and statistics, and industry and production (Table 4.4).

Upon completion of four to six years of university, students may obtain a degree of *licenciado* (first university degree), followed by a *bachiller, doctor, experto*, or *técnico* (three years); *procurador, bachiller*, or *técnico* (four years); *arquitecto, ingeniero*, or *doctor* (five years); and *ingeniero, notario*, or *doctor* (six years). There are also technical and teacher training institutions at tertiary level.

Table 4.4. **Enrolment in tertiary education in Uruguay by area of study in public and private institutions (2011)**

Subject	Enrolment	Share of total
Social and Behavioural Sciences	5 399	20.9%
Medicine	4 656	18.0%
Business and Administration	3 661	14.2%
Law	2 005	7.8%
Computer Science	1 280	5.0%
Journalism	1 218	4.7%
Arts	997	3.9%
Agriculture and Fisheries	864	3.3%
Engineering and similar	828	3.2%
Education and Learning	785	3.0%
Architecture	754	2.9%
Humanities	707	2.7%
Physical Sciences	667	2.6%
Life Sciences	649	2.5%
Veterinary Science	578	2.2%
Personal Services	327	1.3%
Industry and Production	219	0.8%
Mathematics and Statistics	176	0.7%
Social Services	82	0.3%

Source: MEC (2012), *Anuario Estadístico de Educación.*

Like most OECD countries (OECD, 2008a), Uruguay has traditionally placed greater emphasis on equity of access to tertiary education than on equity of outcomes[16] (Table 4.5).

Table 4.5. **Trend in gross enrolment ratios, tertiary education in Uruguay, 1974-2008**

Year	1974	1977	1980	1983	1989	1991	1996	1999	2005	2007	2008
Gross enrolment ratio. ISCED levels 5 and 6	12.3%	17.6%	15.5%	24.1%	29.6%	30.0%	29.4%	33.7%	45.3%	63.7%	64.6%

Source: UNESCO UIS Statistics.

Alongside these rising enrolment rates, probably the biggest challenge confronting the public higher education sector in Uruguay is the high rate of student drop-out (66% in 2011; Figure 4.6). Anecdotal evidence from the site visits suggests that dropping out for a few years and then enrolling again is common practice.

There are very large disparities in graduation rates between faculties (Figure 4.7). For example in 2011, 48% of the 2007 enrolment cohort graduated from the faculty of architecture and construction, 46% in the faculty of law, 41% in agriculture and in medicine. In the same year, 52% of the students who enrolled to study personal services (*servicios personales*) were able to graduate. In contrast, only 2% of the students who enrolled in mathematics and statistics stayed the course. The rate of success was similarly low for educational sciences (6%) and humanities (7%), and only slightly better in administration and commerce (15%) and arts (16%). These numbers do not necessarily indicate drop-outs, as some of the students who failed to graduate in these subjects might have changed their field of study or decided to go for a lower level academic credential. The numbers do, however, suggest that, for whatever reasons, some faculties are considerably more successful than others in retaining their students and maintaining attendance and learning. Other countries are also seeing the expansion of tertiary participation accompanied by a downward trend in graduation rates (OECD, 2008a), although seldom as low as in Uruguay. For the sake of comparison, in 2011 the average rate of non-graduation in the OECD area was 32% (OECD, 2013a).

Figure 4.6. **Tertiary education in Uruguay: Undergraduate enrolment and drop-out rates, 2004-11**

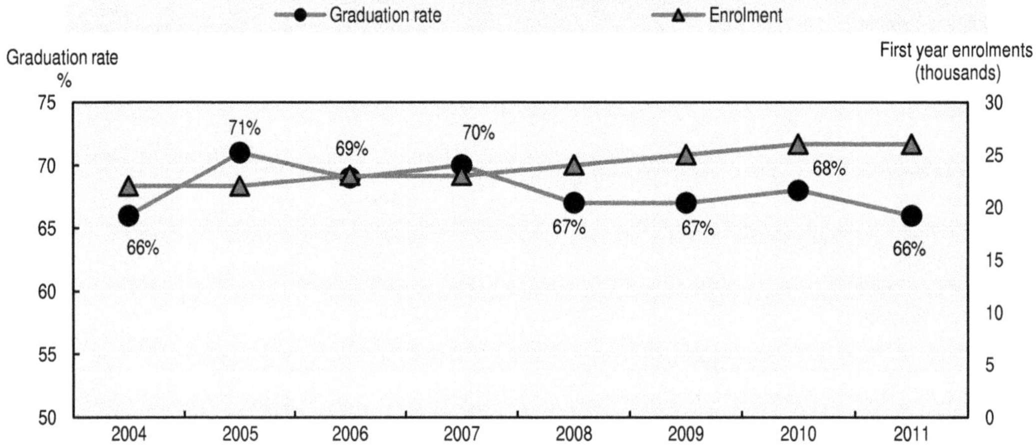

Note: Average for all institutions, assuming a theoretical duration of undergraduate education of four years.

Source: OECD calculations based on MEC (2012), Anuario Estadístico de Educación.

StatLink http://dx.doi.org/10.1787/888933330291

Figure 4.7. **Graduation rate in tertiary education in Uruguay by area of study (public and private institutions), 2013**

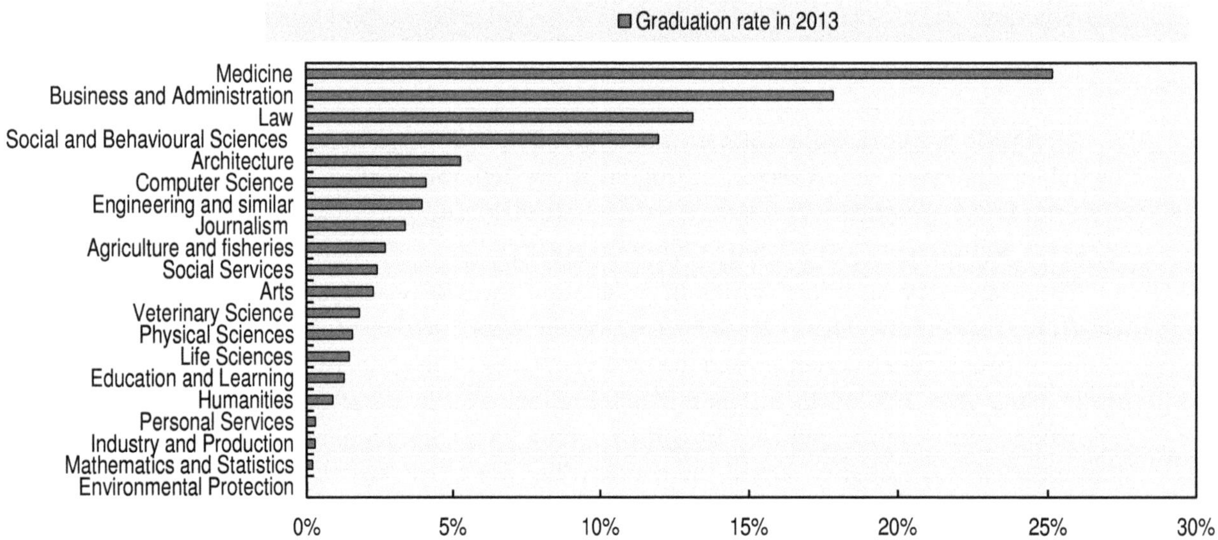

Source: Authors' calculations based on MEC (2013), *Anuario Estadístico de Educación, www.mec.gub.uy/innovaportal/v/11078/5/mecweb/publicaciones_?3colid=927.*

StatLink http://dx.doi.org/10.1787/888933330304

How to balance equity of access with equity of outcomes?

For some years now the balance between equity of access and equity of outcomes has posed a serious challenge which seems to be difficult to address, perhaps because Uruguay still lacks adequate mechanisms to support students as they progress through university. The expansion of the tertiary sector has had some side effects for the public university. According to information provided during the site visits, the enrolment boom has started to put a serious strain on the capacity of UdelaR to accommodate new students while upholding its traditional standards of academic work. It has meant gaps in the supply of teachers, created shortages in learning materials and infrastructure availability, and most importantly, has meant a difficult-to-manage diversity of students, both in terms of academic preparation and socio-economic background.

The first step in designing adequate institutional and sector-wide responses to this challenge should be to identify (and agree) the reasons behind the unsatisfactory rate of student success. The following sub-sections discuss this question in some detail.

Students need greater flexibility

To facilitate student mobility and make study more flexible, universities in Europe and the United States make use of modular study components and rely on systems of transferable academic credits that are awarded for each successfully attended course. In contrast, the organisation of studies in Uruguay follows the *carrera* system, in which students take their classes in only one faculty and course and within the same field, where they stay together as a group for most lectures and seminars in the four years until graduation (ISEP, 2013).

Groups are also the norm when students prepare and study for exams. This seems to be a necessary approach in order to cope with daily life at university. The scope and complexity of classes in public higher education are not necessarily proportionate to the number of contact hours allocated for teaching or to the frequency with which classes take place. More demanding classes might in fact meet for fewer hours and less often, but have higher expectations about the amount of time students will invest outside of class. It is rare for professors to spend time providing advice to students during regular office hours (ISEP, 2013); instead quite a few of them seem to attend to other day jobs,[17] as we saw during the site visits. Consequently if a student has a problem, he or she would be expected to turn elsewhere – to his peers or family – for help. It is therefore a widespread practice for students to distribute the burden of studying between themselves, for example by missing lectures and using someone else's notes instead, preparing group versions of individual written assignments and oral presentations, and in general doing their best to compete against the system and not against each other (ISEP, 2013). While all students provide each other with collegial help, in Uruguay this also includes selective approaches to compulsory course content, which are tolerated by the system. For example, the only consequence of a failure to attend lectures, seminars and exams is a natural prolongation of the overall duration of undergraduate studies, most recently to an average of six years instead of four.[18]

The opt-in, opt-out approach to studying is practical not only because of the particular ways in which the lecturing routine is organised, but also because a considerable share of the undergraduate student population has daytime jobs. According to information provided by UdelaR, 60% of students work to support themselves, and of these more than half work for more than six hours a day. This leaves very little time for active participation in study groups.

Students could be better prepared for the demands of tertiary education

Another factor hindering success in Uruguay are the poor links between upper secondary and tertiary levels of education. These mean that secondary and first year tertiary curricula are misaligned, schools and universities differ in their views on the preparedness of secondary school graduates, and schools lack information about university courses and their professional outlook. The latter problem means that school graduates in Uruguay enrol in university without much prior information or guidance on their choice of study. As higher education institutions become more differentiated, the number of courses to choose from increases, and courses become more differentiated in content between institutions, the need grows for information and advice to help young people decide what and where to study. Asymmetries of information between insiders and outsiders of the tertiary education system all too often lead students along the wrong track, incurring large costs in terms of motivation, self-confidence, time and financial investments. This risk is particularly high for students from low socio-economic backgrounds. It is not enough to provide information on tertiary education opportunities – prospective students also need information on the skill requirements, demands and labour market outcomes of the various programmes to make informed decisions and limit the chances of choosing the wrong path (OECD, 2008b).

Even if their choice was informed, the poor co-ordination between education sectors implies that the first year of study is likely to require skills and knowledge that the final years of secondary schooling and the *ciclo diversificado* have failed to provide them with. Far too many university entrants in Uruguay are reported to lack the minimum set of skills in mathematics, reading and science needed for studying. As mentioned above, the 2012 PISA results show that at the age of 15, only a few years before graduation from secondary school, around 56% of students were not able to reach proficiency Level 2 in mathematics (Figure 4.8).

There are no direct data on how many of these low-performing and hence vulnerable students will enrol at university, but the barrier-free access to higher education implies that the decision on who is qualified enough to study is left entirely to the secondary schools. The reportedly poor quality of new study entrants might be an indication that the graduation criteria applied by schools are different or maybe less demanding than those that UdelaR would wish for. Interviews with representatives from the tertiary sector suggest that graduation from secondary education is an achievement, but that it is not a guarantee of good quality learning outcomes. For UdelaR in particular the main challenge arising from this situation is to balance the commendable mandate of giving a fair chance to everyone with the need to foster academic excellence so that the country and its tertiary sector remain regionally and globally competitive. While this challenge remains to be addressed, the privately managed universities (which enjoy the liberty of preselecting their students) are increasingly establishing themselves as models of high academic quality.

This disconnect between education levels is further complicated by the absence of a central body responsible for higher education that could act as a counterpart to the Secondary Education Council. In the absence of such a body, the burden of tertiary co-ordination rests with UdelaR, the country's sole public provider of higher education. It is not really within UdelaR's mandate to improve co-ordination with the secondary education sector, so each of these education levels continues to do their best within the limits of their own mandates. The public university, for example, is engaging in ANEP-led initiatives for improving the learning outcomes of secondary school graduates, some of which (i.e. the *Compromiso Educativo*) also allow for tutoring by university students.

Figure 4.8. **Proficiency in mathematics 2012: Percentage of students at each level of PISA proficiency**

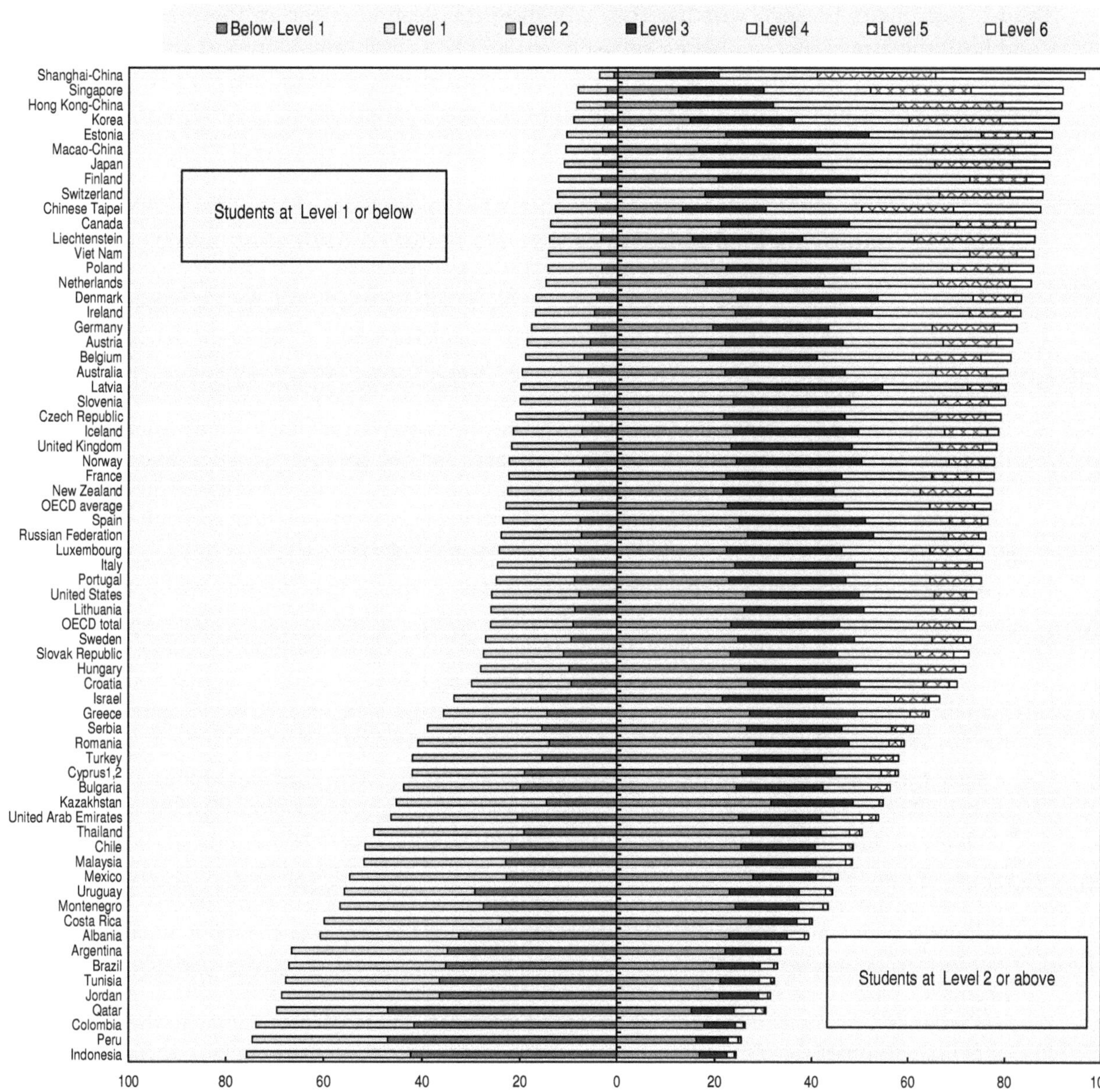

Notes: Countries and economies are ranked in descending order of the percentage of students at Levels 2, 3, 4, 5 and 6.

1. Note by Turkey

The information in this document with reference to "Cyprus" relates to the southern part of the Island. There is no single authority representing both Turkish and Greek Cypriot people on the Island. Turkey recognises the Turkish Republic of Northern Cyprus (TRNC). Until a lasting and equitable solution is found within the context of the United Nations, Turkey shall preserve its position concerning the "Cyprus issue".

2. Note by all the European Union Member States of the OECD and the European Union

The Republic of Cyprus is recognised by all members of the United Nations with the exception of Turkey. The information in this document relates to the area under the effective control of the Government of the Republic of Cyprus.

Source: OECD calculations based on PISA 2012 database, *http://pisa2012.acer.edu.au/*.

StatLink *http://dx.doi.org/10.1787/888933330310*

These project-type initiatives are a step in the right direction, but they are all remedial in nature and do not aim at improving the education system. They are also relatively new and it remains to be seen whether they will have the desired effect. In the meantime, and until the articulation problems between levels of education are addressed in a more systemic fashion (e.g. see Box 4.5), the misalignment of information, learning content and expectations will continue to cause a long-lasting transition shock to newly enrolled students, affecting their graduation outlook.

Box 4.5. **Improving graduation rates through better co-ordination among education levels – an OECD perspective**

Improving graduation rates by closing the gap between upper secondary and tertiary education is a challenge for OECD countries too. Countries resort to different actions to enhance study completion. One approach is to change the upper secondary school curriculum so that it is better aligned with tertiary education. In countries which have a national or state upper secondary curriculum, involving tertiary academics in curriculum design or reform is an obvious option. This approach is used in Australia and Croatia, where university academics are involved in advising on school curriculum and assessment processes. Likewise, changes in the United Kingdom's upper secondary school curriculum are discussed with both schools and higher education institutions.

Another approach has been to revise upper secondary curricula to better prepare upper secondary graduates for tertiary studies. In the Netherlands for instance, policy measures have focused on shifting teaching methods from passive to active learning, as a way to build students' information gathering skills. In Norway and Sweden the general education content of upper secondary vocational curricula has been expanded, while in New Zealand, the government supports a national Curriculum Alignment Project.

Some countries have also introduced extension programmes offered by higher education institutions to upper secondary students. Dual enrolment programmes allow high-school students to enrol in a tertiary course prior to graduation, giving them first-hand exposure to the requirements of tertiary-level work while gaining tertiary credits. Traditionally, these programmes have been reserved for high-achieving students, but some educators encourage their spread to middle- and low-achieving students given the potential impact of advanced coursework on student motivation and future success in tertiary education. Extension programmes are found – albeit not systematically – in Australia, China, the Netherlands, Norway and Sweden where upper secondary students may complete their final project or participate in research projects at a higher education institution.

Source: OECD (2008b), *Tertiary Education for the Knowledge Society, Volume I, http://dx.doi.org/10.1787/9789264046535-en.*

Uruguay is not a passive observer of these developments; for a while now its tertiary sector has been engaging in a range of institutional responses, echoing practices in other countries in the region and the OECD which are confronted with similar problems (Box 4.6). UdelaR's responses to the diversity challenge range from "in-house" solutions such as remedial courses for new study entrants and increasing horizontal mobility,[19] to interventions in the system of provision of tertiary education, such as opening university campuses in remote parts of the country and diversifying the network of public higher education institutions.

Box 4.6. **Increasing equity in outcomes in Norway and Mexico**

Norway's Quality Reform Initiative has seen an increasing focus on equity in study outcomes. More emphasis is now being placed on student progression throughout tertiary studies, with special support and follow-up measures to assist those students experiencing greater difficulties. Similarly, in Mexico new attention to equity in outcomes is reflected in the wide availability of tutoring programmes in tertiary education institutions: typically, students' progress is closely followed by a teacher. Those students who have been identified as coming from a disadvantaged background (e.g. recipients of means-tested scholarships) are entitled to specific support.

Source: OECD (2008a), *Tertiary Education for the Knowledge Society, Volume II*, http://dx.doi.org/10.1787/9789264046535-en.

Learning opportunities could be better tailored to regional and employment needs

High drop-out rates and low retention cannot only be blamed on academic challenges and lack of study time. Discussions in UdelaR, for example, suggest that geographical distance and the associated costs might hinder regular attendance by those students who live in the provinces (classes are largely concentrated in the capital, Montevideo). Research confirms that participation and success levels in tertiary education are related to the availability of tertiary education provision within the vicinity of the place of residence (Box 4.7) (OECD, 2008b).

Box 4.7. **The effect of regionalisation on tertiary enrolment in OECD countries**

A number of studies provide evidence that participation levels in tertiary education are related to the availability of tertiary education provision within the vicinity of the place of residence. Frenette (2006) shows that, in Canada, students living "out of commuting distance" from a university are far less likely to attend university than students living "within commuting distance", the effect being particularly marked for students from lower-income families. Two longitudinal surveys of Canadian youth, find that in both British Columbia and Nova Scotia, students in rural areas have lower expectations and attainments compared to other students, even when controlling for parental background, gender and academic stream (Andres and Looker, 2001). Research conducted in Sweden suggests that distance-learning opportunities in remote areas improve the likelihood that young people will participate in tertiary education. They find that many would not have been able to study at tertiary level without the distance-learning centre, this being particularly the case for women and for students coming from "non-academic" homes (Dahllöf, 2003; Roos, 2003).

Source: OECD (2008a), *Tertiary Education for the Knowledge Society, Volume II*, http://dx.doi.org/10.1787/9789264046535-en.

A recent flagship effort that bundles most of these responses in its mission statement is the newly established Technical University of Uruguay (*Universidad Tecnológica del Uruguay* or UTEC). UTEC opened its doors in 2014 and its study offer consists of technical, pragmatically oriented courses that provide the skills needed in key business sectors. The university is headed by a Central Executive Council with a diverse membership, comprising a rector (elected by the faculty, students and alumni), two teachers, two students, a representative of the non-teaching staff, a representative of the business community, and the directors of the Regional Institutes of Technology. As a public tertiary education institution with a technology profile, UTEC is oriented towards research and innovation, and committed to the matching the needs of the productive sector and increasing the access to educational opportunities in the interior of the country. One of the most innovative features of UTEC is the focus on the collective building of knowledge, with high standards of quality management and academic excellence (UTEC 2013).

UTEC is a rather unique entity in the Uruguayan higher education landscape. First, it is the only university to have the business sector heavily involved in both its management and curriculum design. Second, it provides education mostly through regional campuses, which makes it a forerunner of the plan to regionalise higher education in the country. The regional campuses all have different profiles as the content of courses are shaped by the needs of the dominant business sector in each region.[20] Third, through the use of tailored admission exams, UTEC intends to reach out specifically to those students (mostly from the provinces) whose socio-economic and geographic constraints may prevent them from participating in and benefitting fully from more traditional and academic forms of tertiary education.

Box 4.8. **Better skills for better outcomes: Towards a skills strategy for Uruguay**

Skills transform lives and drive economies. Effective skill development and deployment are central to future economic and social development. Skills are defined by the OECD as the bundle of knowledge, attributes and capacities that can be learned and that enable individuals to successfully and consistently perform an activity or task and can be built upon and extended through learning (OECD, 2012d).

However, Uruguay's education system shows relatively low levels of performance, as illustrated by PISA results among other things. While this is just one of the explanatory factors of skills levels in a country, evidence from the demand side confirms that skills are not always pertinent and thus do not match with the demands from the productive sector. In fact, 1 out of 3 firms in Uruguay (30.8%) does not find the skills it needs, similar to the difficulties faced by Latin American firms (35.9%), but well above the levels at the OECD, where around 15% of firms face this kind of difficulties (OECD/CAF/ECLAC, 2014).

Investing in skills represents one of the main policy strategies to pursue development and economic growth. In a globalized and increasingly knowledge-based economy, the capacity of countries to compete is more and more based on their ability to innovate and reap the benefits of technological progress, to add value to their goods and services, or to integrate their productive sector into higher segments of global value chains, among others. This is why skills matter, as they are a unique instrument to foster economic growth through gains in productivity and capacity to compete. Not only this; employment creation, labour market efficiency and job satisfaction are directly related to the capacity of a country to provide its citizens with the right set of skills and to match the skills provided by the education and training systems with those demanded by the production sector.

In this context, the OECD has been working with different countries to develop and implement a Skills Strategy, which aims to provide countries with a strategic approach for building, maintaining and using their human capital to boost employment and economic growth, so as promote social inclusion and participation. In all this, the OECD works collaboratively with countries to develop a strategic assessment tailored to each country's specific skills challenges and needs. The OECD Skills Strategy provides the overall framework for this work, focusing on: 1) Developing relevant skills; 2) Activating skills supply; 3) Using skills effectively; and 4) Strengthening the skills system.

Given the horizontal nature of skills challenges, a national skills strategy project needs to be designed together with all relevant government authorities and stakeholders. This means taking a whole-of-government approach, with dialogue and collaboration across ministerial portfolios, and engaging stakeholders to build a national consensus and commitment to action.

Source: OECD (2012d), *Better Skills, Better Jobs, Better Lives: A Strategic Approach to Skills Policies*, *http://dx.doi.org/10.1787/9789264177338-en*.

There are high expectations of UTEC and there is no reason to doubt that the new university will not live up to them. Its strength lies in its mission and its bold and unique set of characteristics. Nevertheless, if not managed properly, these very same characteristics that make UTEC a promising undertaking could quickly become its biggest weakness.

The close involvement of the business community in shaping course content, for instance, will be a strong guarantee of the relevance of UTEC studies and the positive employment outlook of its graduates. The connections to the employers' community will also ensure that UTEC's decentralised campuses respond to regional needs – this feature has the potential to make the university an example of best practice far beyond the national borders of Uruguay. However, UTEC will first have to find a way to disperse the deeply rooted public mistrust of private sector involvement in matters of public education.[21] Otherwise the new institution, whose creation was driven partly by regional political agendas, risks being taken hostage by local political interests. Establishing and promoting equity as a guiding principle of its work may be a way forward.

Another point is that UTEC's technical, shorter, more labour market relevant courses will fill a niche in the country's educational landscape by bridging the gap between vocational post-secondary and academic tertiary education. This suggests creating a much more promising employment outlook for UTEC graduates than any other post-secondary institution in Uruguay. However, UTEC's reputation (and with it the chances of success of its graduates) will take time to build, at least until the first wave of graduations. Until then much will depend on the ability of the new institution to balance the technical-vocational and academic "halves" of its identity. Too much focus on the technical-vocational half might "disqualify" UTEC's students from access to more academically oriented study content (i.e. courses offered at UdelaR) and might also diminish the attractiveness of UTEC's offer to UdelaR students, thus turning UTEC's "niche" into an educational dead-end. This is a plausible concern. According to the OECD, inter-institutional transfers between academic and more vocationally oriented higher education institutions are limited in most OECD education systems (OECD, 2008b). In Uruguay, it would be important to put in place formal arrangements for inter-institutional teacher and student transfers, in particular between UTEC and UdelaR, to facilitate a flow of students and ensure that the new university is fully integrated in the tertiary education sector and accepted as a viable tertiary education alternative by prospective students and their families.

Too much focus on the academic dimension of its work might, on the other hand, leave UTEC struggling to compete for academic recognition, stretched between academic ambitions and the needs and expectations of its main "customers" – the students and their potential employers, for whom an "academic drift" (Box 4.9) might bring little (if any) added value. The causes of academic drift are multiple and are often linked to the tendency of young or more technically and vocationally oriented institutions to strive towards the status of older and well established universities, their staff and students (OECD, 2008b). UTEC might or might not be different in this respect, but in the first years of its operation the new university should be supported in developing ownership of its special mission and discouraged from emulating UdelaR and its research outlets. This could be done through incentives and rewards for achievement, and by encouraging and promoting innovation in the study process.

Box 4.9. **The move towards vocational tertiary provision across the OECD**

Over the past 15 years, numerous OECD countries have faced similar diversity challenges, and have resorted to similar solutions, notably the creation of vocationally and technically oriented tertiary institutions (OECD, 2008b). Examples include the university colleges in Norway, the *Instituts Universitaires de Technologie* in France, the polytechnics in Finland and Portugal, the professional higher education institutions in Estonia, the professional institutes and technical training centres in Chile, and the technological universities and institutes in Mexico. In order to establish themselves as viable education alternatives, all of these education providers had to find a way around some common pitfalls. These include tendencies towards "academic drift" – the "widespread, persistent and inappropriate aspiration of more vocationally oriented institutions to emulate the mission and practices of established and generally 'elite' universities" (OECD, 2008b); the danger of slipping into isolation due to limitations in teacher and student mobility from/to more academically oriented tertiary institutions; and the lack of guidance on the appropriate involvement in academic life and research for a university with a technical-vocational profile.

Recommendations

In striving to meet the educational needs of every student in the country, Uruguay has removed all barriers to access. Public education is free and open to everyone, at all levels. Once enrolled, however, numerous students discover that their educational path gets narrower and more slippery the further they progress in the education system. The excessively high rates of repetition and drop-out are a vivid reminder of how limited the value of free access to education can be if struggling students are left without support. To give every student in the country a fair chance not only of enrolling, but also of graduating, effective support mechanisms should be put in place as a matter of priority.

This is a complex task that requires deep and far-reaching interventions in key areas of education policy. Uruguay is certainly not starting from scratch. The groundwork for these interventions has been done – in education development plans and promising pilots, such as the Full Time School. The right choices are now needed for what to do next: where to best focus limited resources, which initiatives merit being scaled-up nationwide; and – most of all – where to start in order to make a difference, quickly and for as many as possible.

The following sections outline a package of measures to target the equity challenge discussed in this chapter. The recommendations try to build on existing reform initiatives and/or good practice so as to capitalise on what has already been achieved. The fourteen recommendations are summarised in Table 4.6.

Secondary education

Secondary education needs to:

- improve the mechanisms for identifying students who are struggling academically
- empower teachers to mobilise their full potential as professionals
- individualise the learning process.

Below we outline recommended measures to achieve each of the three objectives.

Identify students in need of support

The most effective strategy to address learning gaps and avoid repetition (and drop-out) is to pre-empt students' learning problems by tackling them as they emerge during the school year (OECD, 2012e). No-one is in a better position to detect such problems than the teachers. The minimum that timely and reliable detection takes is a sound combination of classroom and external assessments, and know-how to use the results for both summative and formative purposes. A reform to improve support for students who struggle academically should therefore start by revising the assessment system and practices in secondary education so as to identify problems more quickly:

1. Redefine classroom assessment by specifying classroom assessment procedures and objective criteria to guide the assessments administered by teachers. This will remove arbitrariness and allow students' learning to be assessed against clearly defined, collectively developed criteria that are known in advance to all participants of the process (teachers, students, their parents, education school administrators). Criteria-based classroom assessment is likely to be more transparent and fair than the currently predominant norm-based approach. The choice of criteria should allow for tracking students' success or failure over time, identify knowledge and skills gaps, and communicate reliable information on success and failure (including on decisions about repeating years) to parents and the students themselves.
2. Promote the use of assessment results for formative purposes, so that the responses of students are used not only to mark success or failure, but also to identify problems with learning and determine corresponding adjustments in teaching and, if possible and necessary, in the learning environment.
3. Triangulate the results of classroom assessments with external standardised examinations. The National Learning Assessment of the primary level is a good, home-grown example of the information potential of standardised testing built on a rich, externally maintained pool of multiple-choice and open-ended questions, complemented by questionnaires on the socio-economic context of students. The fact that teachers can use the external test for the development of their own tests shows the added value which external testing can have for the design of classroom assessments.
4. Make use of the good practice existing in the national education system. For many years now, assessment practices in primary education follow the best of international developments, combining summative and formative elements, and standardised external assessments. The rich experience of primary schools and ANEP can (and should) guide and inspire the long overdue improvements in assessment on secondary school level.

Empower teachers

Designing a state-of-the-art assessment system is only half the battle in increasing equity. Teachers also need to be empowered to make regular use of the assessment findings in their work, and provided with incentives to do so. This will require technical interventions – such as the provision of training in applying criteria-based classroom assessments – and longer-term efforts to upgrade the status of the teaching profession:

5. Improve the conditions for teaching by giving teachers more time with the same students, primarily by curbing the detrimental practice of teaching multiple shifts in different schools. As discussed earlier, this exposes teachers to an unmanageable number of students and deprives the students, especially the weaker ones, of the attention they

might require to succeed. Interventions to regulate the practice of multi-shift, multi-school teaching must be planned and executed with caution because working more hours is probably the only legitimate way for teachers to compensate for their low income. However, rather than focusing primarily on the issue of salary increases (a contentious topic), a suitable response might involve better regulation, such as permitting teachers to teach more than one shift up to a certain ceiling as long as it is in the same school with the same students, and barring them from teaching in more than one school. In this way students will be able to benefit from longer exposure to the same teachers and from a more personal approach to their learning needs.

6. Develop and implement a realistic plan for scaling-up the Full Time School model nationwide as soon as possible. The pilot has shown its value for both teachers and students. An added value of this intervention is that it will create the conditions for those who are already in the teaching profession to rediscover the vocation of teaching.
7. Develop a package of measures to encourage young teachers without a teaching certificate to obtain one and to stay in the profession. The incentives could be both financial (such as a salary premium upon certification) as well as non-income related, such as work time flexibility, greater autonomy in teaching the curriculum, and greater job security. The certification procedure could be redesigned to include a new "fast certification track" which recognises hands-on experience as a professional asset that can be tested and credited in their favour.

Individualise the learning process

PISA data suggest that schools in Uruguay with greater autonomy to adjust curricula and teaching to theirs and their students' needs tend to perform better in the survey (see section on "Conditions of schooling"). Experiences from OECD countries confirm that a certain degree of autonomy to adjust the organisation of the instruction time, the class composition and teaching can lead to more personalised and effective learning environments which benefit disadvantaged students (OECD, 2012e):

8. Initiate peer learning among secondary schools on experiences with greater teaching and curricular autonomy with a view to:
   - setting guidelines on how to balance student-centred instruction with aligned curricular and assessment practices (OECD, 2012e).
   - increasing school autonomy gradually.

Higher education

Public higher education in Uruguay faces similar equity challenges to the rest of the public education system. Here access rates are in stark contrast with success rates, especially for disadvantaged students. The recommendations are similar to those suggested for secondary education, concentrating on ways to create a more supportive academic environment which meets students' learning needs and is flexible enough to allow for adjustments in their academic career. The recommendations can be summarised under the headings "mobility", "support" and "coherence".

Facilitate mobility

International practice points towards a growing awareness of the benefits of more flexible student pathways and student mobility within and between tertiary institutions.[22] Universities in Europe and the United States offer a modular approach in which students can accumulate transferable academic credits for each successfully attended course. In Uruguay the learning ethos and environment differs strongly between primary and secondary and between secondary and tertiary education; secondary school graduates are not necessarily well prepared for and informed about their further education options. It is only when they are exposed to the new academic environment that they can make informed choices about their interests and strengths. Allowing for a certain degree of mobility within the tertiary institution will allow them to change or fine-tune their initial study choices and concentrate on subjects that really interest them, which will be a win-win solution for all sides.

9. Promote student mobility by revising the *carrera* system in favour of a modular approach to study content and awarding of credits.

Strengthen support for students

The massive scale of home-grown student support is an indication of the scarcity of "official" academic support at UdelaR and the extent to which it is in demand. The self-help groups operate without much contact and co-ordination with the academic staff responsible for the lectures, exercises and the exams. The availability of professors for advice and consultations is also limited.

10. Foster stronger connections and better co-ordination between the self-help groups and the "official" academic world at UdelaR. One way of doing this would be to recognise and institutionalise them as an academic instrument by providing them with content and instructions sanctioned directly by the faculty, and requesting the faculty to take ownership and responsibility for their respective self-help groups. This will ensure some minimum standards of academic preparation, harvest their potential as multipliers of academic support, and reassure their members that they are doing the right thing.

Improve the coherence and links between secondary and tertiary education levels

The disconnect between upper secondary and tertiary levels of education means misalignments between secondary and first year tertiary curricula, diverging expectations of schools and universities regarding the preparedness of secondary school graduates, and lack of information in schools about university courses and professional career paths. This results in a massive transition shock for new university entrants.

11. Improve alignment between secondary and tertiary levels (perhaps drawing on the examples provided in Box 4.5). Consider introducing transition support in the form of induction and remedial courses for first year students.

UTEC

The newly established Technical University of Uruguay (*Universidad Tecnológica del Uruguay* – UTEC) is a key initiative for addressing some of the higher education issues discussed in this chapter. Ensuring UTEC fulfils its potential will require it to:

12. Deal with public distrust of private sector participation in public education. This will require continuously investing in fulfilling the institutional mission statement and in demonstrating to the public the commitment to it.

13. Establish a good reputation through incentives and rewards for achievement, and by encouraging and promoting innovation in the study process.

14. Keep the focus on UTEC's special mission, and avoid emulating UdelaR and its research outlets to ensure that the new university is fully integrated in the tertiary education sector, and is accepted as a viable tertiary education alternative by prospective students and their families. This can be done through: preserving the more technical, shorter, labour market-relevant character of its courses; and formalising arrangements for inter-institutional teacher and student transfers between UTEC and UdelaR to facilitate a flow of students.

Table 4.6. **Summary of recommendations**

	Sections and main recommendations	Target	Area of policy intervention
Secondary education			
1	Redefine classroom assessment by specifying procedures and objective criteria to guide the assessments administered by teachers	Improve identification mechanisms	Assessment
2	Promote the use of assessment results for formative purposes		
3	Triangulate the results of classroom assessments with external standardised examinations		
4	Make use of the good practice existing in the national education system		
5	Improve the conditions for teaching by giving teachers more time with the same students	Empower teachers	School organisation
6	Develop a realistic plan for scaling-up the Full Time School model nation-wide, and commence with its implementation as soon as possible		
7	Develop a package of measures tailored to the expectations and needs of young teachers without a teaching certificate, which provide them with incentives to obtain one and to stay in the profession		Teacher policies
8	Initiate peer learning between secondary schools on experiences with greater teaching and curricular autonomy	Individualise instruction	Governance
Higher education			
9	Promote student mobility by revising the *carrera* system in favour of a modular approach to study content and awarding of credits.	Facilitate mobility	Governance
10	Recognise, institutionalise and support self-help study groups as an instrument of academic preparation and work	Strengthen student support	
11	Improve alignment between secondary and tertiary levels and introduce transition support for first year students	Improve coherence and co-ordination	
UTEC			
12	Invest in meeting the institutional mission statement and in demonstrating to the public that there is commitment to it.		
13	Set up incentives and provide rewards for achievement, and encourage and promote innovation in the study process.		
14	Put in place formal arrangements for inter-institutional teacher and student transfers between UTEC and UdelaR to facilitate a flow of students, ensure that the new university is fully integrated in the tertiary education sector, and is accepted as a viable tertiary education alternative by prospective students and their families		

Notes

1. Prepared by Mihaylo Milovanovitch on behalf of the OECD Directorate for Education and Skills.
2. In the region, Chile was top performer in all three subjects in 2012, followed by Mexico in mathematics and reading and Uruguay in science.
3. At Level 2, students can interpret and recognise situations in contexts that require no more than direct inference. They can extract relevant information from a single source and make use of a single representational mode. Students at this level can employ basic algorithms, formulae, procedures, or conventions to solve problems involving whole numbers. They are capable of making literal interpretations of the results (OECD, 2014a).
4. As measured by PISA.
5. Calculations available only for 2009.
6. Middle of the performance distribution in the education system, or 50th percentile.
7. Census-based national assessments are those in which all (or most) schools and students in the target population participate; sample-based national assessments are those in which a representative sample of students or schools takes part.
8. See for example *www.anep.edu.uy/sea/?page_id=2542*.
9. As implied by the high rates of repetition and drop-out.
10. This phenomenon is not exclusive to Uruguay, as other Latin American countries have introduced reforms for the improvement of the teaching profession (see OECD, 2014e).
11. The precise term used in PISA is "resources". The index of quality of school resources is constructed from school principals' reports and measures the extent to which the lack of certain resources hinders the school's ability to provide instruction. High levels in the index indicate more resources. The resources captured by the index include class size, instruction time, participation in after-school lessons, availability of extracurricular activities, teacher shortages, and lack of material resources that can adversely affect instruction.
12. In terms of statistically significant correlation.
13. The governance domains captured by PISA are resource allocation, curriculum and assessment, competition for students, form of management (public or private).
14. Except for teacher training.
15. While universities offer a wider range of study subjects, university institutes are limited to only few.
16. This distinction is important. Equity of access relates to equality of opportunities to enter tertiary education. Equity of outcomes stands for opportunities to progress and complete tertiary education (OECD, 2008a).
17. The latter also influences the frequency with which classes take place. Due to their loaded schedules, professors might opt for longer sessions once a week instead of shorter meetings several times a week, and set the classes for the evening.
18. The figures were provided during site visits to UdelaR.
19. Meaning that students can change their subject of study if they discover that their initial choice was not right.
20. The first three careers covered will be milk production, industrial chemistry and informatics.
21. For example by establishing and promoting equity as a guiding principle of its work. Concerns about the private involvement in UTEC have been raised already in the Parliamentary session of 12 November 2012, which endorsed the UTEC project (see *http://brecha.com.uy/index.php/politica-uruguaya/900-al-final-salio*).
22. See for example (OECD, 2008b), Chapter 3.

References

Andres, L. and D. Looker (2001), "Rurality and Capital: Educational Expectations and Attainments of Rural, Urban/Rural and Metropolitan youth", *The Canadian Journal of Higher Education*, 31(2).

Avendano. R., Barrera, F., Nieto-Parra, S., Vever, F (2016), Understanding student performance beyond traditional factors: Evidence from PISA 2012. OECD Development Centre Working Papers (forthcoming).

Benveniste, L. (2000), *Student Assessment as a Political Contruction: The Case of Uruguay*, The World Bank, Washington, DC.

Bianchi, R. (2013), *Global Issues*, retrieved from URUGUAY: Personal Touch Gets Kids Back in, 27 December, *www.globalissues.org/news/2009/12/09/3832.*

Bogliaccini, J. A. (2006), "Primary Education: Changing Mainstay of Uruguay". In Noblit-Pink, *International Handbook of Education*, University of North Carolina and Marquette University.

Dahllöf, Urban (2003), "Vägar till högre utbildning med länen i Småland som titthål" ("Pathways to higher education with the county of Småland as a peep hole"), in L. Kim and P. Mårtens (eds.), *Den vildväxande högskolan*, Nya Doxa, Nora.

EPPI (2002), "A Systematic Review of the Impact of Summative Assessment and Tests on Students' Motivation for Learning". Review conducted by the Assessment and Learning Synthesis Group, Evidence for Policy and Practice Information and Co-ordinating Centre, London.

Ferrer, G. (2006), *Educational Assessment Systems in Latin America: Current Practice and Future Challenges*, Partnership for Educational Revitalization in the Americas, Washington DC.

Field, S., M. Kuczera and B. Pont (2007), *No More Failures: Ten Steps to Equity in Education*, Education and Training Policy, OECD Publishing, Paris, *http://dx.doi.org/10.1787/9789264032606-en.*

Filardo, V. and Mancebo, M. E. (2013), Universalizar la educación media en Uruguay: ausencias,tensiones y desafíos. Article 2 Collection, University fund for the contribution to the public comprehension of general interest topics.

Frenette, M. (2006), "Too Far to Go On? Distance to School and University Participation", *Education Economics*, 14(1).

Guiney, E. (2001), "Coaching Isn't Just For Athletes: The Role of Teacher Leaders", *Phi Delta Kappan, 82(10)*, 740-743.

ISEP (2013), *International Student Exchange Programs*, 14 December. Retrieved from *www.isep.org/students/Placed/handbook_education.asp?country=43.*

MEC (2013), *Anuario Estadístico de Educación*, Ministerio de Educación Y Cultura, Montevideo, *www.mec.gub.uy/innovaportal/v/11078/5/mecweb/publicaciones_?3colid=927.*

MEC (2012), *Anuario Estadístico de Educación*, Ministerio de Educación Y Cultura, Montevideo, *www.mec.gub.uy/innovaportal/v/11078/5/mecweb/publicaciones_?3colid=927.*

Melguizo, A. y J.R. Perea (2016), "Mind the skills gap! Regional and industry patterns in emerging economies", OECD Development Centre Working Paper No. 329. OECD Publishing, Paris.

Ministerial Council on Education of Australia, (2003), *Demand and Supply of Primary and Secondary School Teachers in Australia*, Ministerial Council on Education, Employment, Training and Youth Affairs, Melbourne.

Mizala, A. and H. Ñopo (2011), *Teachers' Salaries in Latin America: How Much Are They (Under or Over) Paid?* Institute for the Study of Labor, Bonn.

OECD (2014a), *PISA 2012 Results: What Students Know and Can Do (Volume I, Revised edition, February 2014): Student Performance in Mathematics, Reading and Science*, PISA, OECD Publishing, Paris, *http://dx.doi.org/10.1787/9789264208780-en.*

OECD (2014b), *PISA 2012 Results: What Makes Schools Successful? (Volume IV): Resources, Policies and Practices*, PISA, OECD Publishing, Paris, *http://dx.doi.org/10.1787/9789264201156-en.*

OECD (2014c), *Reviews of National Policies for Education: Secondary Education in Kazakhstan*, OECD Publishing, Paris, *http://dx.doi.org/10.1787/9789264205208-en.*

OECD (2014d), *PISA 2012 Results: Excellence through Equity (Volume II): Giving Every Student the Chance to Succeed*, PISA, OECD Publishing, Paris, *http://dx.doi.org/10.1787/9789264201132-en.*

OECD (2014e), *Latin American Economic Outlook 2015: Education and Skills for Development*. OECD, Paris.

OECD (2013a), *Education at a Glance: OECD Indicators*, OECD Publishing, Paris, *http://dx.doi.org/10.1787/eag-2013-en*.

OECD (2013b), *Synergies for Better Learning. An International Perspective on Evaluation and Assessment*, OECD Reviews of Evaluation and Assessment in Education, OECD Publishing, Paris, *http://dx.doi.org/10.1787/9789264190658-en*.

OECD (2012a), *Learning beyond Fifteen: Ten Years after PISA*, PISA, OECD Publishing, Paris, *http://dx.doi.org/10.1787/9789264172104-en*.

OECD (2012b), *Public and Private Schools: How Management and Funding Relate to their Socio-economic Profile*, PISA, OECD Publishing, Paris, *http://dx.doi.org/10.1787/9789264175006-en*.

OECD (2012c), *Grade Expectations: How Marks and Education Policies Shape Students' Ambitions*, PISA, OECD Publishing, Paris, *http://dx.doi.org/10.1787/9789264187528-en*.

OECD (2012d), *Better Skills, Better Jobs, Better Lives: A Strategic Approach to Skills Policies*, OECD Publishing, Paris, *http://dx.doi.org/10.1787/9789264177338-en*.

OECD (2012e), *Equity and Quality in Education: Supporting Disadvantaged Students and Schools*, OECD Publishing, Paris, *http://dx.doi.org/10.1787/9789264130852-en*.

OECD (2010a), *PISA 2009 Results: Overcoming Social Background: Equity in Learning Opportunities and Outcomes (Volume II)*, PISA, OECD Publishing, Paris, *http://dx.doi.org/10.1787/9789264091504-en*.

OECD (2010b), *PISA 2009 Results: What Makes a School Successful?: Resources, Policies and Practices (Volume IV)*, PISA, OECD Publishing, Paris, *http://dx.doi.org/10.1787/9789264091559-en*.

OECD (2008a), *Tertiary Education for the Knowledge Society*, Volume II, OECD Publishing, Paris, *http://dx.doi.org/10.1787/9789264046535-en*.

OECD (2008b), *Tertiary Education for the Knowledge Society*, Volume I, OECD Publishing, Paris, *http://dx.doi.org/10.1787/9789264046535-en*.

OECD (2005), *Teachers Matter: Attracting, Developing and Retaining Effective Teachers*, Education and Training Policy, OECD Publishing, Paris, *http://dx.doi.org/10.1787/9789264018044-en*.

Orellana, N. (2011), *Diversity Between Higher Education Institutions: The Cases of Argentina, Chile and Uruguay*, Global University Network for Innovation, Barcelona.

Pebé, P. J. (2013), *Tuning America Latina*, 28 December, retrieved from the Sistema Nacional de Educacion Superior de la Republica Oriental del Uruguay, *http://tuning.unideusto.org/tuningal/images/stories/presentaciones/uruguay.pdf#sthash.Ns56RGsY.dpuf*.

Roos, G. (2003), "Lokala studiecentra i Hälsingland – en inkörsport till högre utbildning" ("Local study centers in Hälsingland – a gateway to higher education"), in L. Kim and P. Mårtens (eds.), *Den vildväxande högskolan*, Nya Doxa, Nora.

Santiago, P. (2004), "The Labour Market for Teachers" in G. Johnes and J. Johnes (eds.), *International Handbook on the Economics of Education*, Edward Elgar Publishing, Cheltenham.

SEA (2013), *Sistema de Evaliación de Aprendizaje*, 3 December, retrieved from *www.anep.edu.uy/sea/?p=4278*.

UNESCO (2014), *Unesco Institute for Statistics, Global Education Digest*, 3 January, retrieved from *http://stats.uis.unesco.org/unesco/ReportFolders/ReportFolders.aspx*.

UNESCO Regional Bureau for Education in Latin America and the Caribbean (2013), 3 December. Retrieved from Interview with Andrés Peri, LLECE national coordinator in Uruguay: *www.unesco.org/new/en/santiago/press-room/single-new/news/interview_with_andres_peri_llece_national_coordinator_in_uruguay/#.UqEPBPRDtns*

UTEC (2013), Universidad Tecnológica del Uruguay, 15 December, retrieved from *www.utec.edu.uy/itr/*.

World Bank (2014), *World Development Indicators*, 3 January, retrieved from World Data Bank, *http://databank.worldbank.org/data/databases.aspx*.

ORGANISATION FOR ECONOMIC CO-OPERATION AND DEVELOPMENT

The OECD is a unique forum where governments work together to address the economic, social and environmental challenges of globalisation. The OECD is also at the forefront of efforts to understand and to help governments respond to new developments and concerns, such as corporate governance, the information economy and the challenges of an ageing population. The Organisation provides a setting where governments can compare policy experiences, seek answers to common problems, identify good practice and work to co-ordinate domestic and international policies.

The OECD member countries are: Australia, Austria, Belgium, Canada, Chile, the Czech Republic, Denmark, Estonia, Finland, France, Germany, Greece, Hungary, Iceland, Ireland, Israel, Italy, Japan, Korea, Luxembourg, Mexico, the Netherlands, New Zealand, Norway, Poland, Portugal, the Slovak Republic, Slovenia, Spain, Sweden, Switzerland, Turkey, the United Kingdom and the United States. The European Commission takes part in the work of the OECD.

OECD Publishing disseminates widely the results of the Organisation's statistics gathering and research on economic, social and environmental issues, as well as the conventions, guidelines and standards agreed by its members.

OECD DEVELOPMENT CENTRE

The OECD Development Centre was established in 1962 as an independent platform for knowledge sharing and policy dialogue between OECD member countries and developing economies, allowing these countries to interact on an equal footing. Today, 26 OECD countries and 24 non-OECD countries are members of the Centre. The Centre draws attention to emerging systemic issues likely to have an impact on global development and more specific development challenges faced by today's developing and emerging economies. It uses evidence-based analysis and strategic partnerships to help countries formulate innovative policy solutions to the global challenges of development.

For more information on the Centre and its members, please see *www.oecd.org/dev*.

OECD PUBLISHING, 2, rue André-Pascal, 75775 PARIS CEDEX 16
(41 2016 02 1P1) ISBN 978-92-64-25165-6 – 2016

www.ingramcontent.com/pod-product-compliance
Ingram Content Group UK Ltd.
Pitfield, Milton Keynes, MK11 3LW, UK
UKHW051503290926
15471UKWH00008B/1397

9 789264 251656